...ying
Witch

Chihiro Ishizuka

10

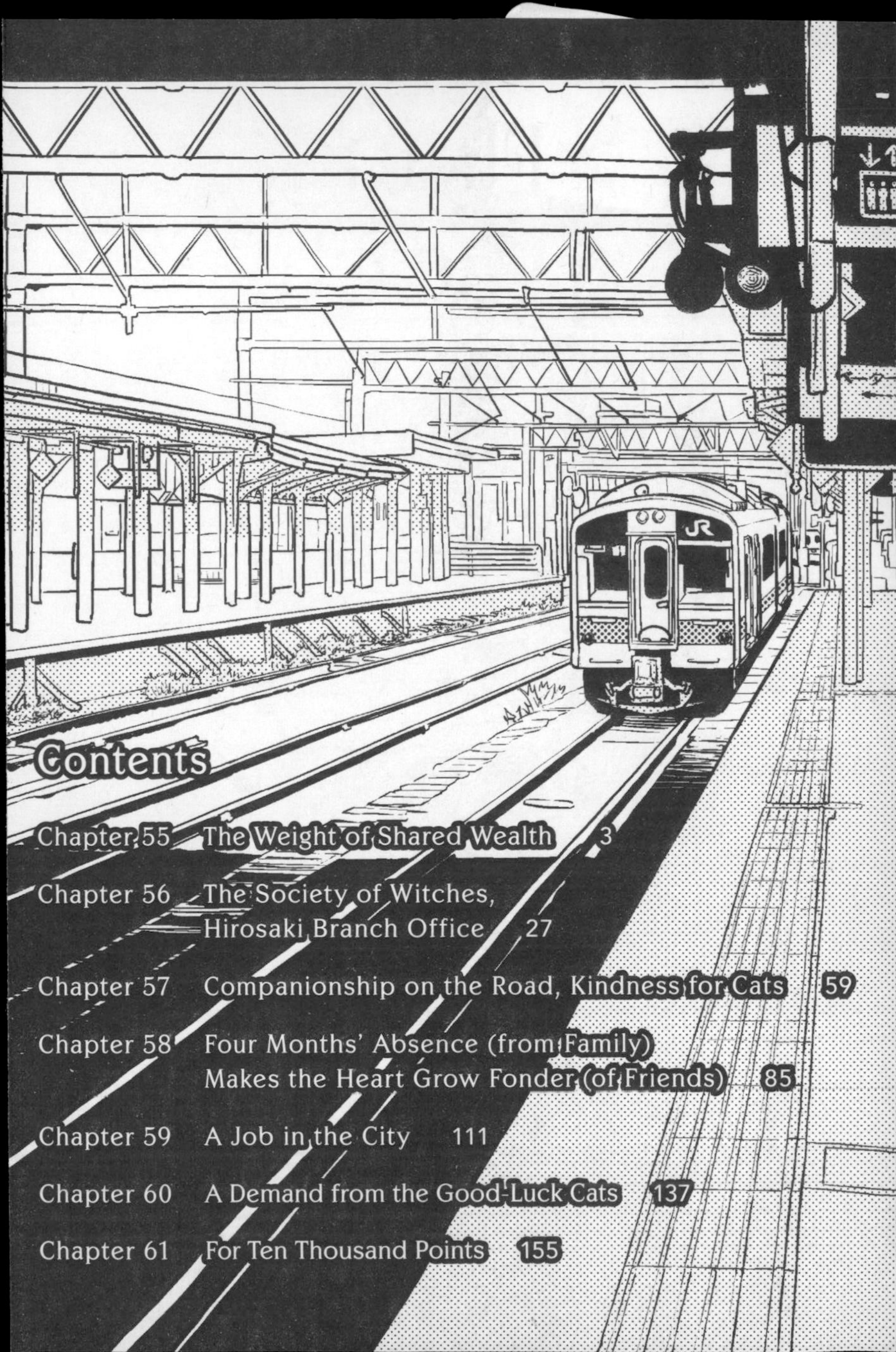
JR

Contents

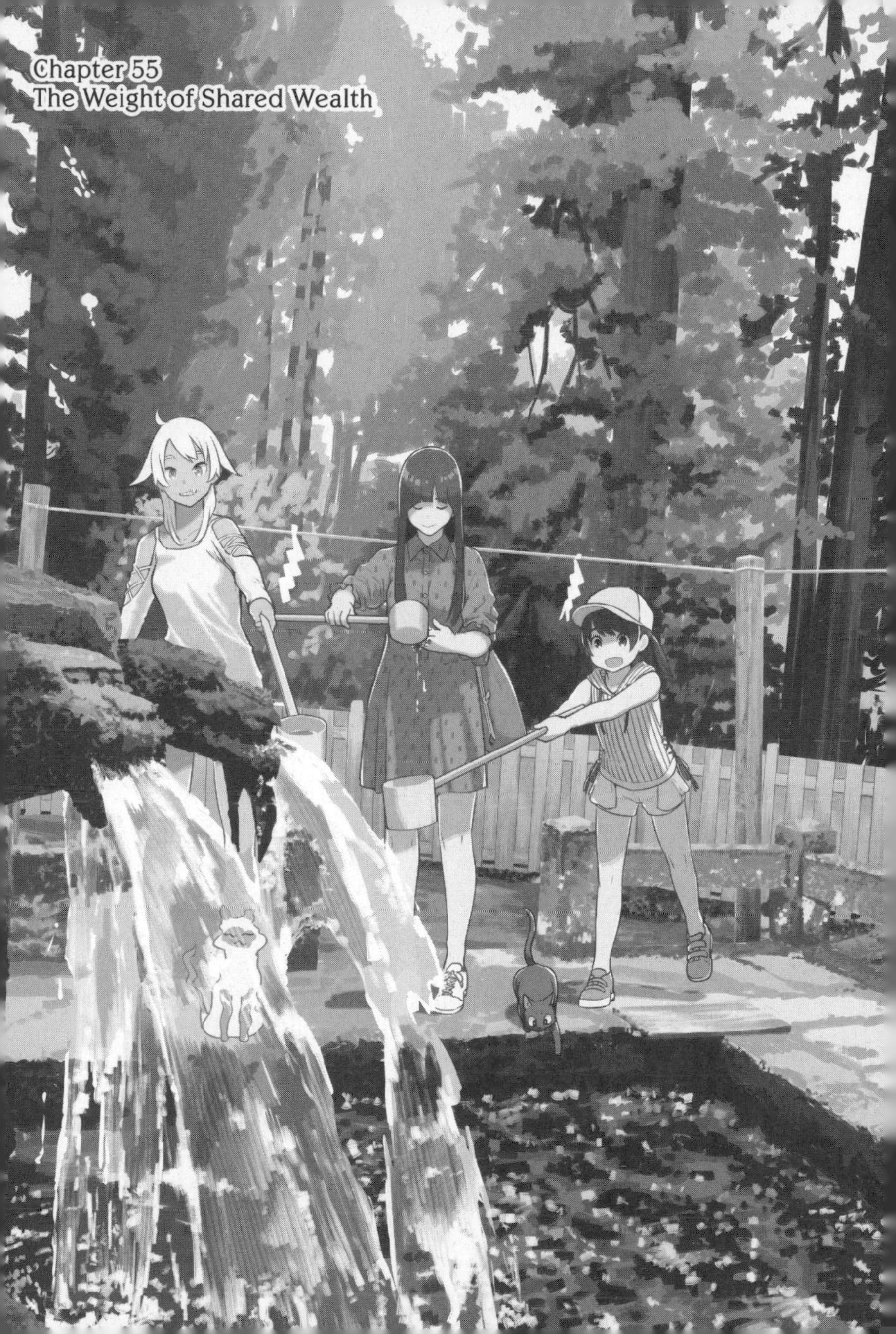
Chapter 55
The Weight of Shared Wealth

Flying
Witch

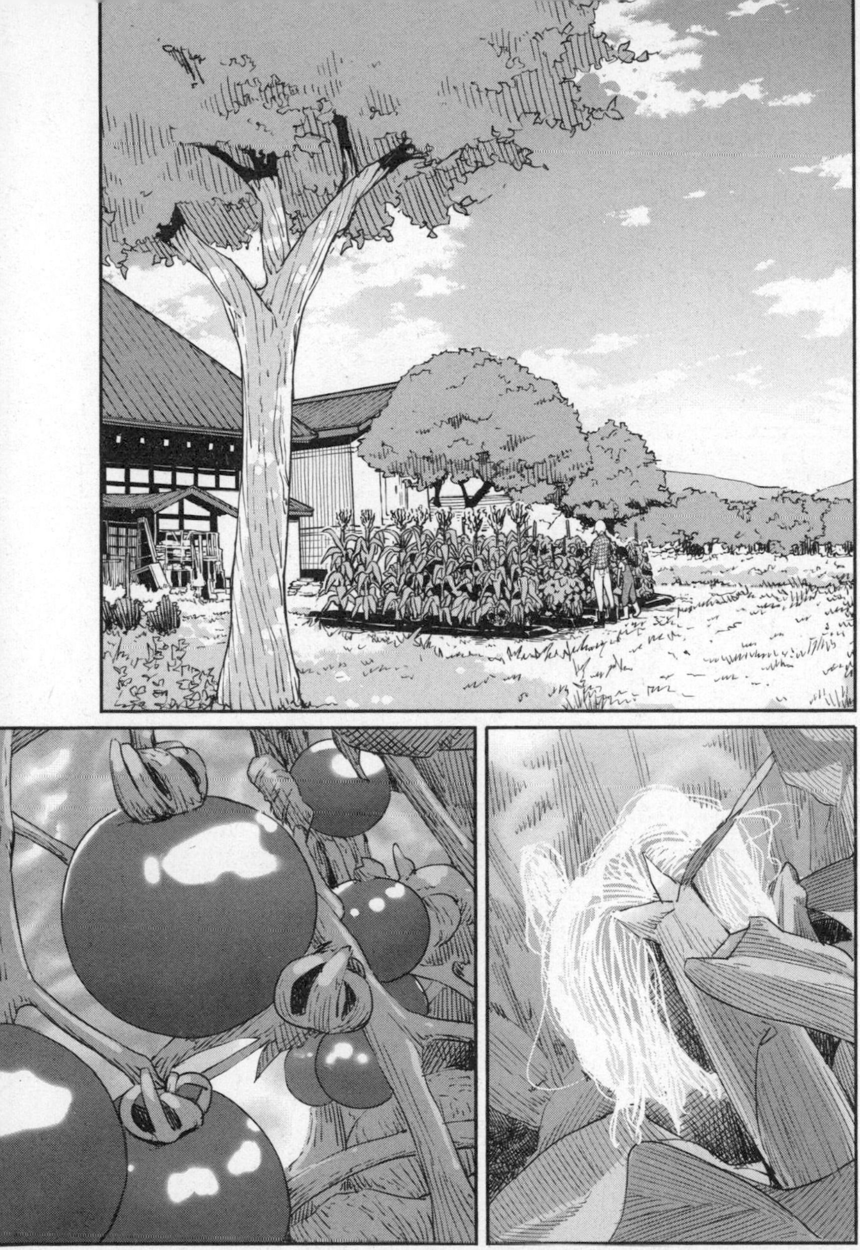

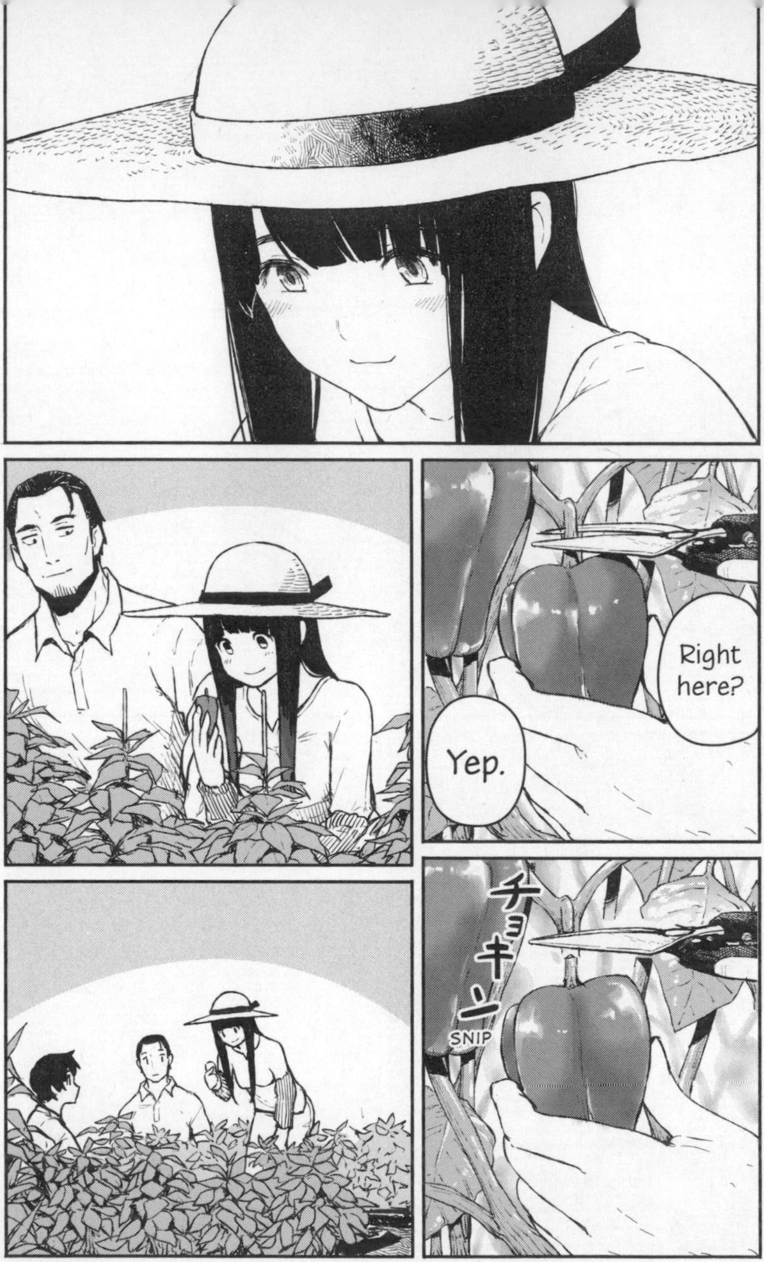
Right here?
Yep.
チョキン
SNIP

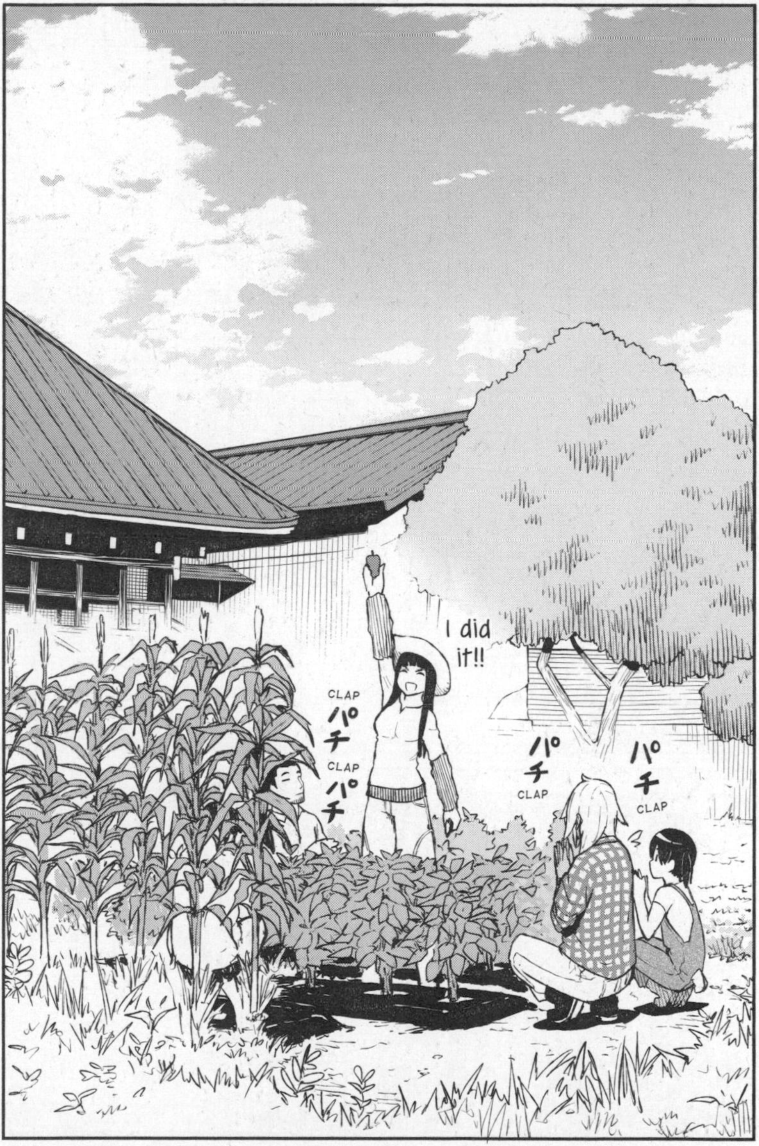
I did it!!
パチ
CLAP
パチ
CLAP
CLAP
パチ
CLAP
パチ

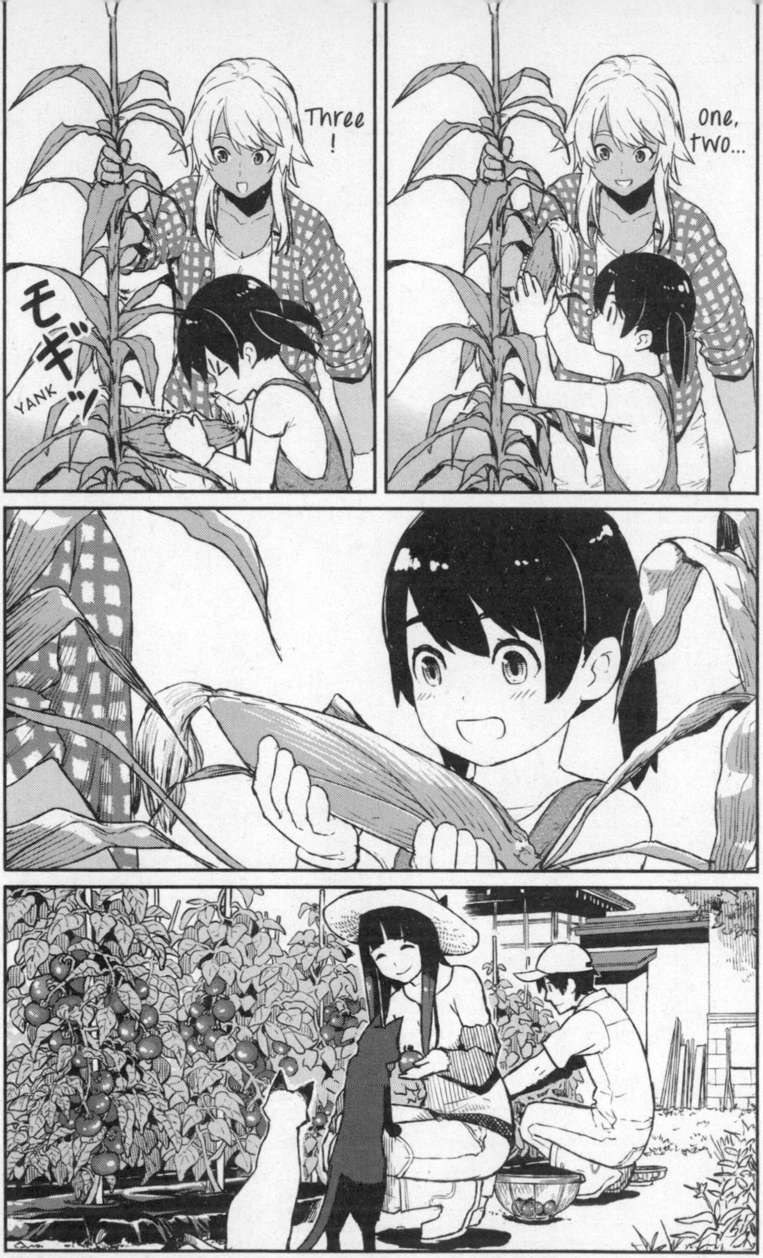
One, two...
Three!
モギッ
YANK

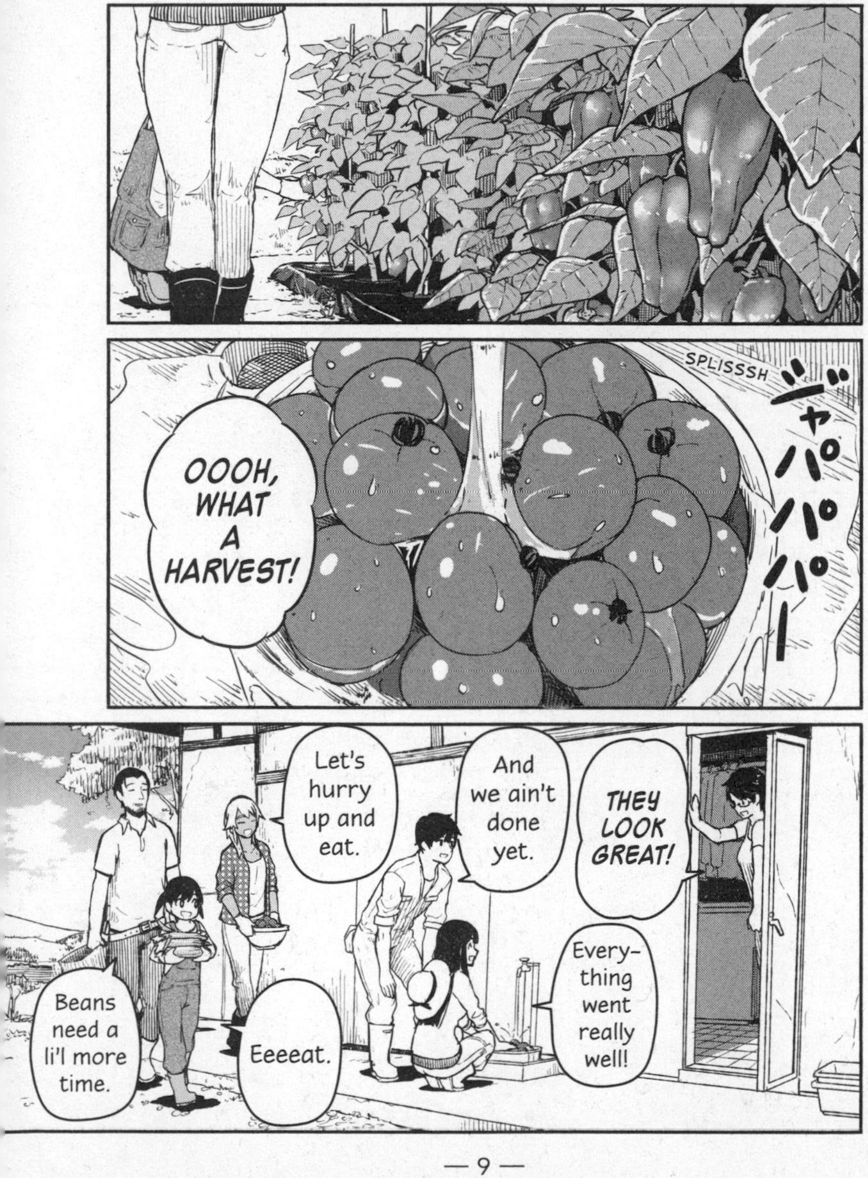
SPLISSSH
ジャパパパー
OOOH, WHAT A HARVEST!
THEY LOOK GREAT!
Every-thing went really well!
And we ain't done yet.
Let's hurry up and eat.
Eeeeat.
Beans need a li'l more time.

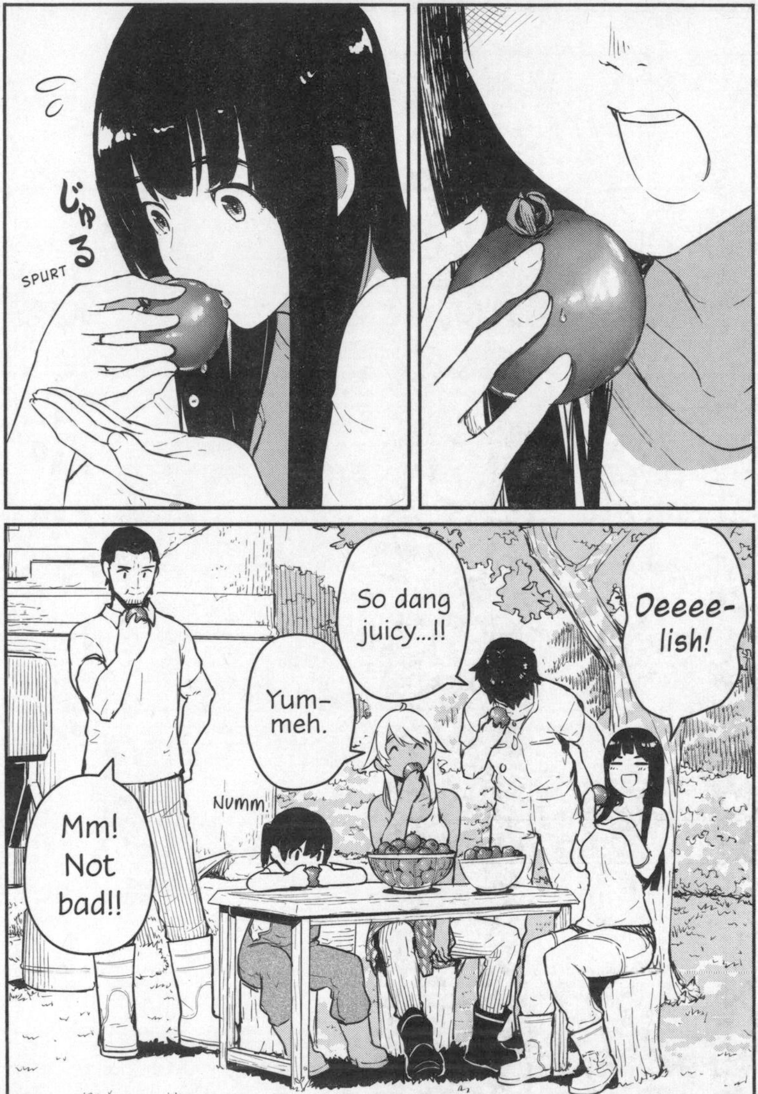
じゅる
SPURT
Deeee-lish!
So dang juicy...!!
Yum-meh.
Numm.
Mm! Not bad!!

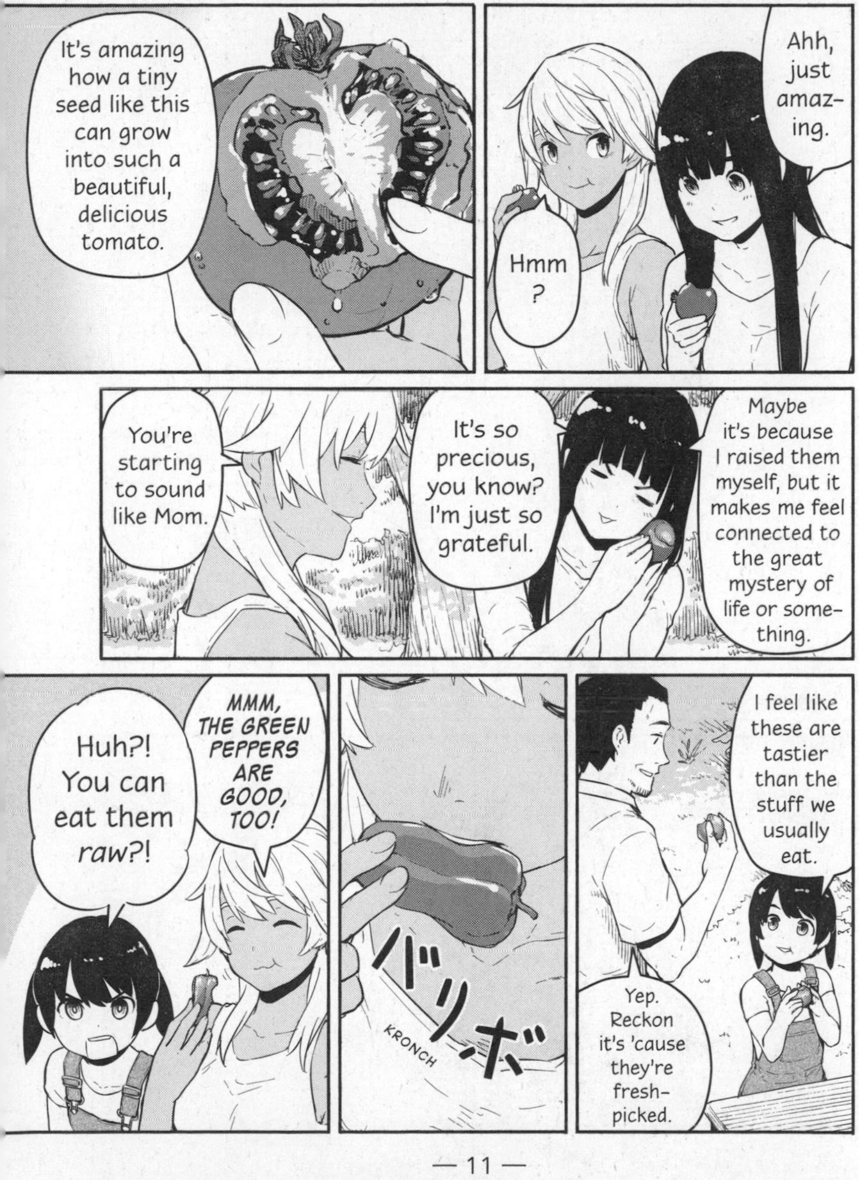
Ahh, just amaz-ing.
Hmm?
It's amazing how a tiny seed like this can grow into such a beautiful, delicious tomato.
Maybe it's because I raised them myself, but it makes me feel connected to the great mystery of life or some-thing.
It's so precious, you know? I'm just so grateful.
You're starting to sound like Mom.
I feel like these are tastier than the stuff we usually eat.
Yep. Reckon it's 'cause they're fresh-picked.
KRONCH
MMM, THE GREEN PEPPERS ARE GOOD, TOO!
Huh?! You can eat them raw?!

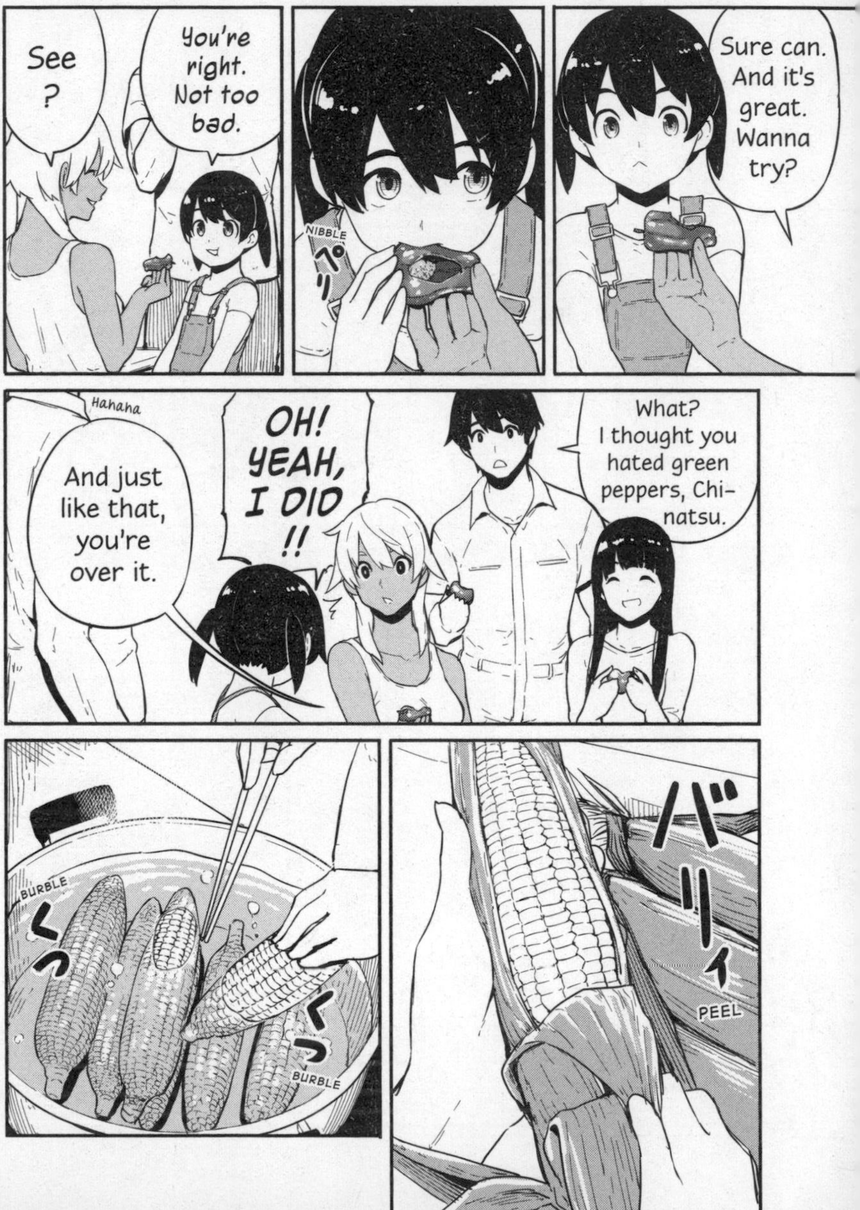

Sure can. And it's great. Wanna try?
NIBBLE
ペリ
You're right. Not too bad.
See?
What? I thought you hated green peppers, Chi-natsu.
OH! YEAH, I DID!!
Hahaha
And just like that, you're over it.
バリィ
PEEL
BURBLE
くつ
くつ
BURBLE

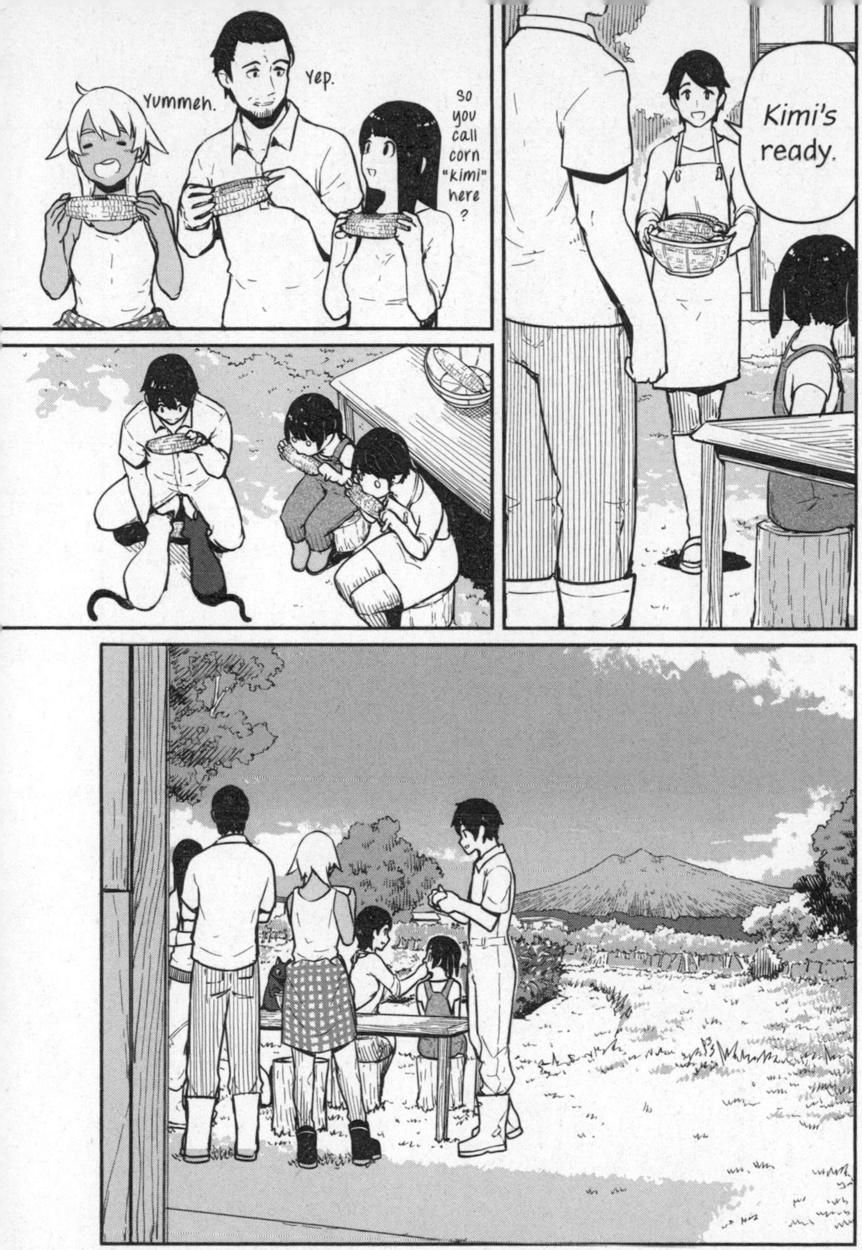
Kimi's ready.
So you call corn "kimi" here?
Yep.
Yummeh.

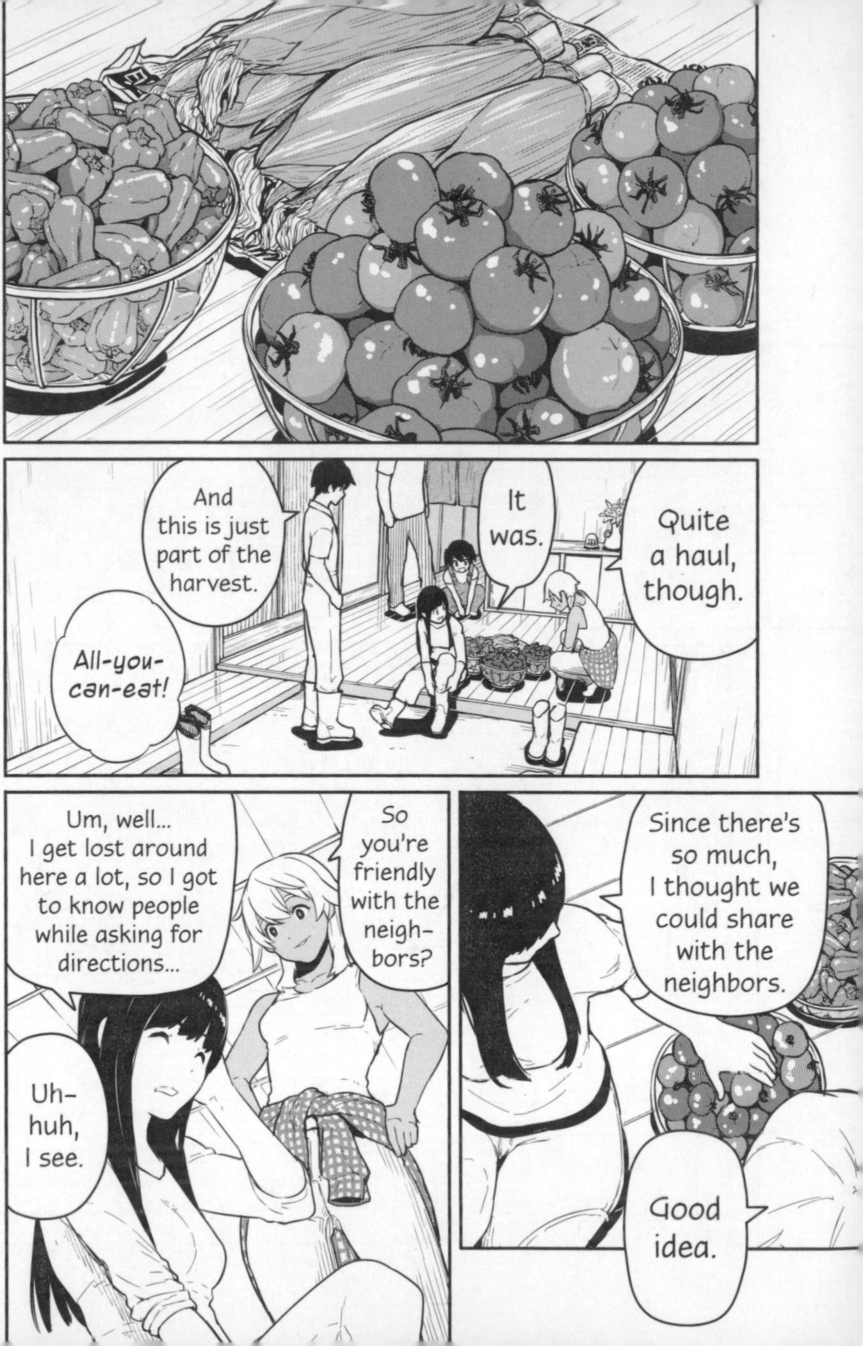
Quite a haul, though.
It was.
And this is just part of the harvest.
All-you-can-eat!
Since there's so much, I thought we could share with the neighbors.
Good idea.
So you're friendly with the neighbors?
Um, well... I get lost around here a lot, so I got to know people while asking for directions...
Uh-huh, I see.

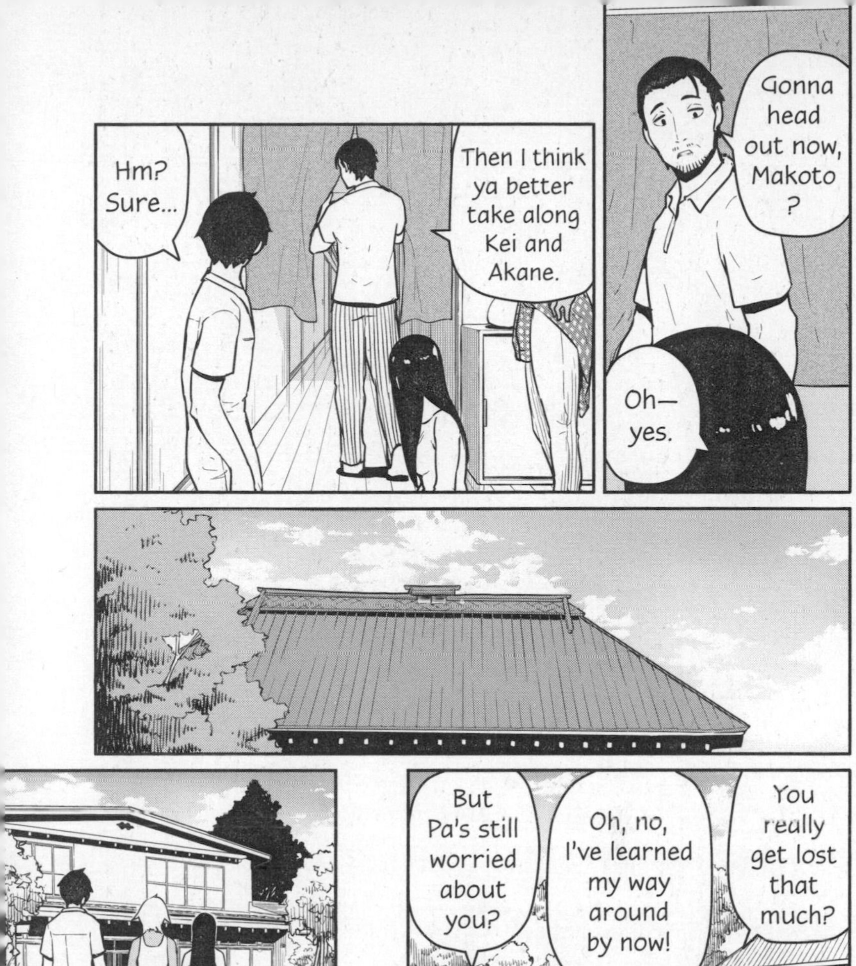
Gonna head out now, Makoto?
Oh— yes.
Then I think ya better take along Kei and Akane.
Hm? Sure...
You really get lost that much?
Oh, no, I've learned my way around by now!
But Pa's still worried about you?
OH, THERE HE IS.

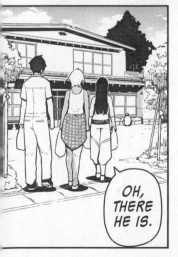

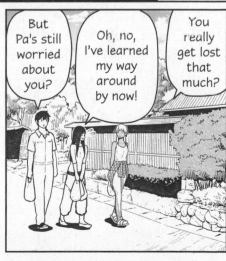

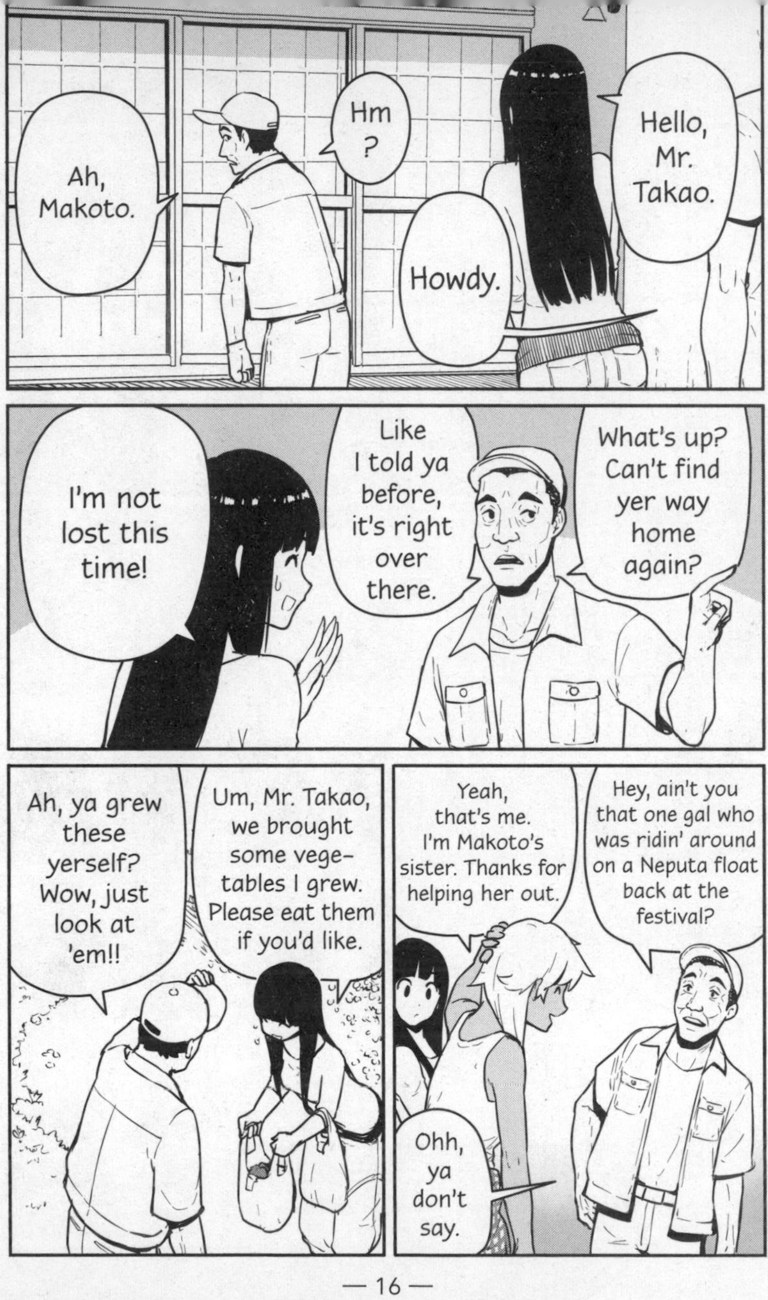
Hello, Mr. Takao.
Howdy.
Hm?
Ah, Makoto.
What's up? Can't find yer way home again?
Like I told ya before, it's right over there.
I'm not lost this time!
Hey, ain't you that one gal who was ridin' around on a Neputa float back at the festival?
Yeah, that's me. I'm Makoto's sister. Thanks for helping her out.
Ohh, ya don't say.
Um, Mr. Takao, we brought some vege-tables I grew. Please eat them if you'd like.
Ah, ya grew these yerself? Wow, just look at 'em!!

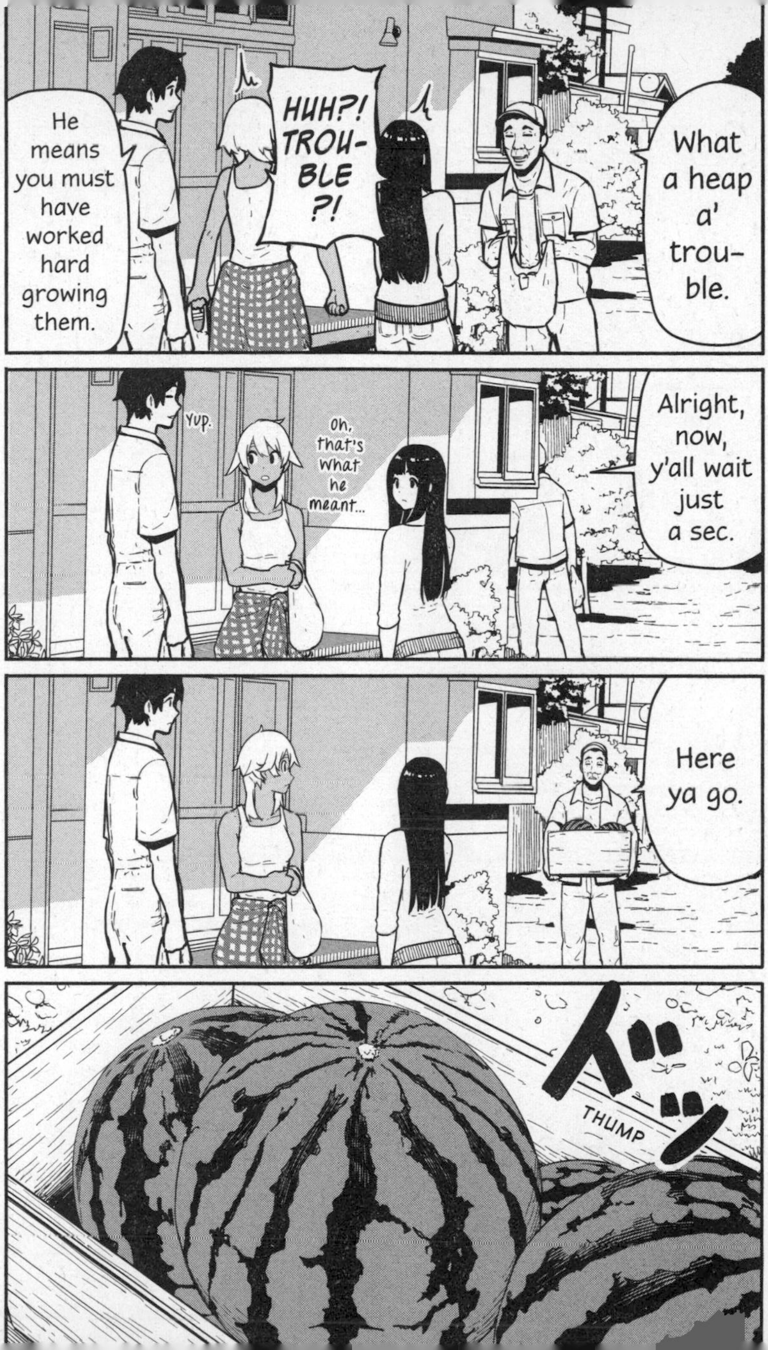
What a heap a' trouble.
HUH?! TROUBLE?!
He means you must have worked hard growing them.
Alright, now, y'all wait just a sec.
oh, that's what he meant...
Yup.
Here ya go.
ズッ
THUMP

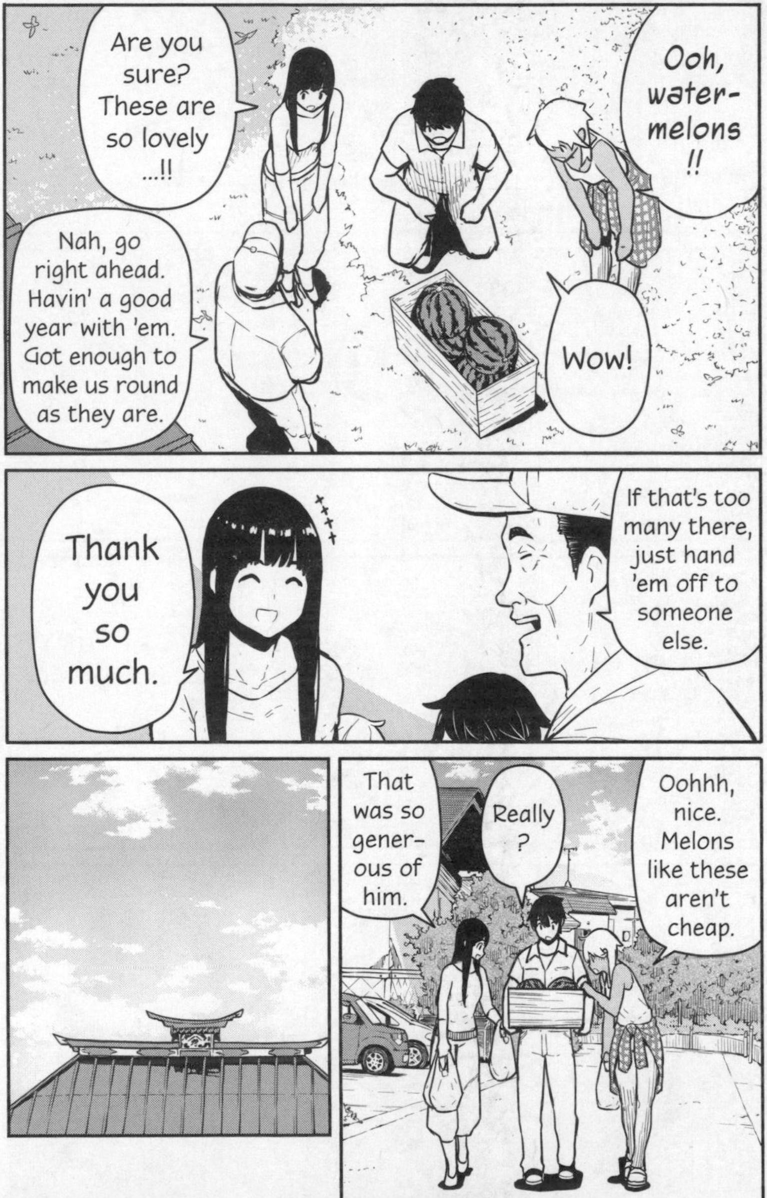
Ooh, water-melons !!
Wow!
Are you sure? These are so lovely ...!!
Nah, go right ahead. Havin' a good year with 'em. Got enough to make us round as they are.
If that's too many there, just hand 'em off to someone else.
Thank you so much.
Oohhh, nice. Melons like these aren't cheap.
Really ?
That was so gener-ous of him.

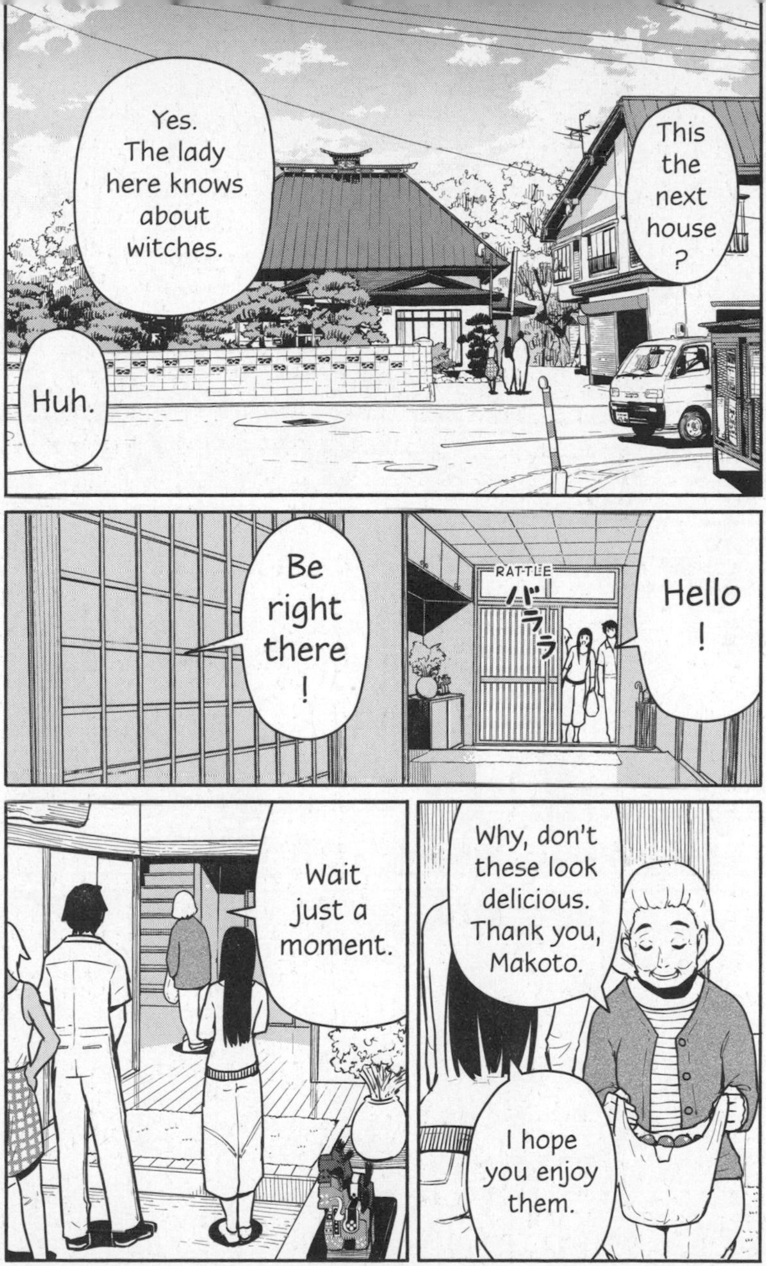
This the next house?
Yes. The lady here knows about witches.
Huh.
RATTLE バララ
Hello!
Be right there!
Why, don't these look delicious. Thank you, Makoto.
I hope you enjoy them.
Wait just a moment.

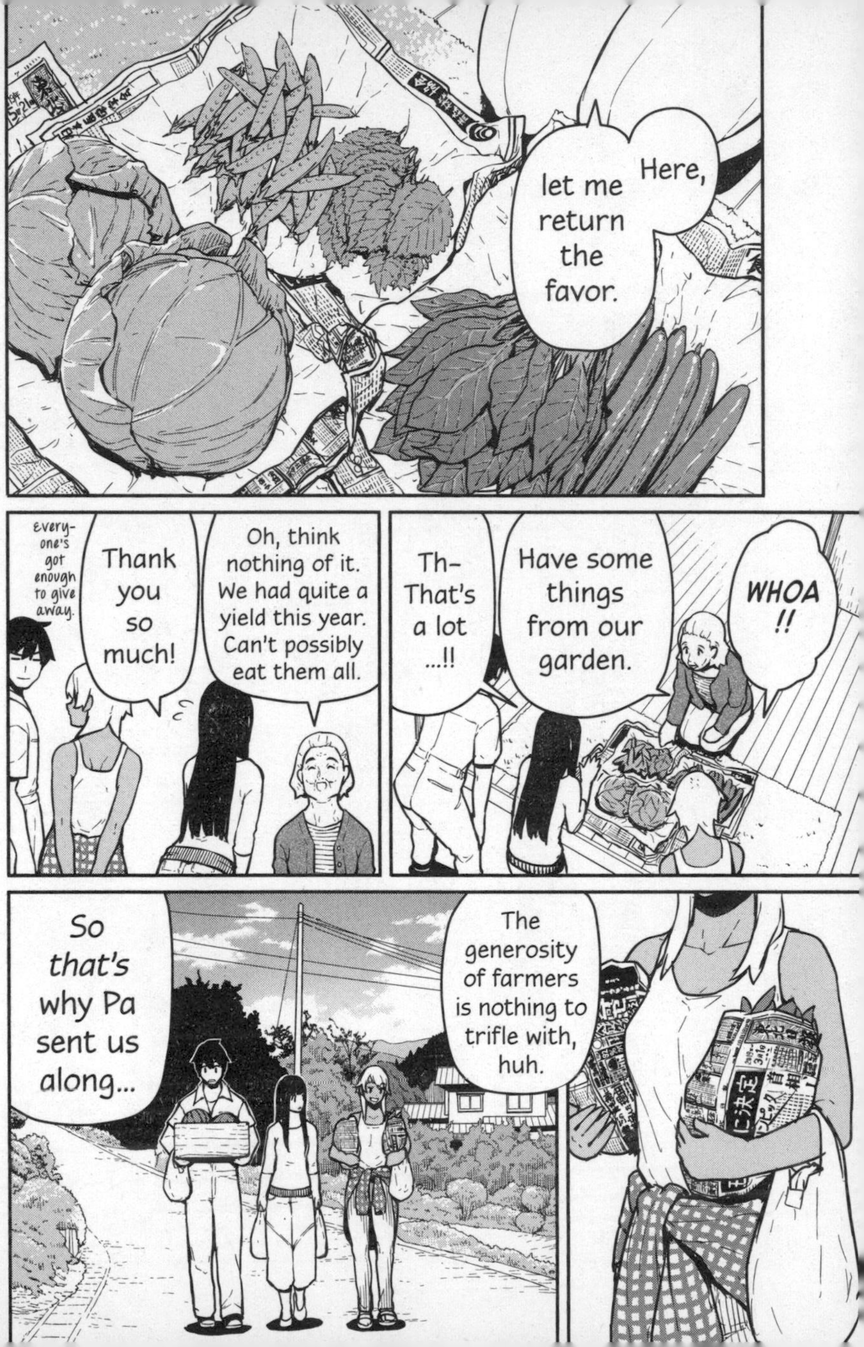
Here, let me return the favor.
WHOA !!
Have some things from our garden.
Th- That's a lot ...!!
Oh, think nothing of it. We had quite a yield this year. Can't possibly eat them all.
Thank you so much!
Every-one's got enough to give away.
The generosity of farmers is nothing to trifle with, huh.
So *that's* why Pa sent us along...

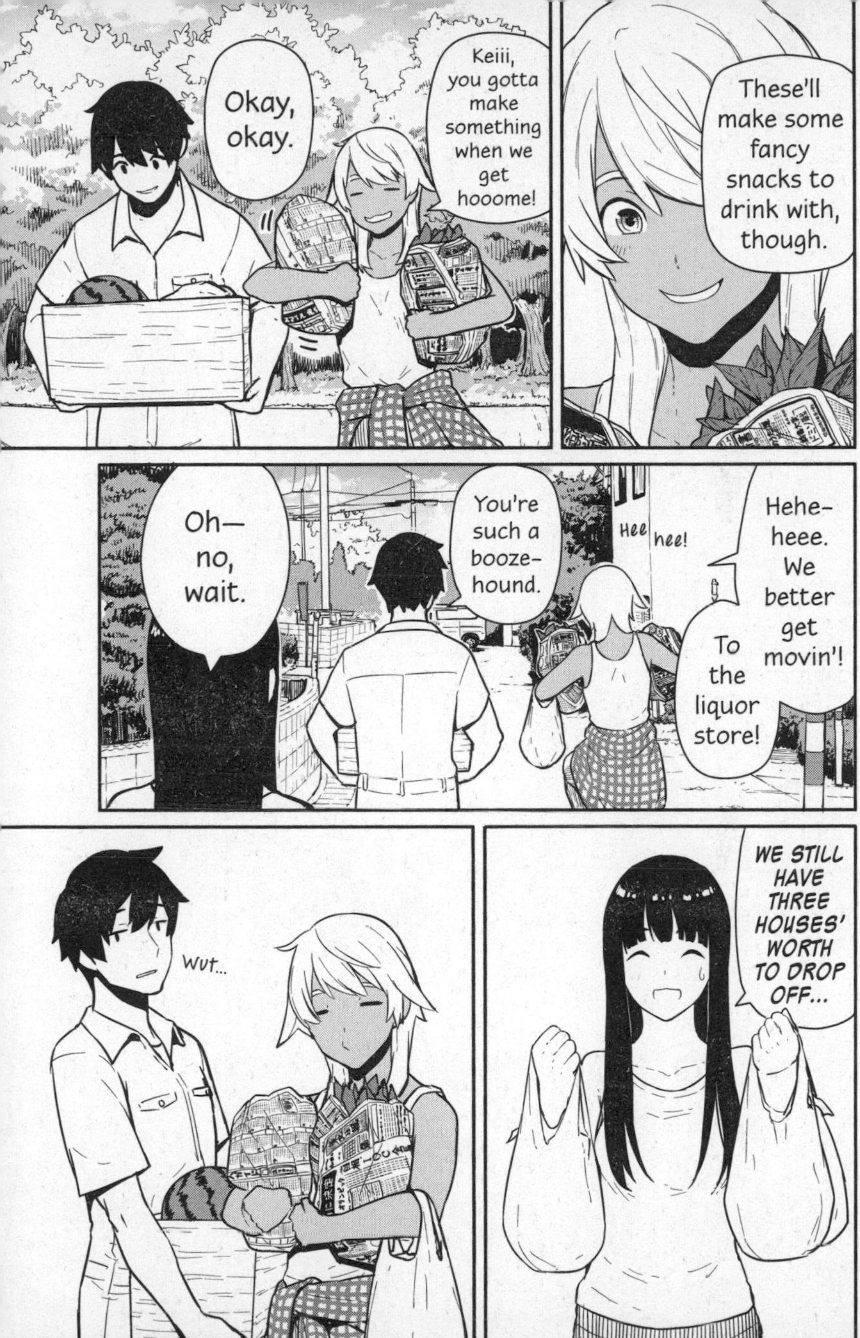
These'll make some fancy snacks to drink with, though.
Keiii, you gotta make something when we get hooome!
Okay, okay.
Hehe-heee. We better get movin'!
To the liquor store!
Hee hee!
You're such a booze-hound.
Oh— no, wait.
WE STILL HAVE THREE HOUSES' WORTH TO DROP OFF...
Wut...

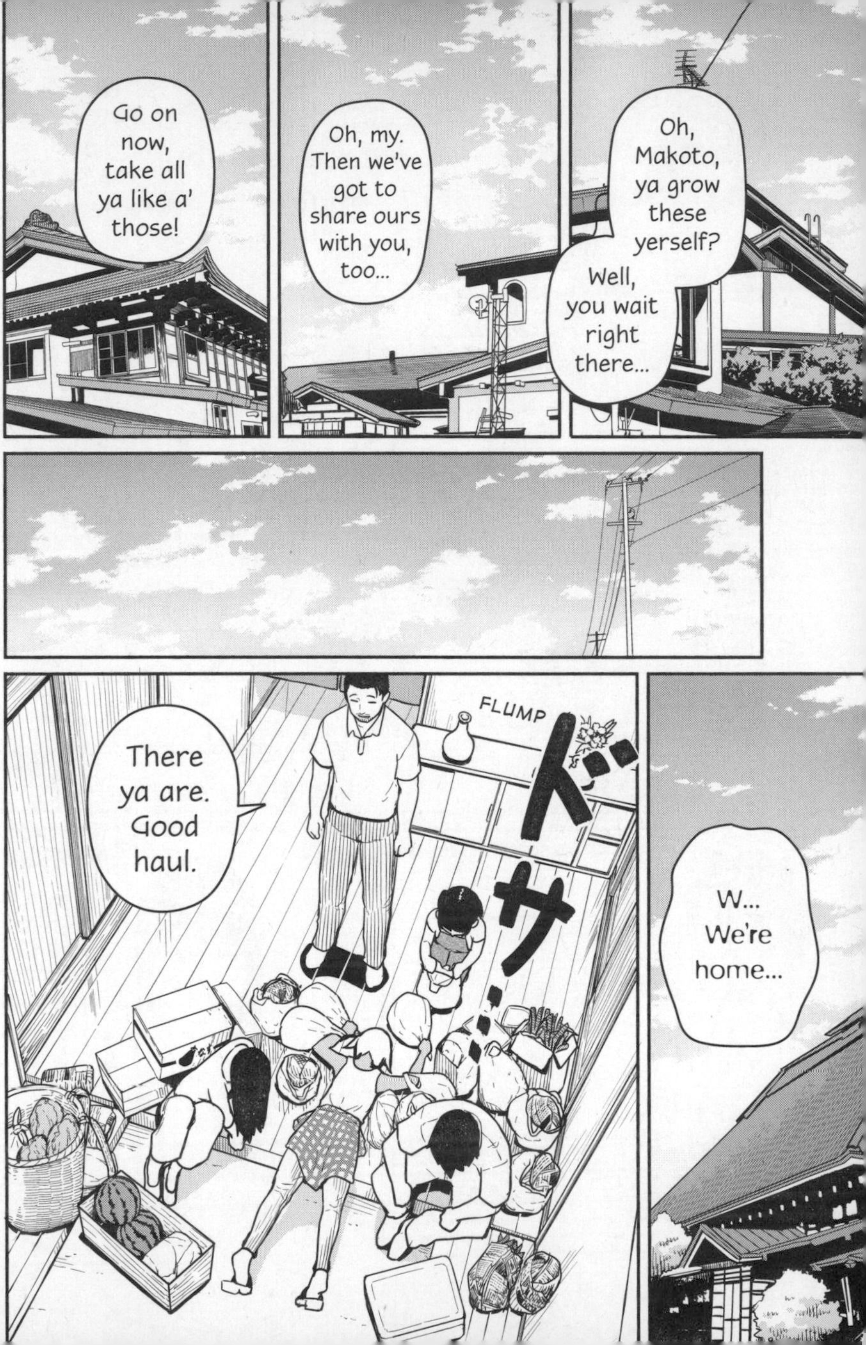
Oh, Makoto, ya grow these yerself?
Well, you wait right there...
Oh, my. Then we've got to share ours with you, too...
Go on now, take all ya like a' those!
W... We're home...
FLUMP
ドサ
There ya are. Good haul.

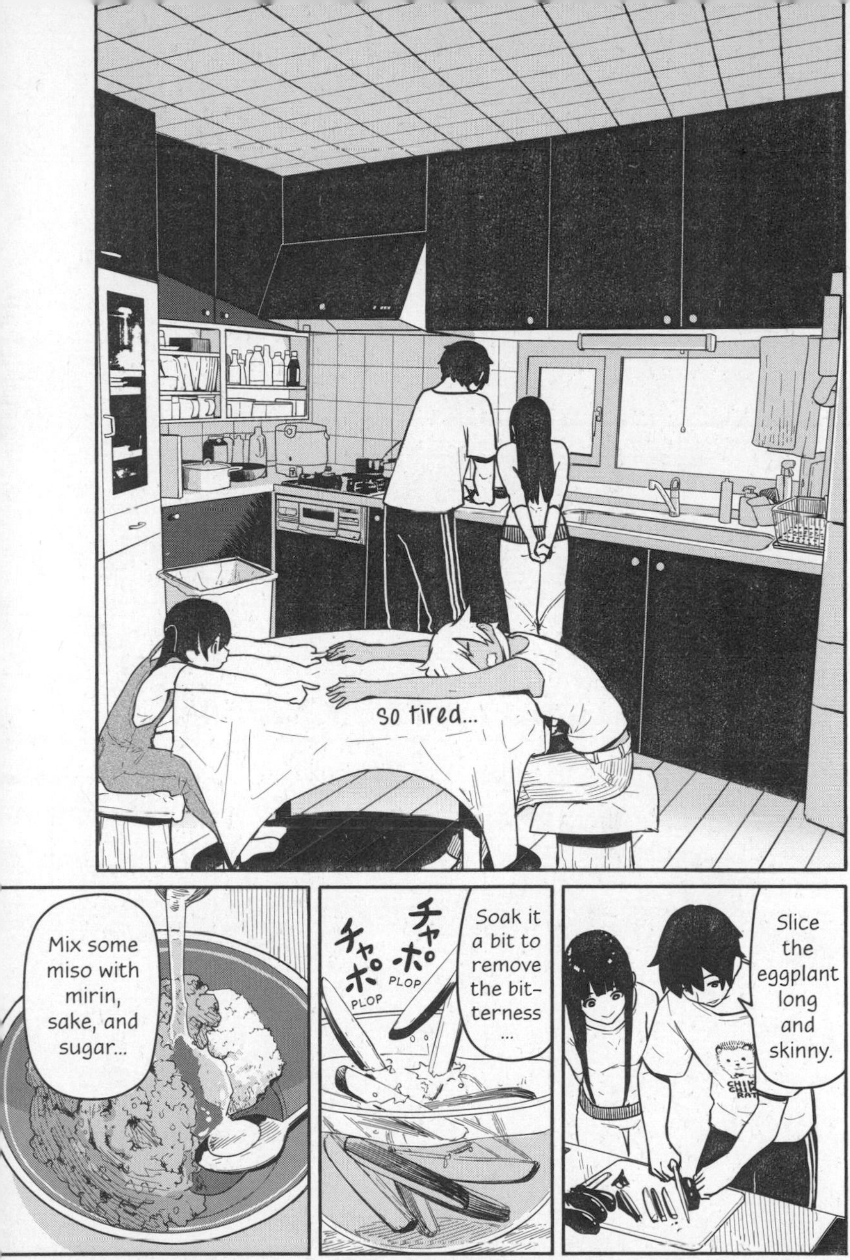
so tired...
Slice the eggplant long and skinny.
Soak it a bit to remove the bit-terness ...
チャポ PLOP
チャポ PLOP
Mix some miso with mirin, sake, and sugar...

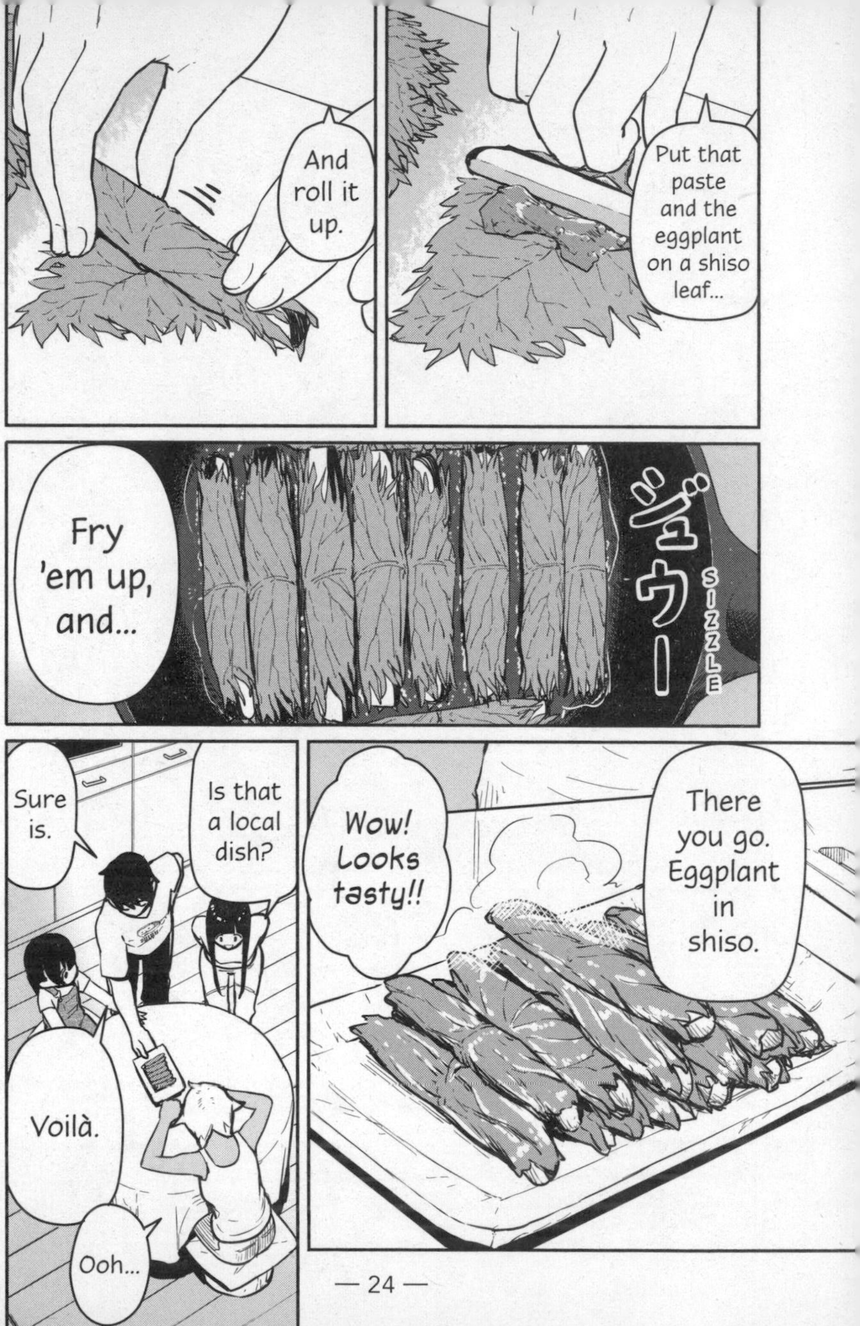
Put that paste and the eggplant on a shiso leaf...
And roll it up.
Fry 'em up, and...
ジュウー
SIZZLE
There you go. Eggplant in shiso.
Wow! Looks tasty!!
Is that a local dish?
Sure is.
Voilà.
Ooh...

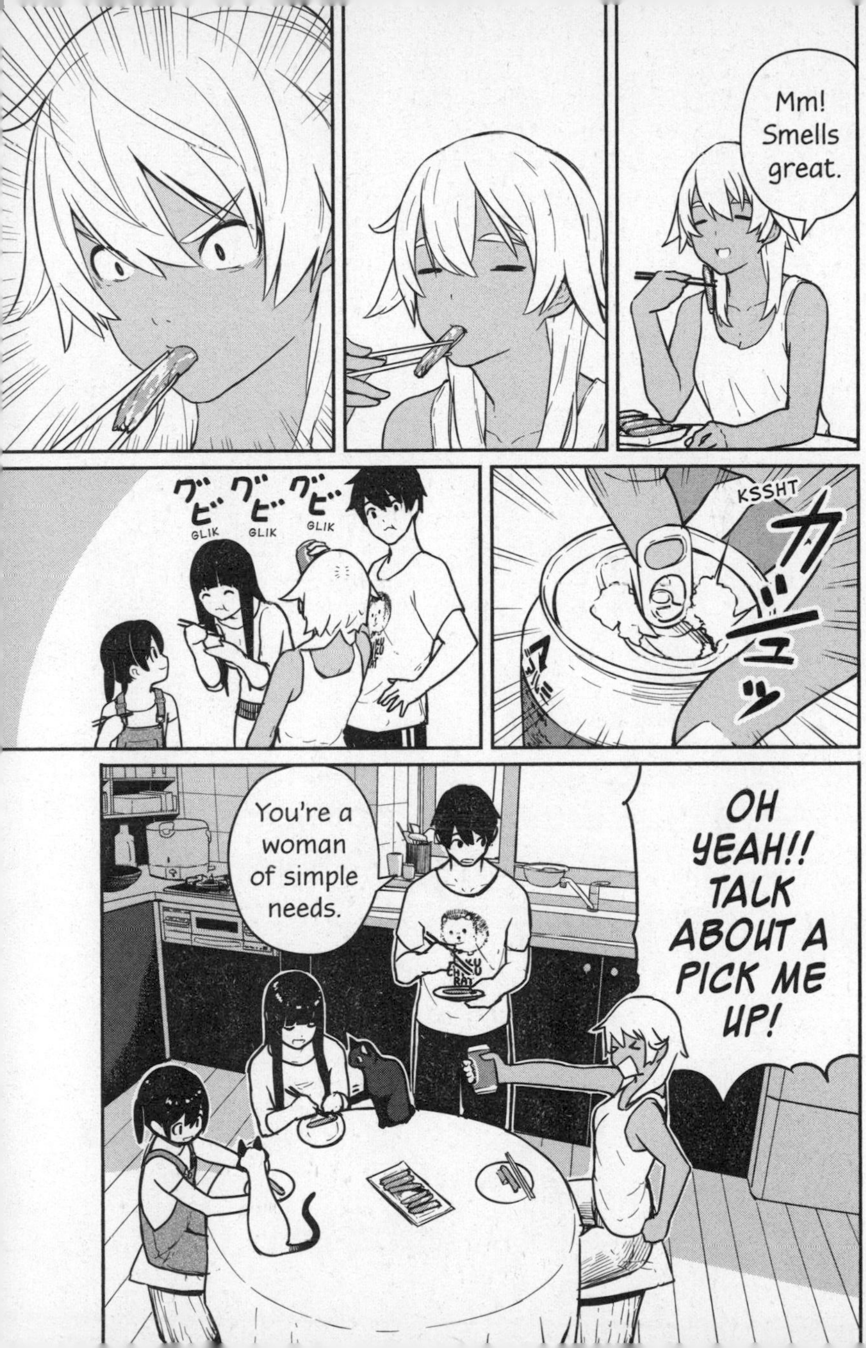
Mm! Smells great.
KSSHT
グビ グビ グビ
GLIK GLIK GLIK
OH YEAH!! TALK ABOUT A PICK ME UP!
You're a woman of simple needs.

BRO COOKING

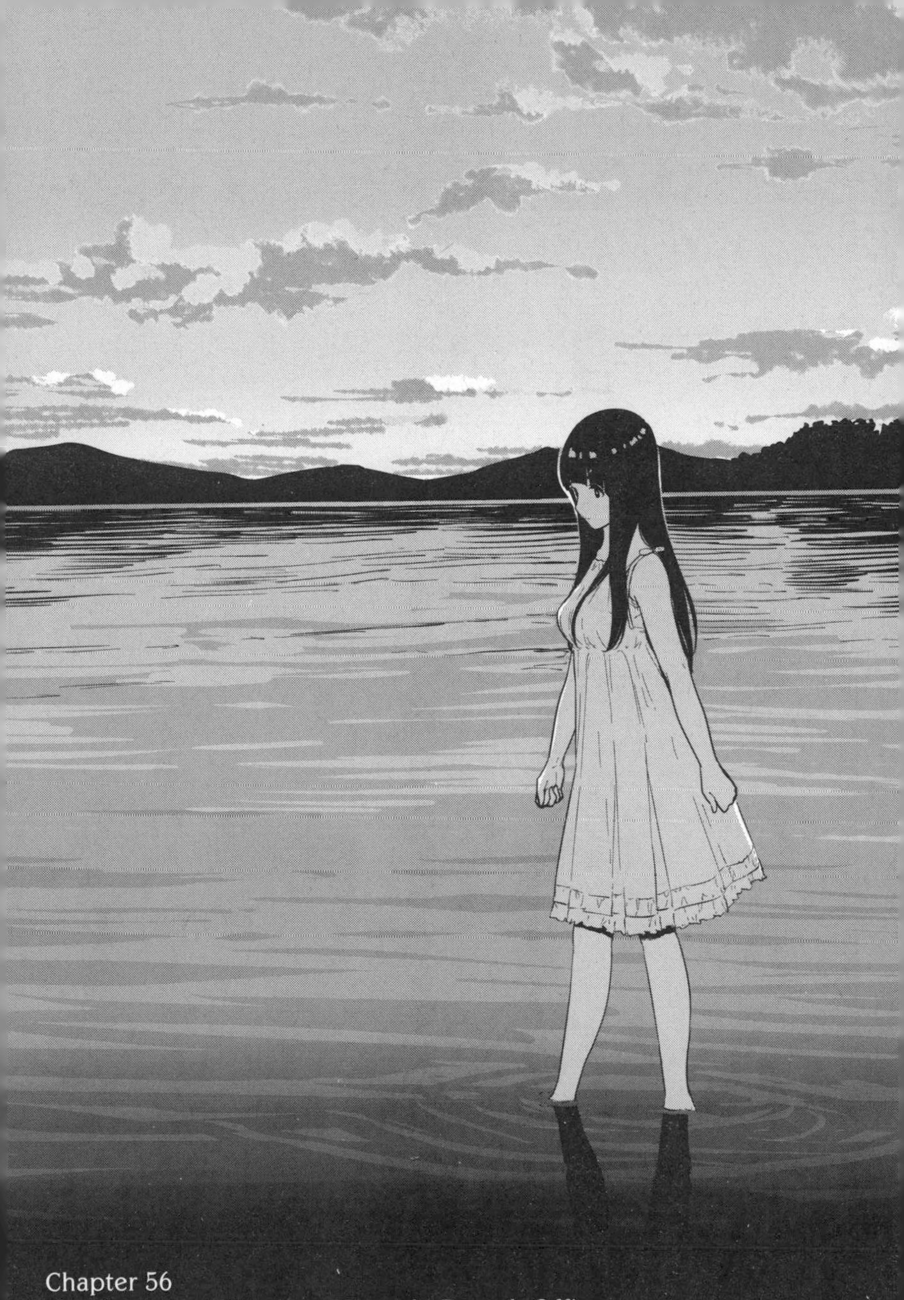

Chapter 56
The Society of Witches, Hirosaki Branch Office

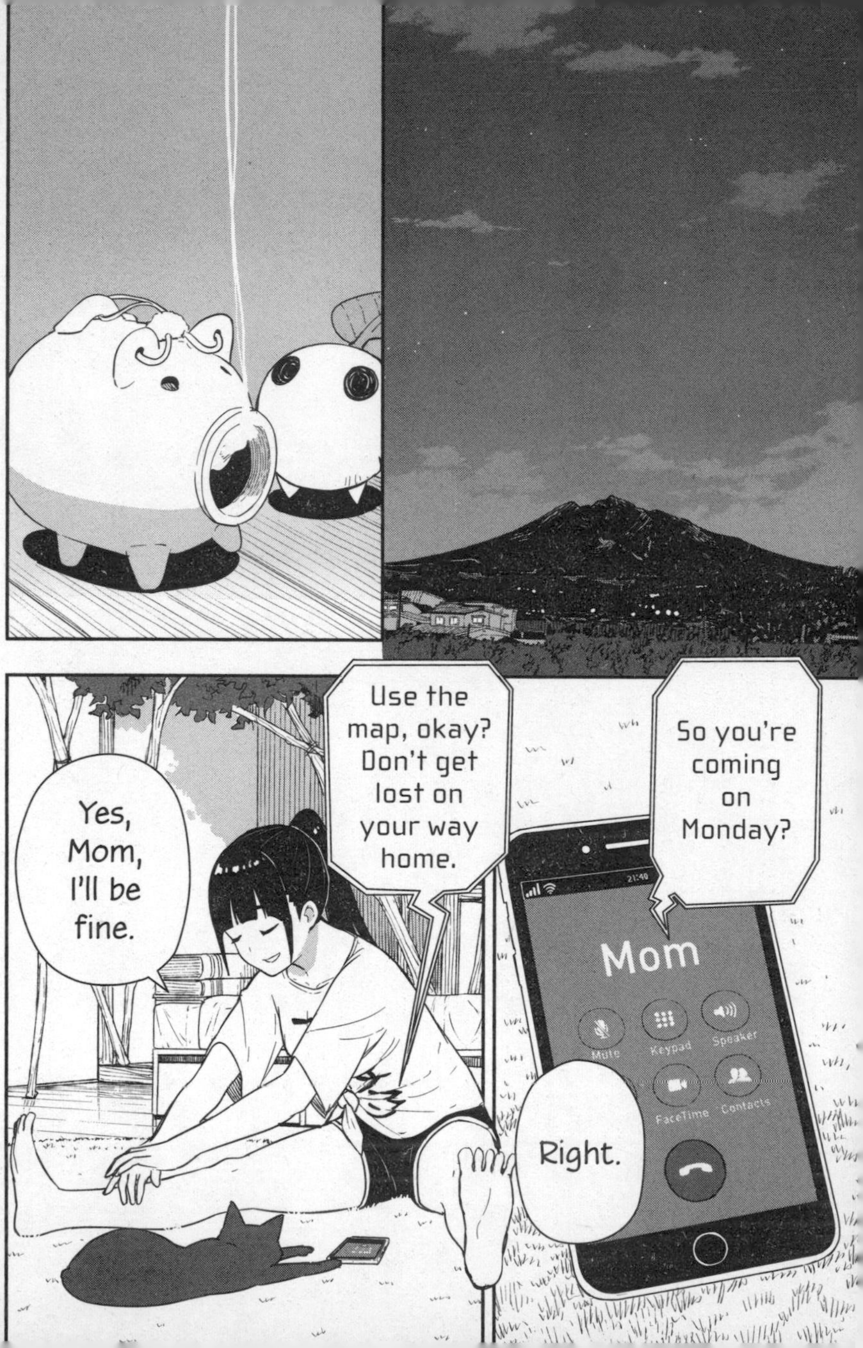
So you're coming on Monday?
Mom
Mute
Keypad
Speaker
FaceTime
Contacts
Right.
Use the map, okay? Don't get lost on your way home.
Yes, Mom, I'll be fine.

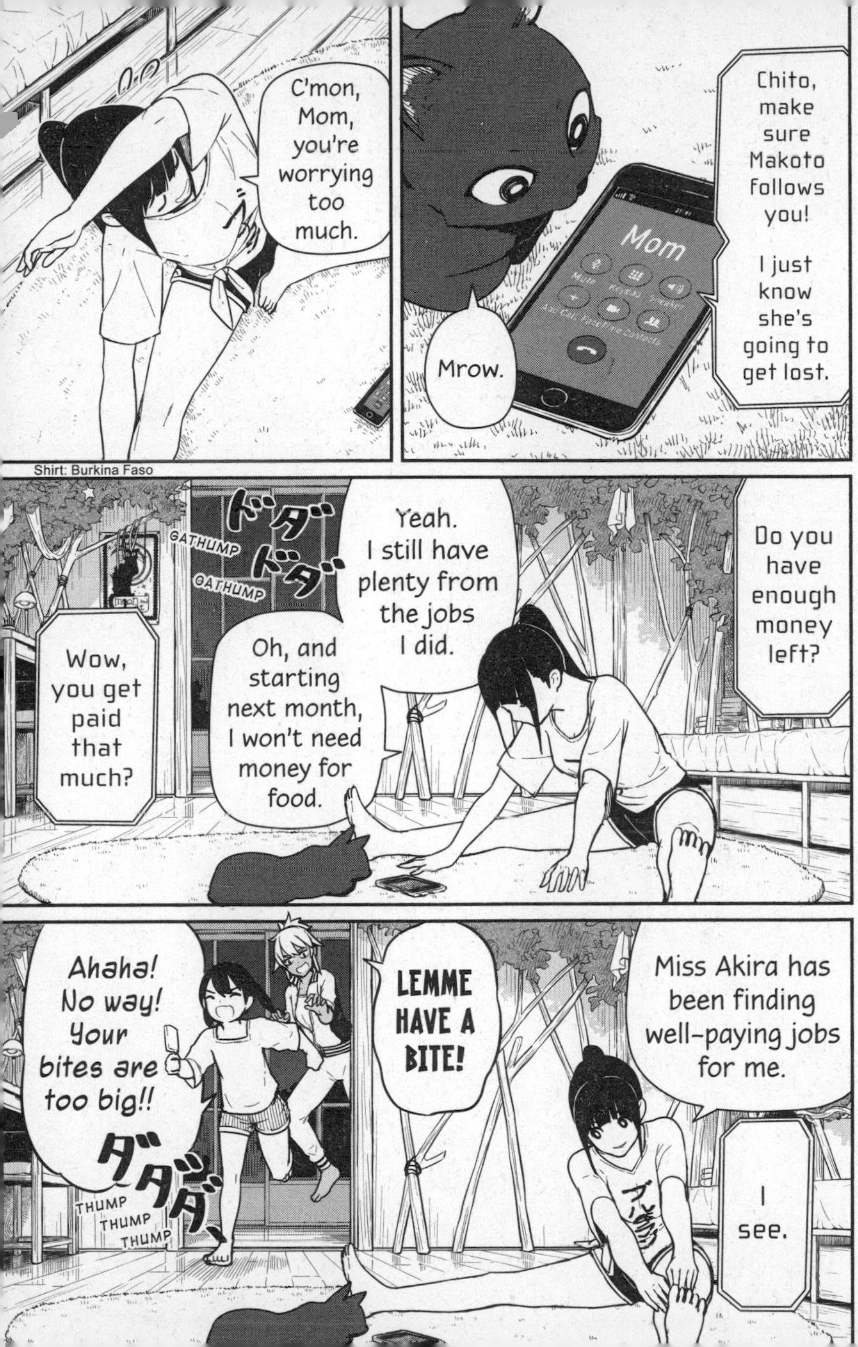
Chito, make sure Makoto follows you! I just know she's going to get lost.
Mom
Mrow.
C'mon, Mom, you're worrying too much.
Shirt: Burkina Faso
Do you have enough money left?
Yeah. I still have plenty from the jobs I did.
Oh, and starting next month, I won't need money for food.
ドダ ドダ
GATHUMP GATHUMP
Wow, you get paid that much?
Miss Akira has been finding well-paying jobs for me.
I see.
LEMME HAVE A BITE!
Ahaha! No way! Your bites are too big!!
ダダダ
THUMP THUMP THUMP

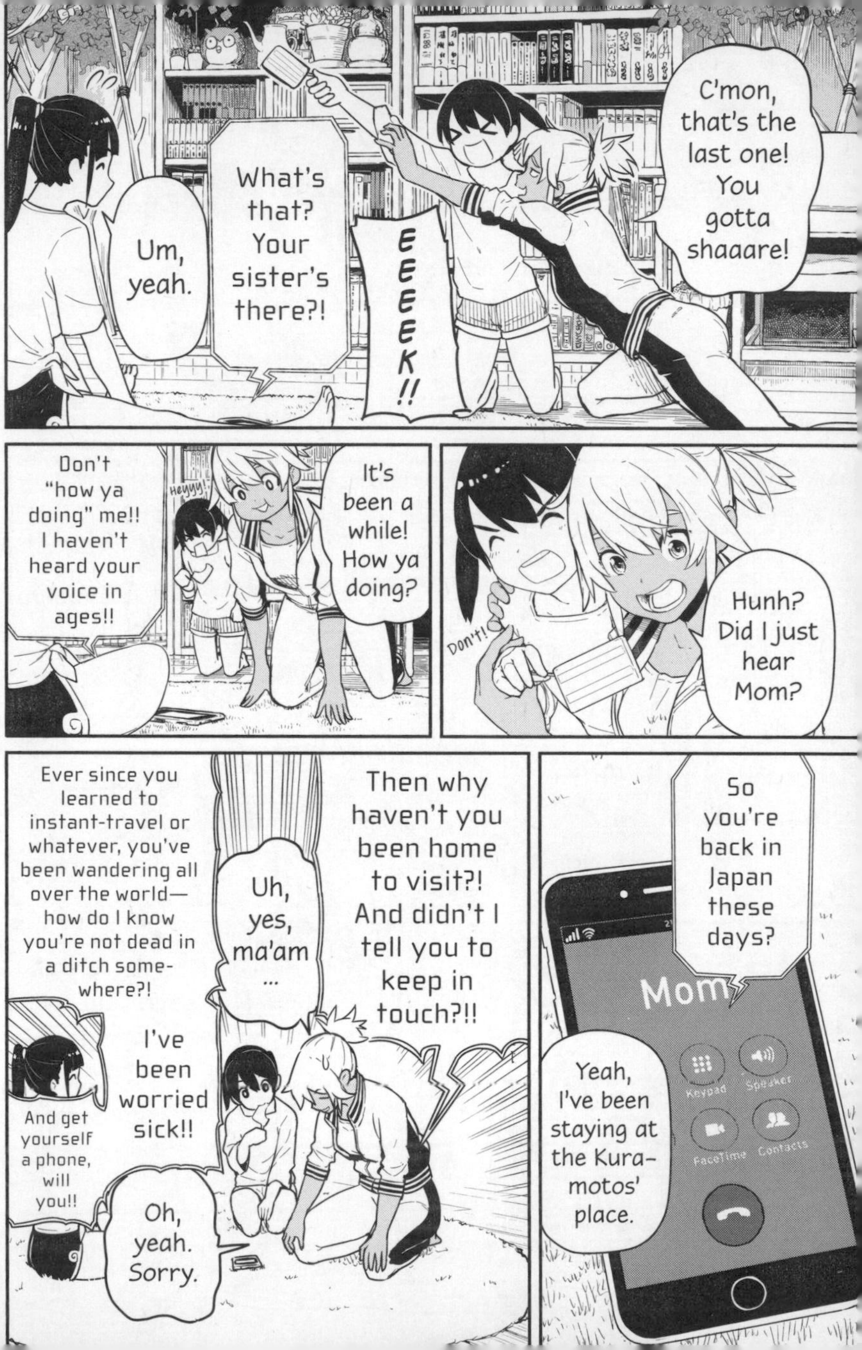
C'mon, that's the last one! You gotta shaaare!
EEEEK!!
What's that? Your sister's there?!
Um, yeah.
Hunh? Did I just hear Mom?
Don't!
It's been a while! How ya doing?
Heyyy!
Don't "how ya doing" me!! I haven't heard your voice in ages!!
So you're back in Japan these days?
Mom
Keypad
Speaker
FaceTime
Contacts
Yeah, I've been staying at the Kuramotos' place.
Then why haven't you been home to visit?! And didn't I tell you to keep in touch?!!
Uh, yes, ma'am ...
Ever since you learned to instant-travel or whatever, you've been wandering all over the world—how do I know you're not dead in a ditch somewhere?!
I've been worried sick!!
And get yourself a phone, will you!!
Oh, yeah. Sorry.

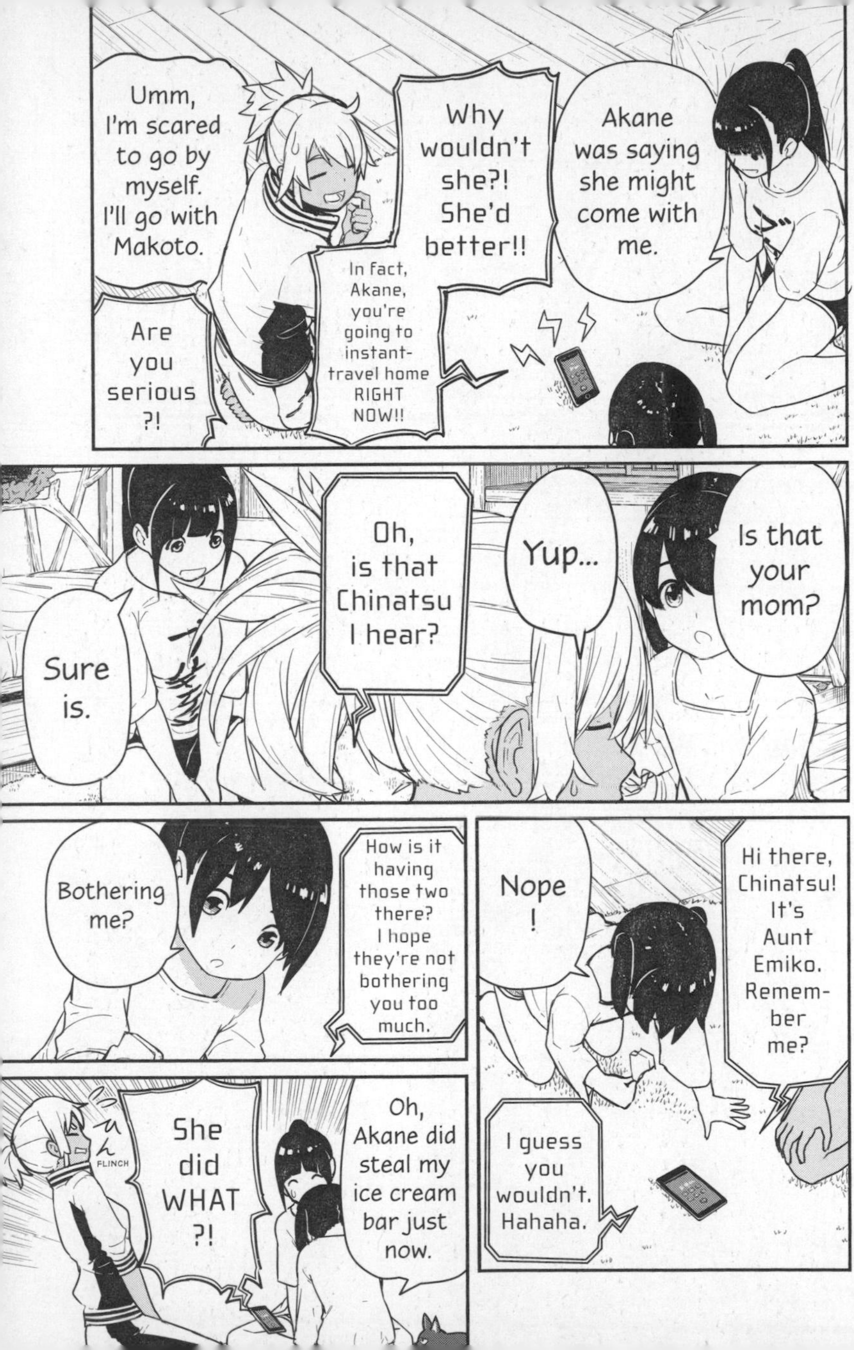
Akane was saying she might come with me.
Why wouldn't she?! She'd better!!
In fact, Akane, you're going to instant-travel home RIGHT NOW!!
Umm, I'm scared to go by myself. I'll go with Makoto.
Are you serious?!
Is that your mom?
Yup...
Oh, is that Chinatsu I hear?
Sure is.
Hi there, Chinatsu! It's Aunt Emiko. Remember me?
Nope!
I guess you wouldn't. Hahaha.
How is it having those two there? I hope they're not bothering you too much.
Bothering me?
Oh, Akane did steal my ice cream bar just now.
She did WHAT?!
FLINCH

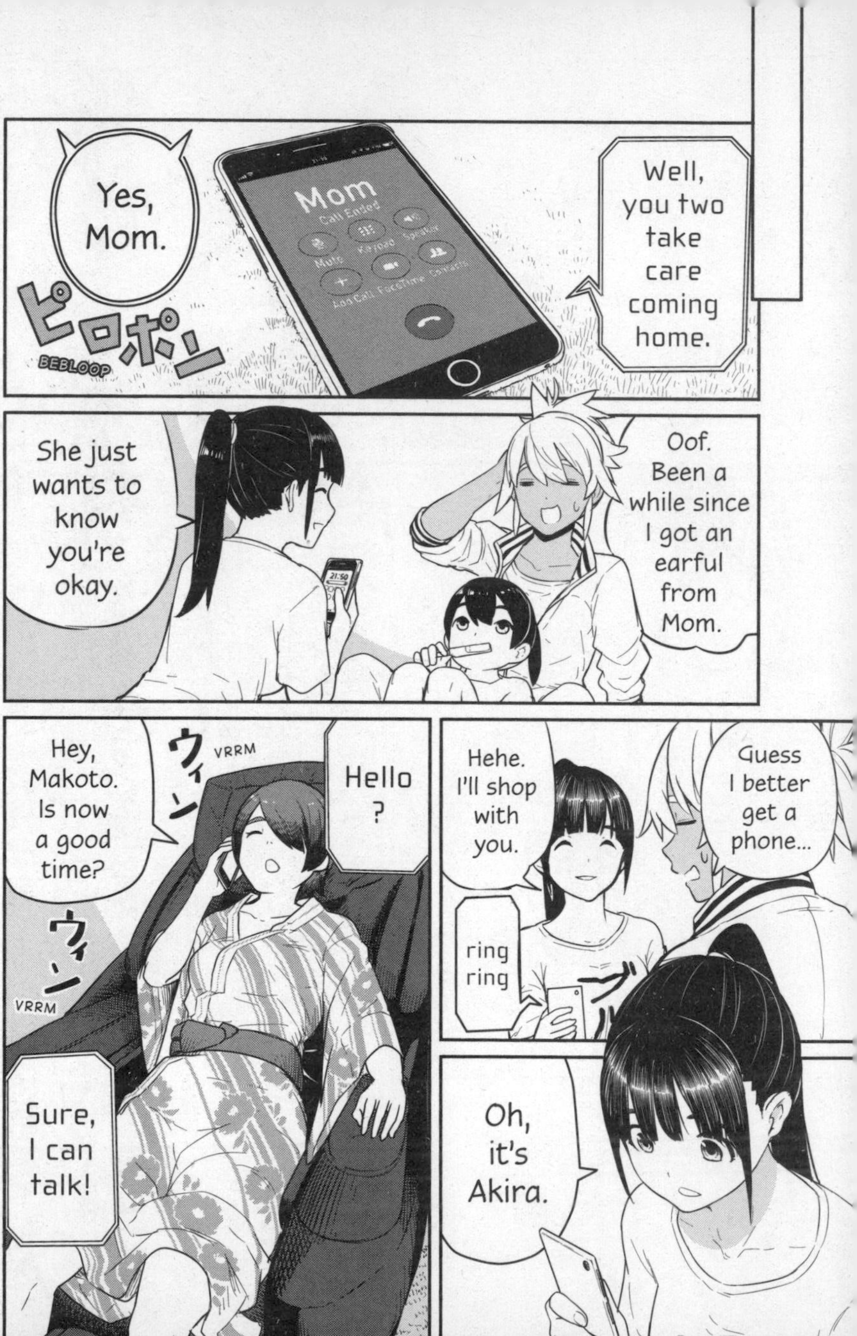
Well, you two take care coming home.
Mom
Call Ended
Mute Keypad Speaker
Add Call FaceTime Contacts
Yes, Mom.
ピロポン
BEBLOOP
Oof. Been a while since I got an earful from Mom.
She just wants to know you're okay.
21:50
Guess I better get a phone...
Hehe. I'll shop with you.
ring ring
Oh, it's Akira.
Hello?
ウィン
VRRM
Hey, Makoto. Is now a good time?
ウィン
VRRM
Sure, I can talk!

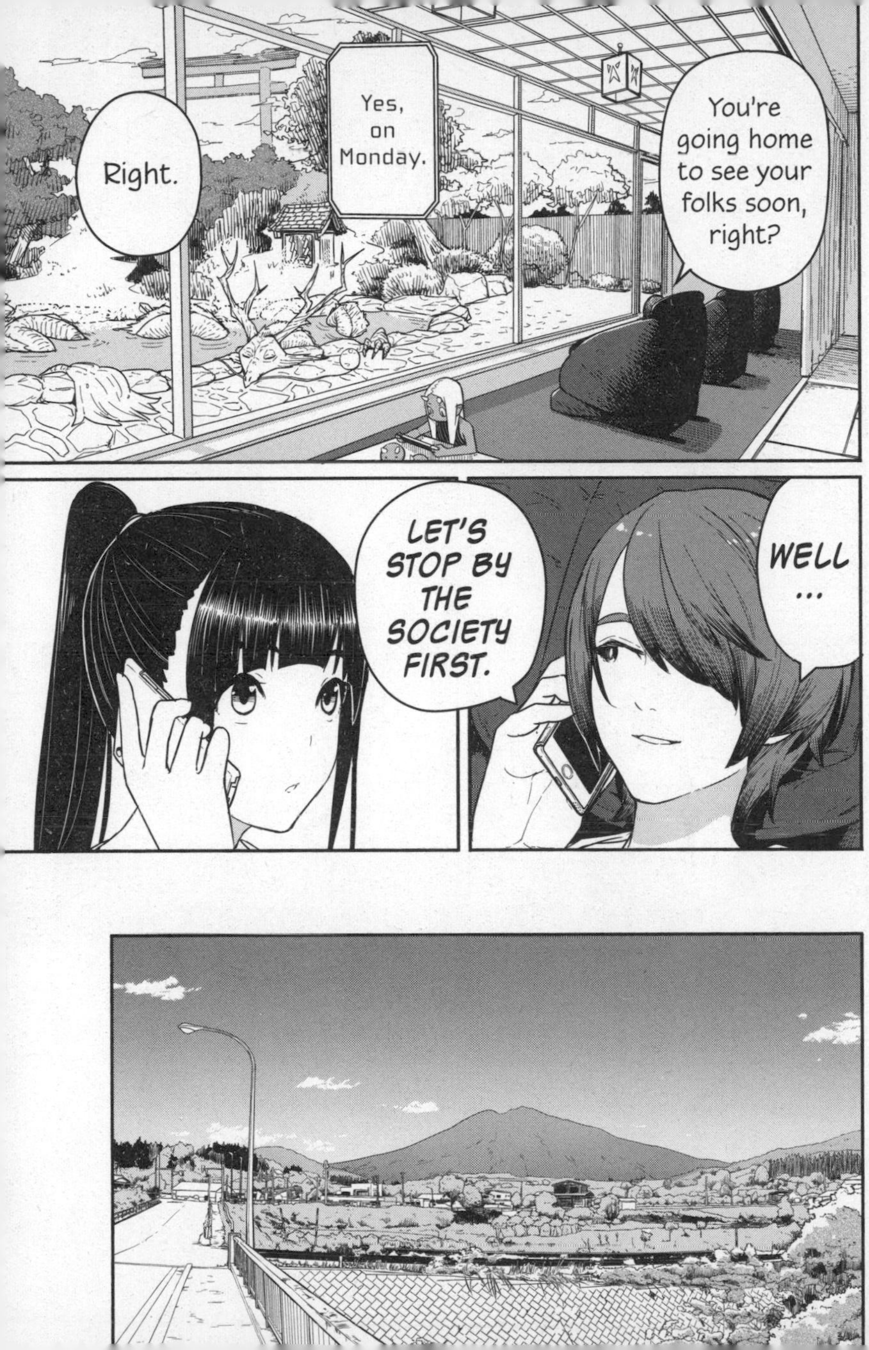
You're going home to see your folks soon, right?
Yes, on Monday.
Right.
WELL ...
LET'S STOP BY THE SOCIETY FIRST.

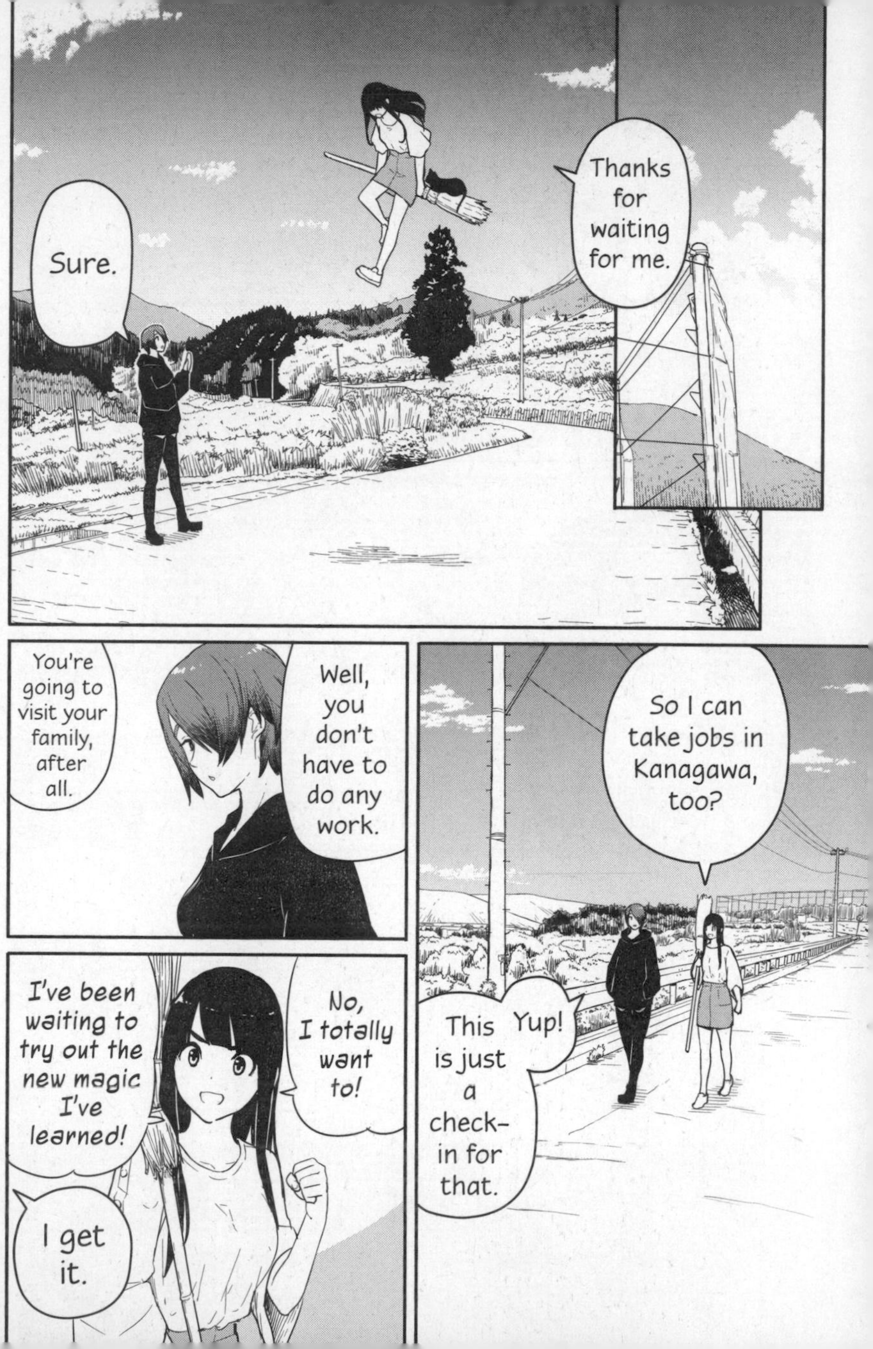
Thanks for waiting for me.
Sure.
So I can take jobs in Kanagawa, too?
Yup!
This is just a check-in for that.
Well, you don't have to do any work.
You're going to visit your family, after all.
No, I totally want to!
I've been waiting to try out the new magic I've learned!
I get it.

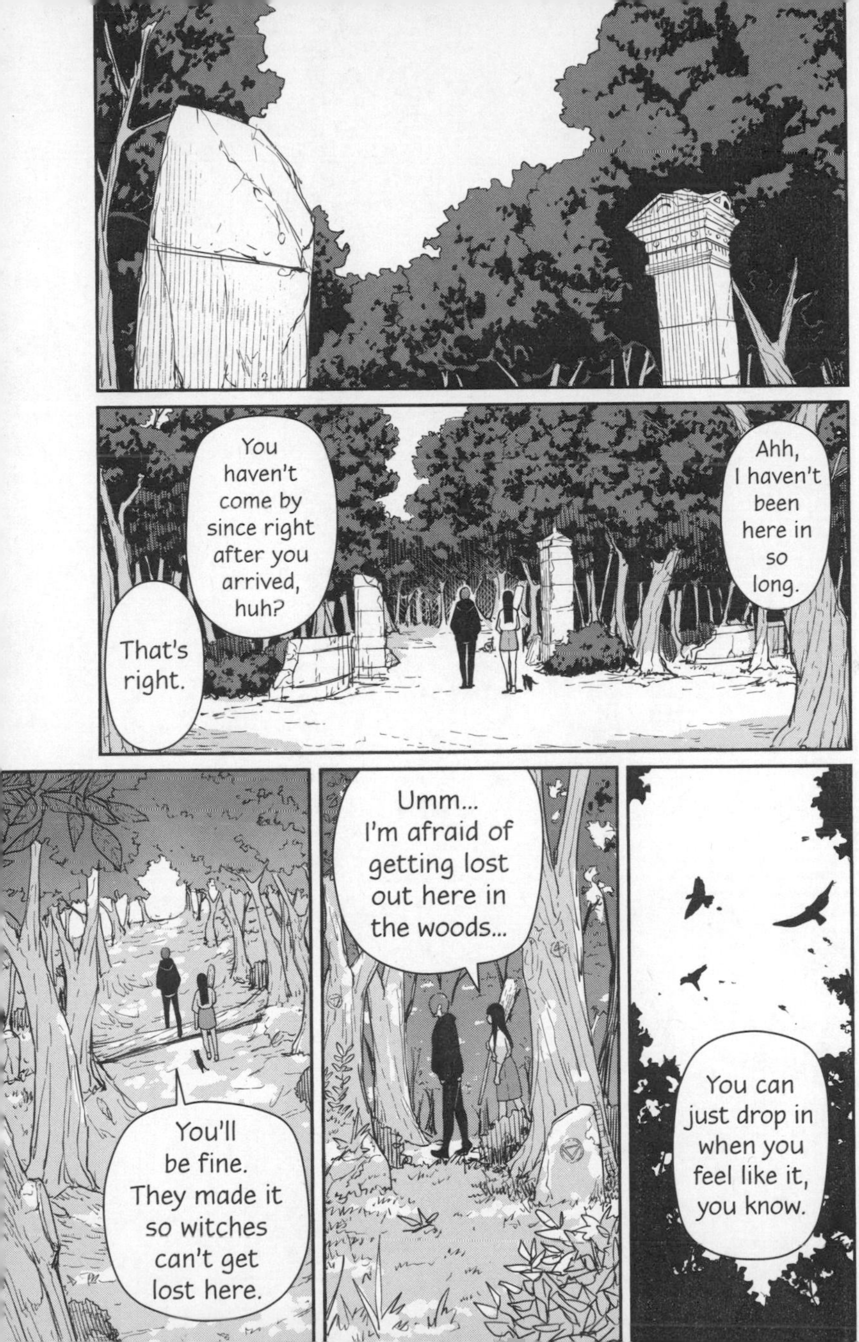
Ahh, I haven't been here in so long.
You haven't come by since right after you arrived, huh?
That's right.
You can just drop in when you feel like it, you know.
Umm... I'm afraid of getting lost out here in the woods...
You'll be fine. They made it so witches can't get lost here.

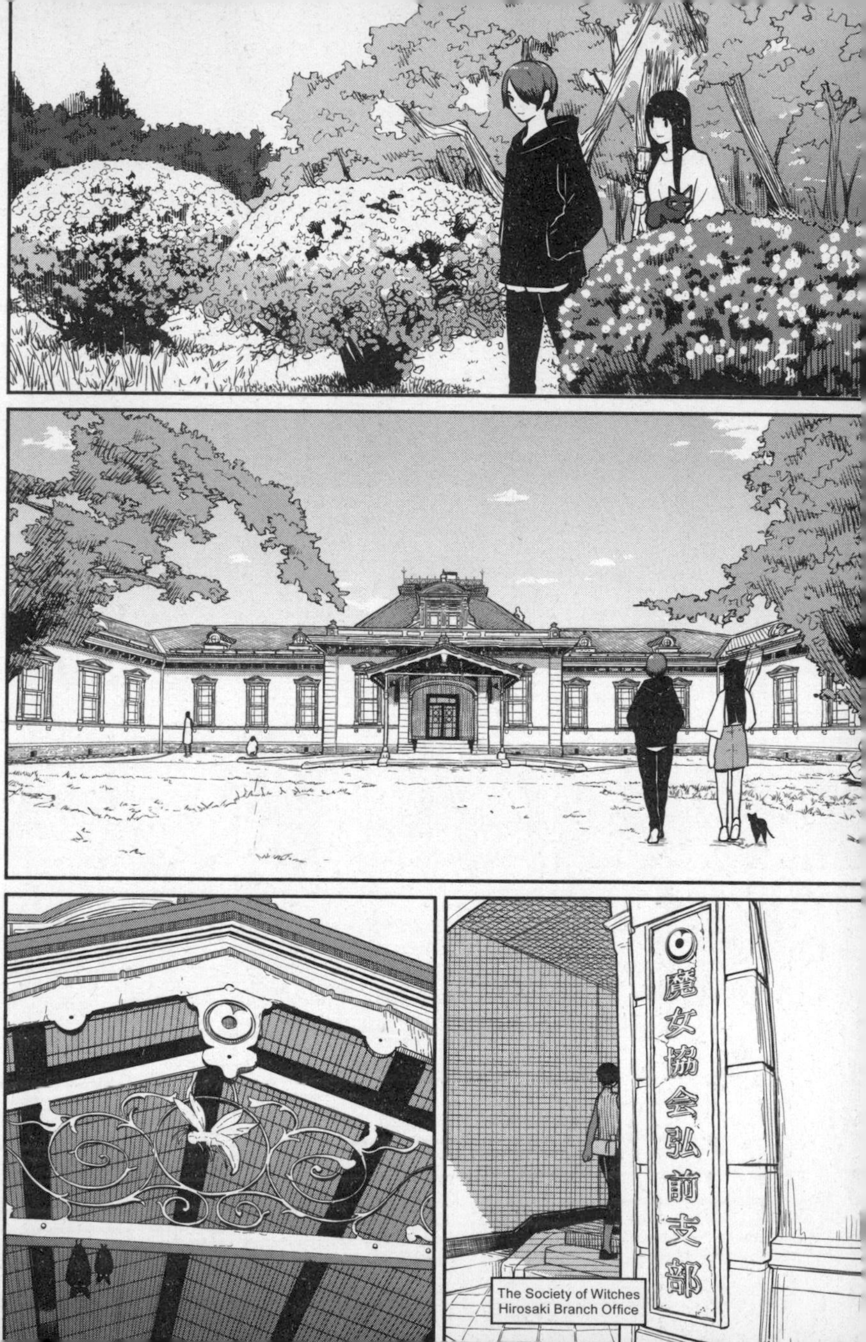
魔女協会弘前支部
The Society of Witches Hirosaki Branch Office

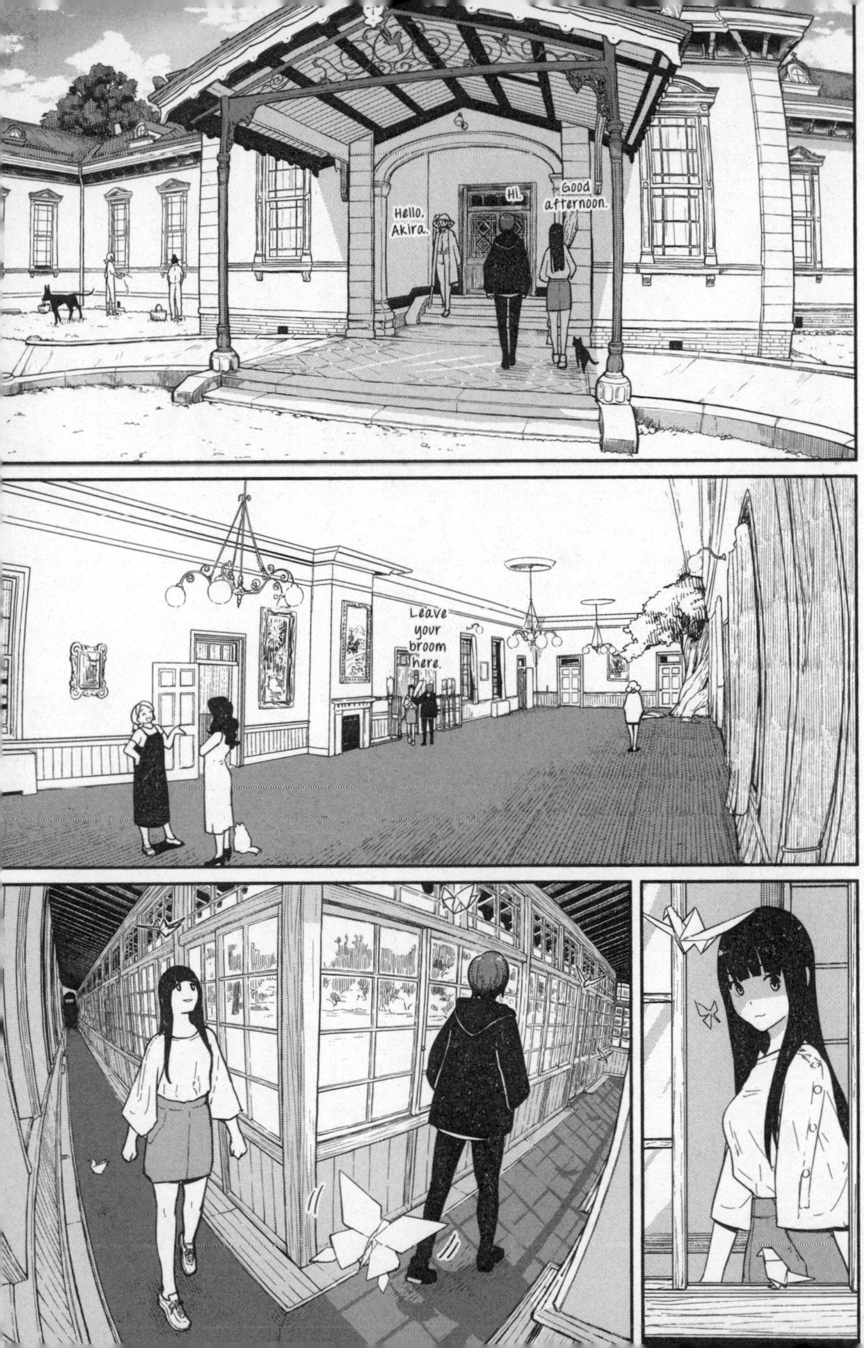
Good afternoon.
Hi.
Hello, Akira.
Leave your broom here.

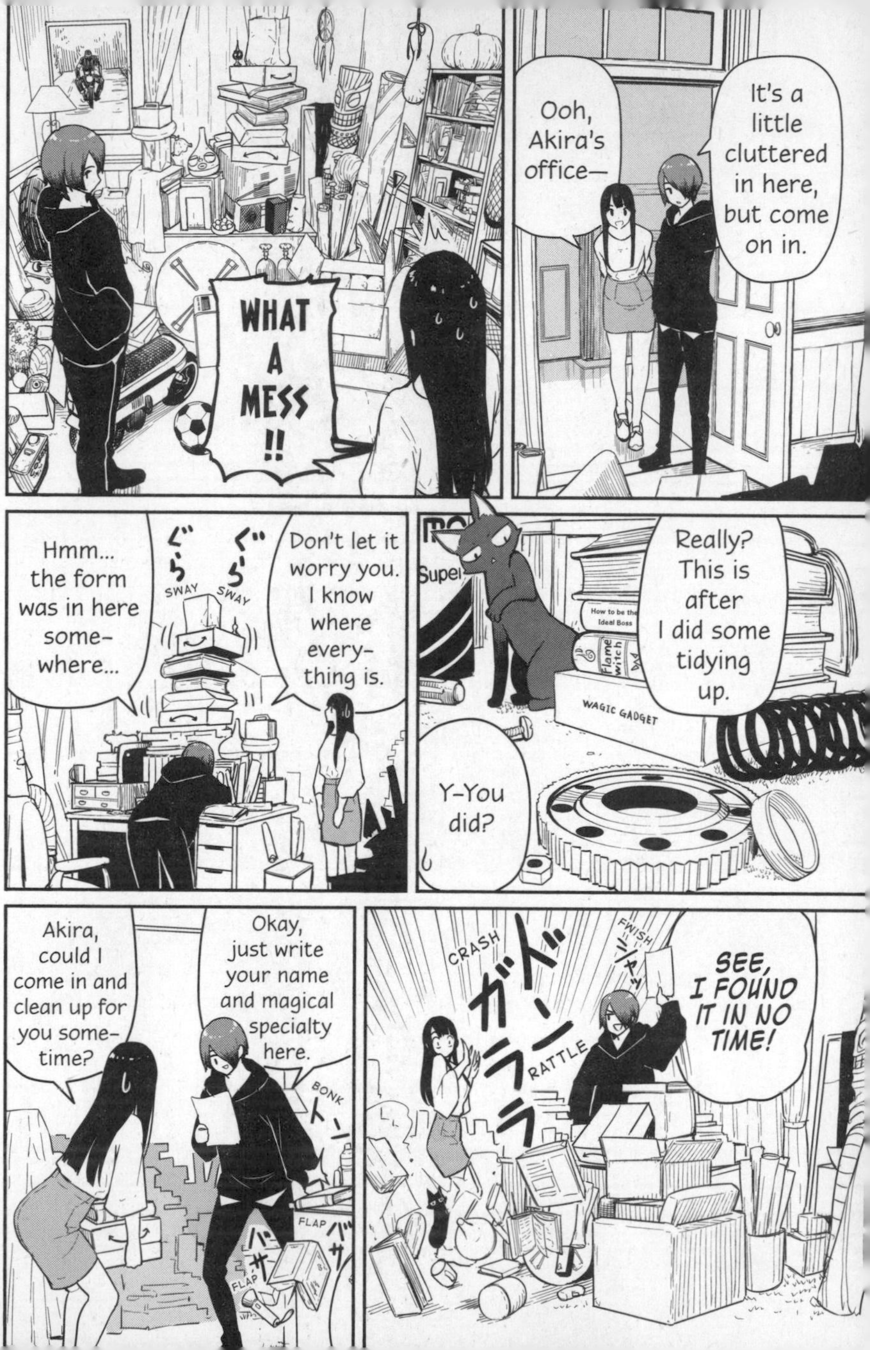
It's a little cluttered in here, but come on in.
Ooh, Akira's office—
WHAT A MESS!!
Really? This is after I did some tidying up.
How to be the Ideal Boss
Flame witch
WAGIC GADGET
Y-You did?
Don't let it worry you. I know where every-thing is.
ぐら ぐら
SWAY SWAY
Hmm... the form was in here some-where...
FWISH
シャッ
CRASH
ドンガラララ
RATTLE
SEE, I FOUND IT IN NO TIME!
Okay, just write your name and magical specialty here.
BONK
トン
FLAP
バサ
FLAP
Akira, could I come in and clean up for you some-time?

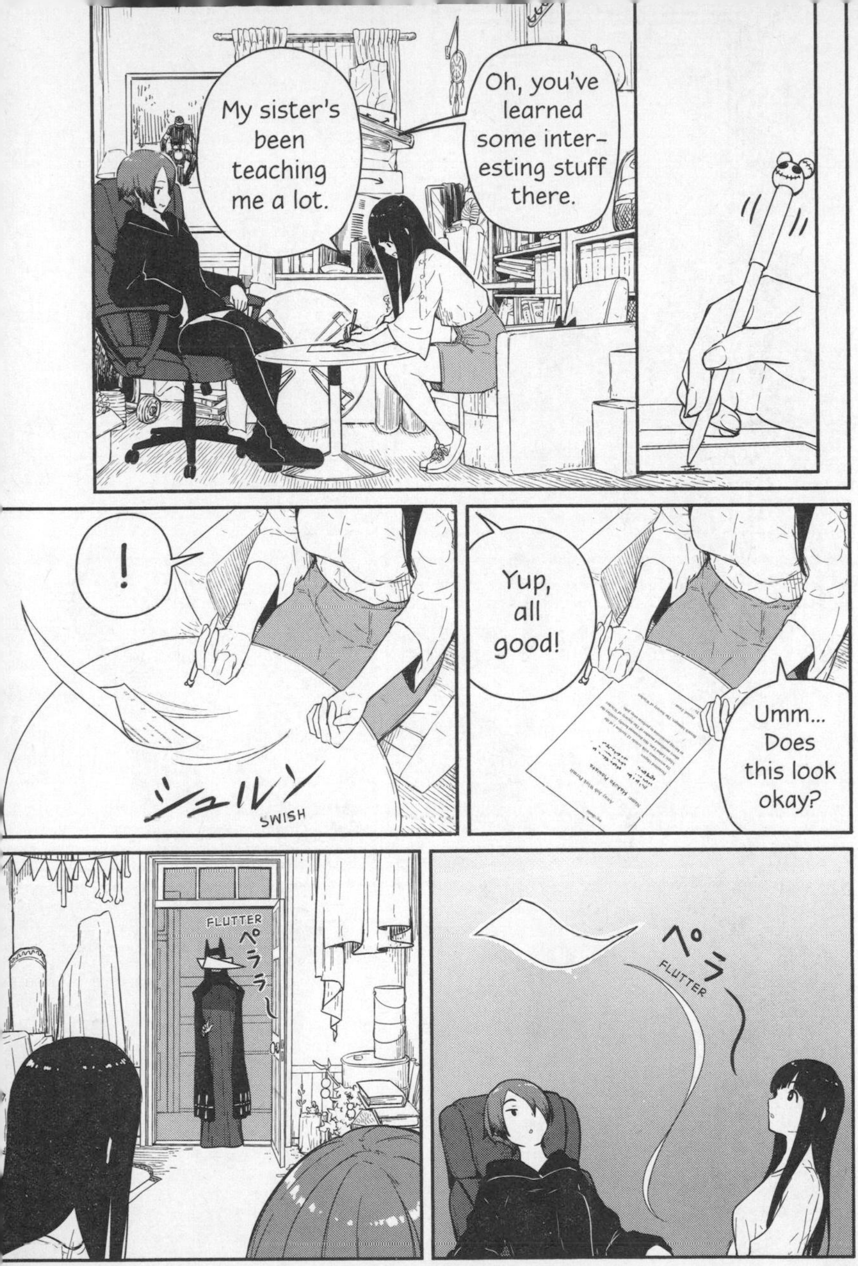
Oh, you've learned some interesting stuff there.
My sister's been teaching me a lot.
Umm... Does this look okay?
Yup, all good!
!
シュルン
SWISH
ペラ
FLUTTER
FLUTTER
ペラララ

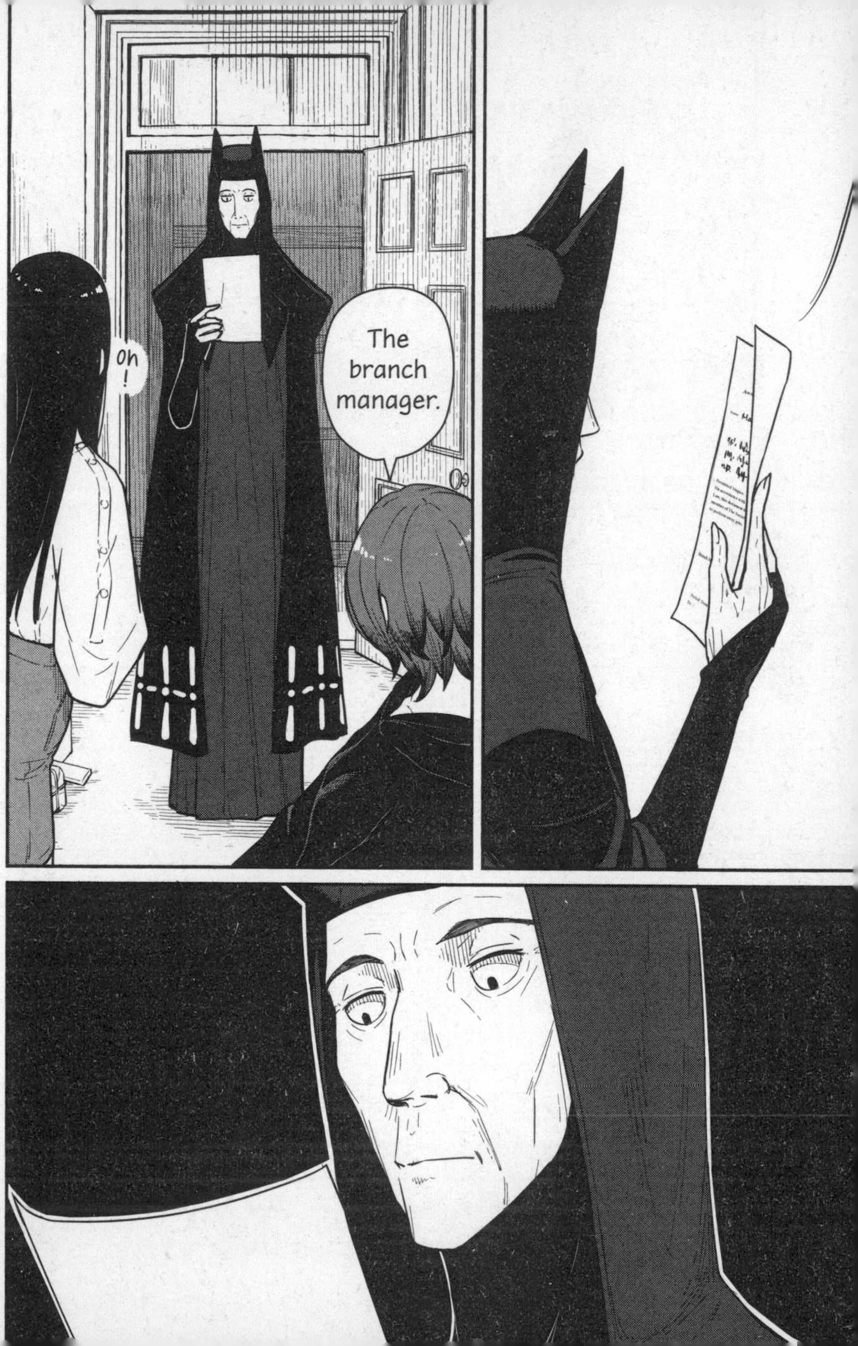
The branch manager.
Oh!

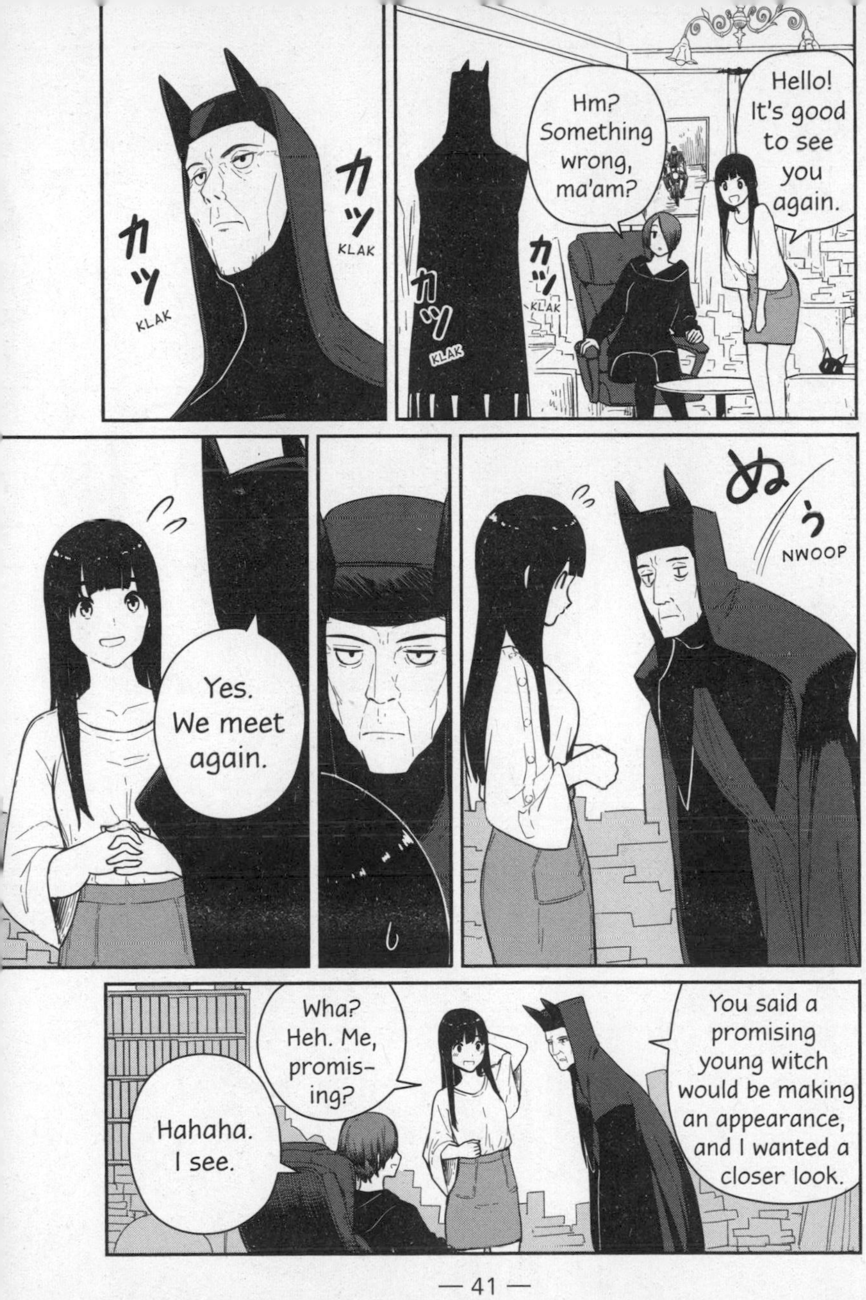
Hello! It's good to see you again.
Hm? Something wrong, ma'am?
カッ
KLAK
カッ
KLAK
カッ
KLAK
カッ
KLAK
ぬぅ
NWOOP
Yes. We meet again.
You said a promising young witch would be making an appearance, and I wanted a closer look.
Wha? Heh. Me, promis-ing?
Hahaha. I see.

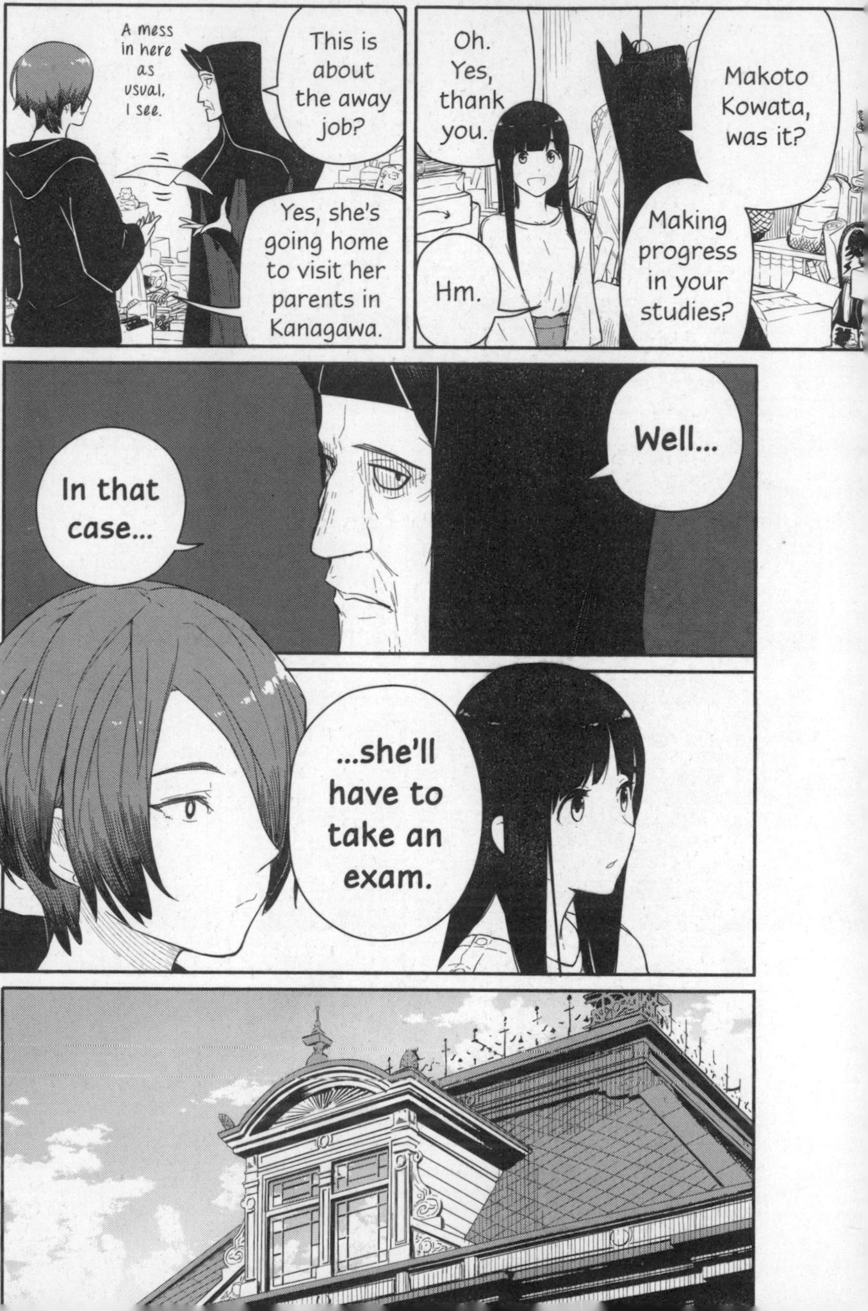
Makoto Kowata, was it?
Oh. Yes, thank you.
Making progress in your studies?
Hm.
This is about the away job?
A mess in here as usual, I see.
Yes, she's going home to visit her parents in Kanagawa.
Well...
In that case...
...she'll have to take an exam.

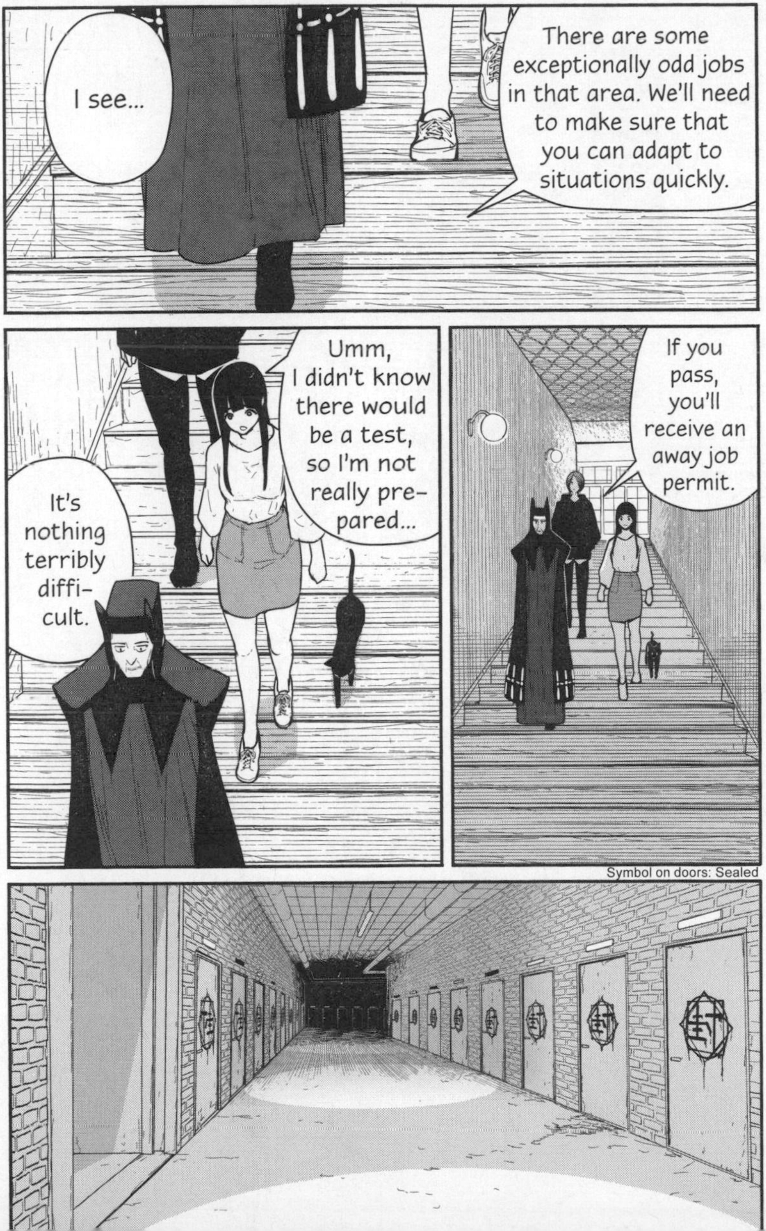
There are some exceptionally odd jobs in that area. We'll need to make sure that you can adapt to situations quickly.
I see...
If you pass, you'll receive an away job permit.
Umm, I didn't know there would be a test, so I'm not really pre-pared...
It's nothing terribly diffi-cult.
Symbol on doors: Sealed

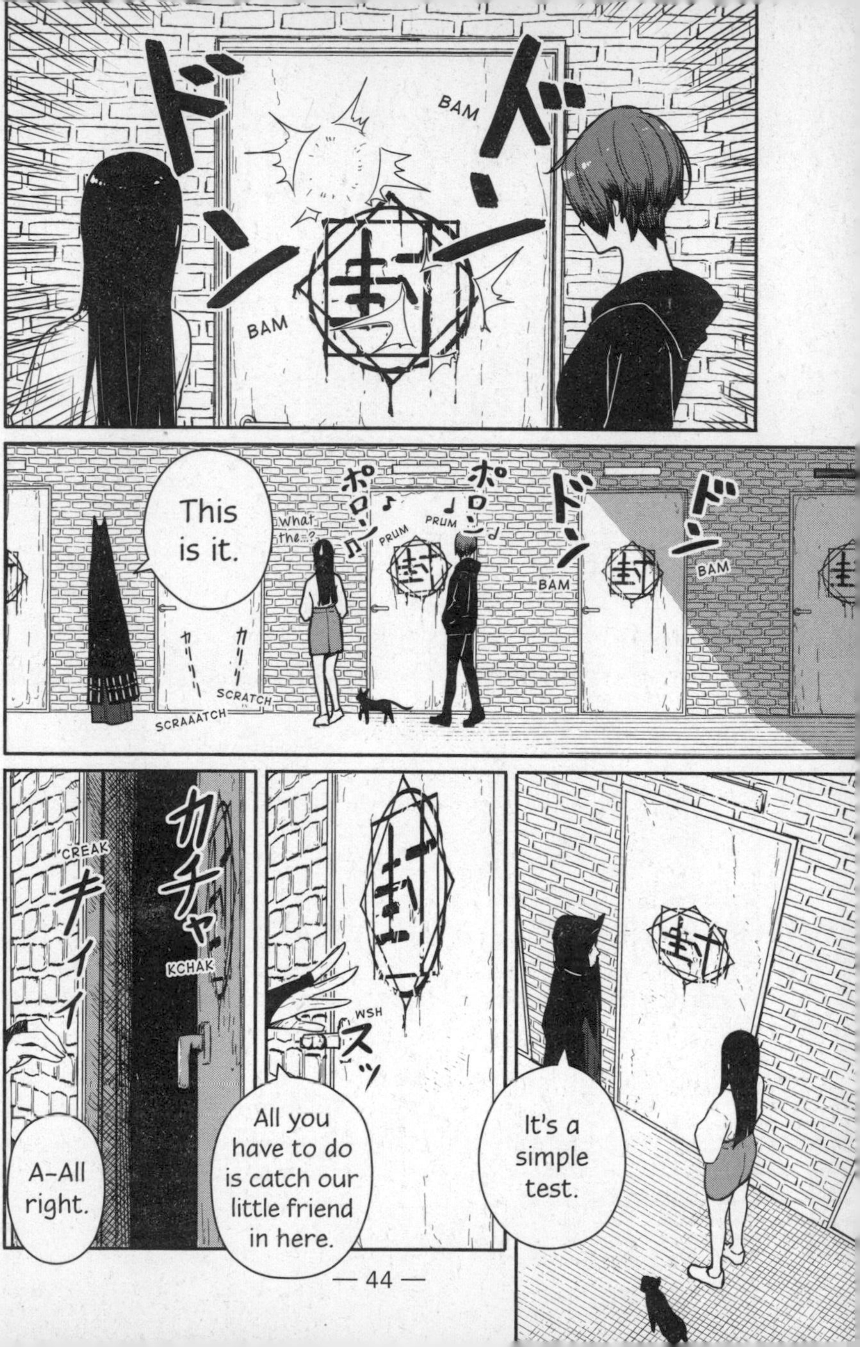
ドン
BAM
ドン
BAM
ドン
BAM
ドン
BAM
ポロン
PRUM
ポロン
PRUM
what the...?
This is it.
カリッ
SCRATCH
カリリ
SCRAAATCH
It's a simple test.
All you have to do is catch our little friend in here.
スッ
WSH
カチャ
KCHAK
ギィイ
CREAK
A-All right.

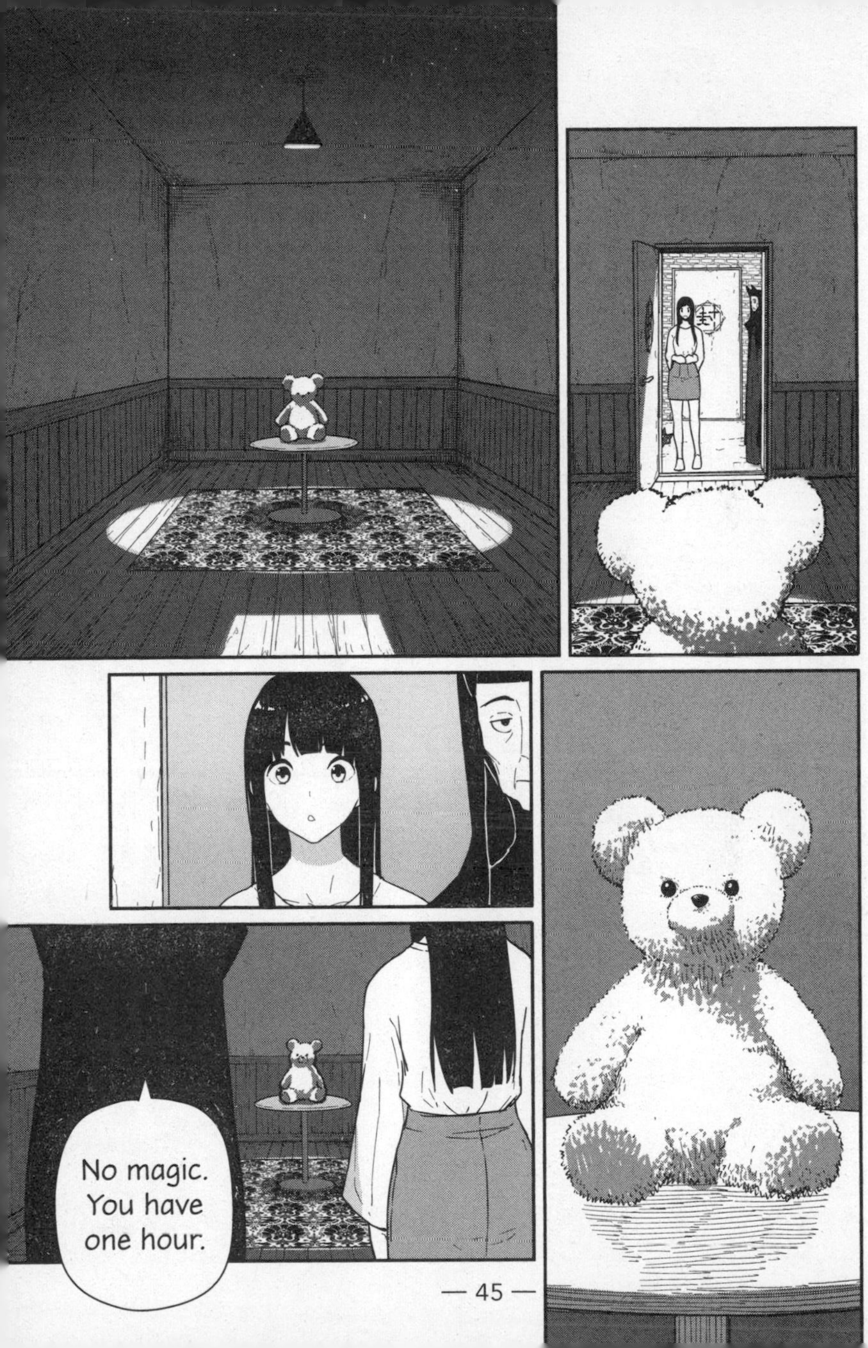
No magic. You have one hour.

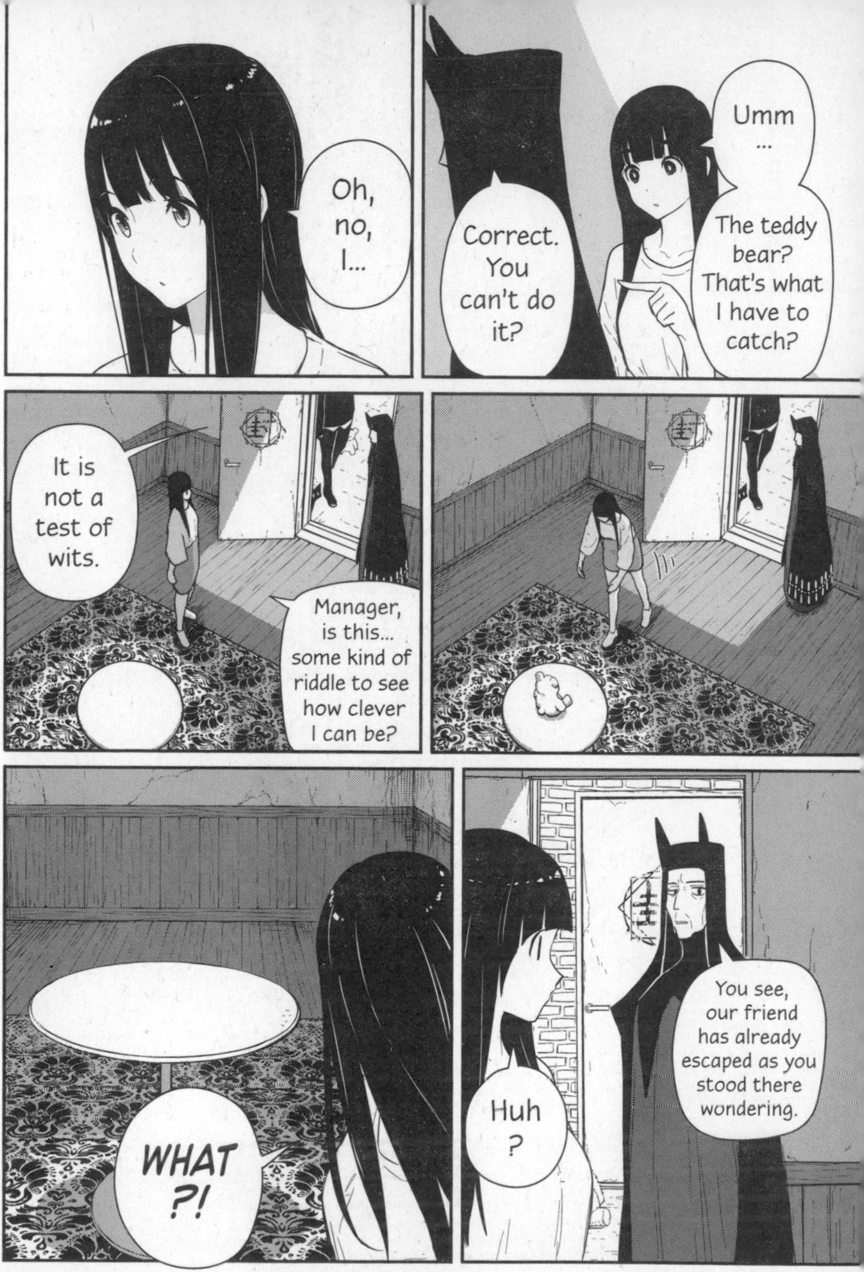

Umm ...
The teddy bear? That's what I have to catch?
Correct. You can't do it?
Oh, no, I...
Manager, is this... some kind of riddle to see how clever I can be?
It is not a test of wits.
You see, our friend has already escaped as you stood there wondering.
Huh ?
WHAT ?!

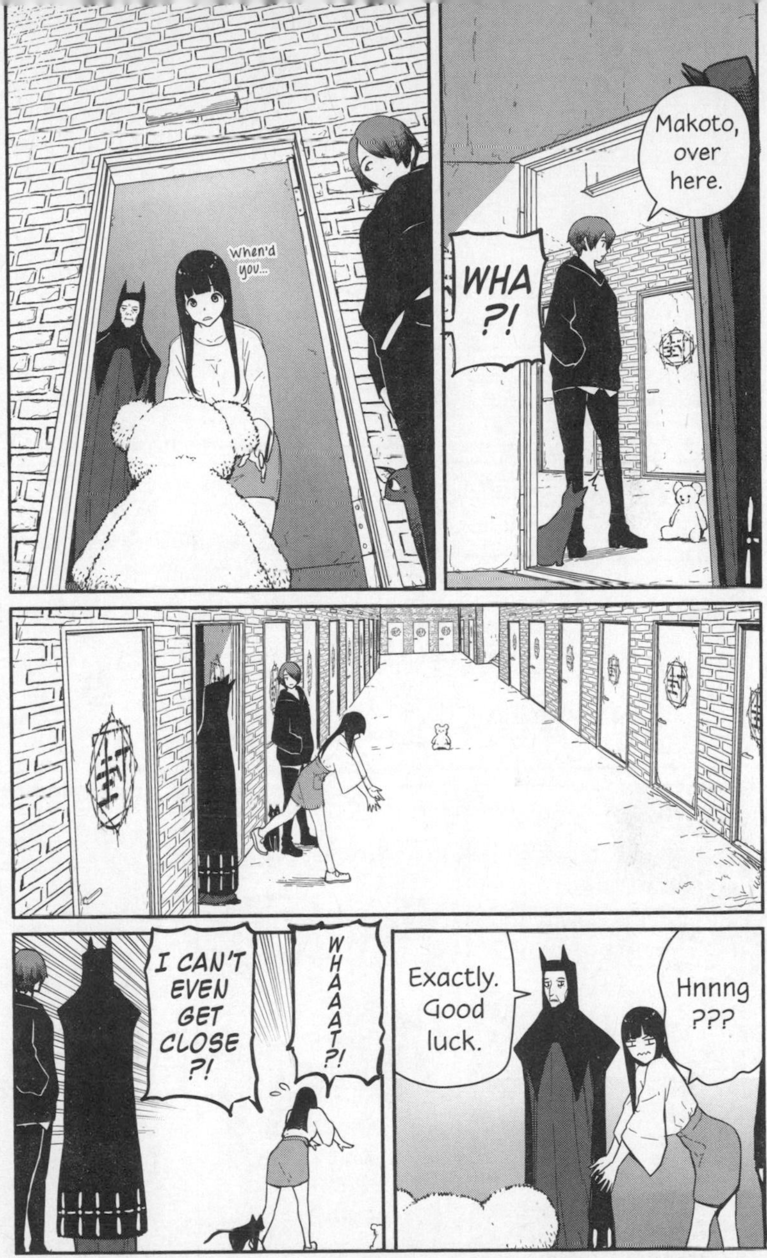
Makoto, over here.
WHA ?!
When'd you...
Hnnng ???
Exactly. Good luck.
WHAAAAT?!
I CAN'T EVEN GET CLOSE ?!

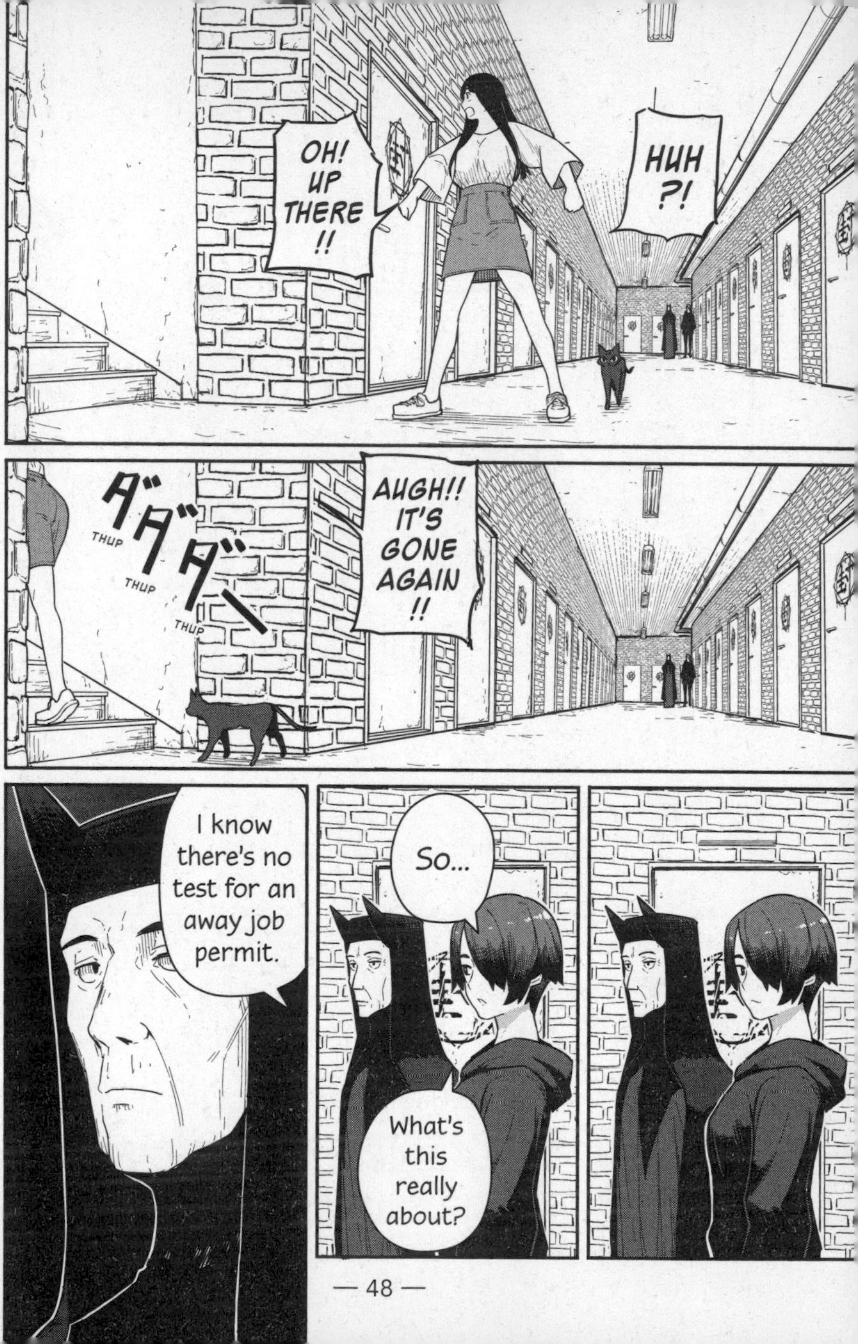
HUH ?!
OH! UP THERE !!
AUGH!! IT'S GONE AGAIN !!
ダダダ
THUP
THUP
THUP
So...
What's this really about?
I know there's no test for an away job permit.

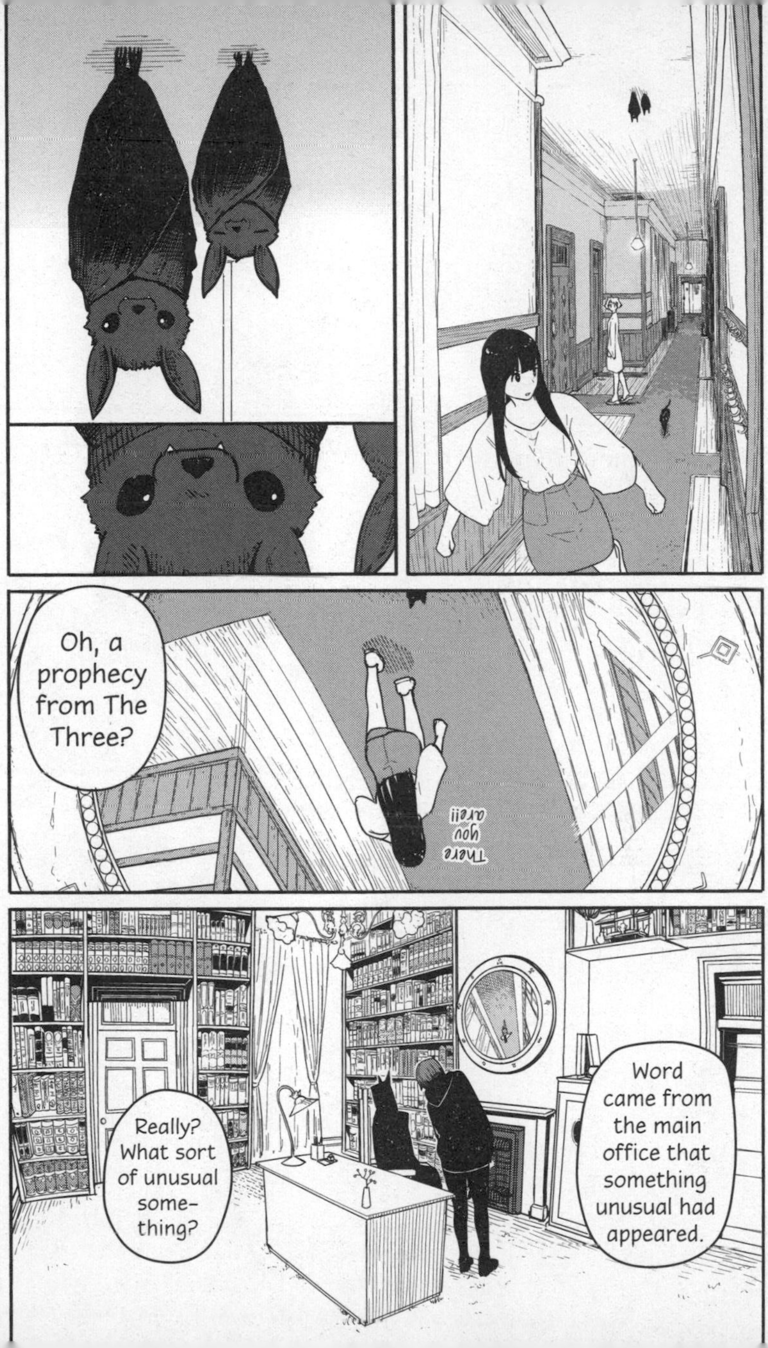
There you are!!
Oh, a prophecy from The Three?
Word came from the main office that something unusual had appeared.
Really? What sort of unusual some-thing?

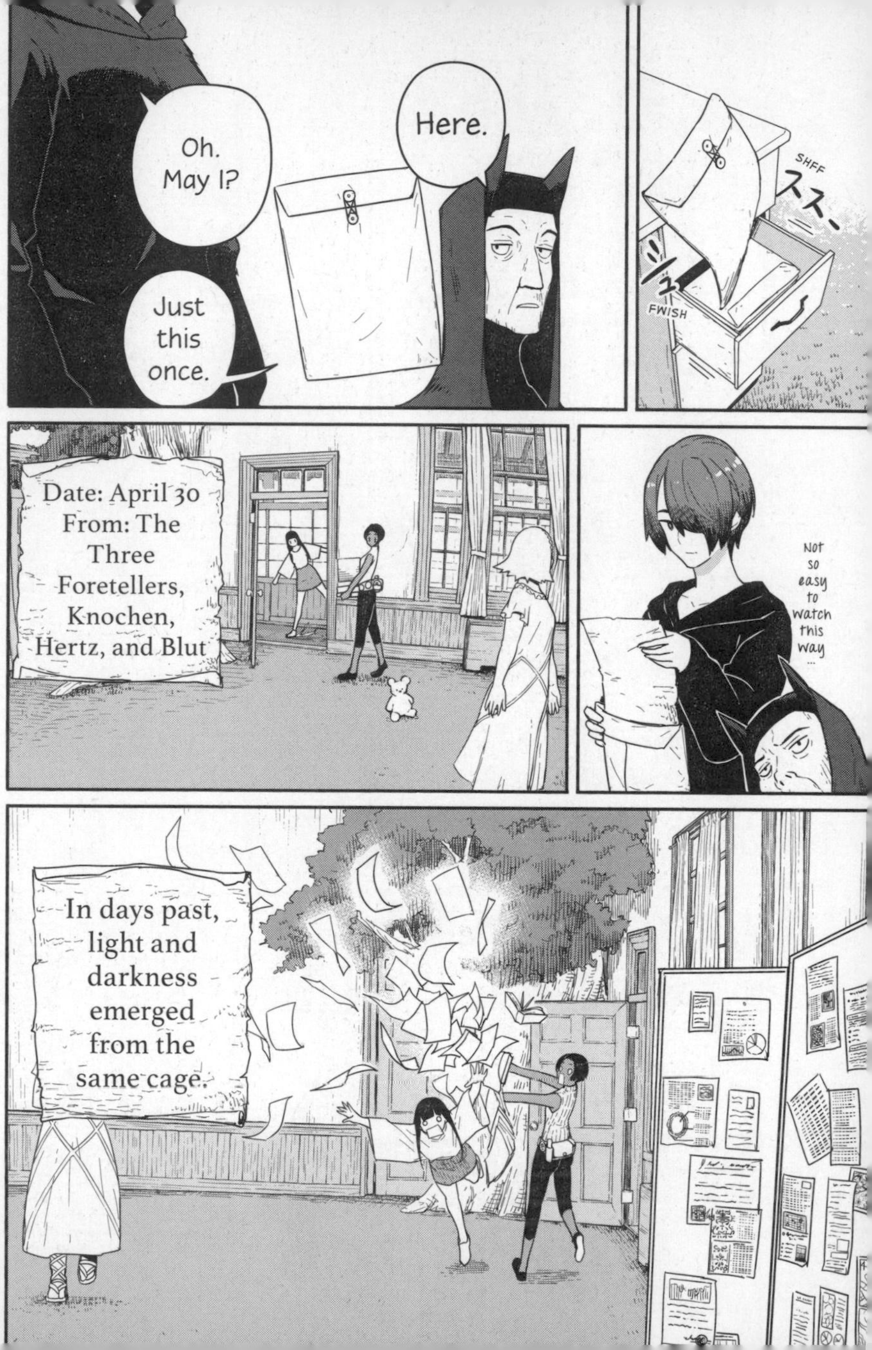
SHFF
スス、
シュ
FWISH
Here.
Oh. May I?
Just this once.
Not so easy to watch this way...
Date: April 30
From: The Three Foretellers, Knochen, Hertz, and Blut
In days past, light and darkness emerged from the same cage.

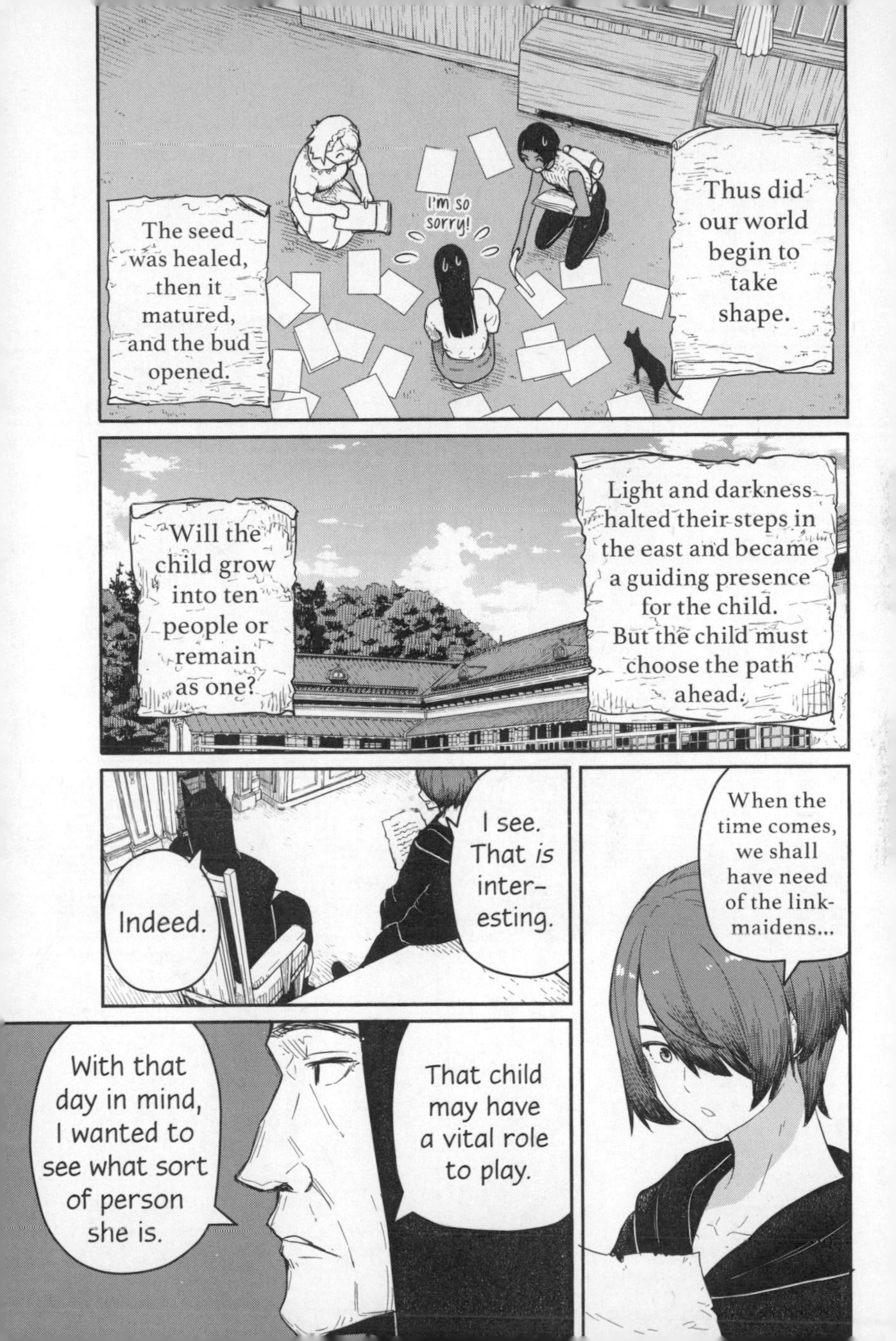

Thus did our world begin to take shape.
I'm so sorry!
The seed was healed, then it matured, and the bud opened.
Light and darkness halted their steps in the east and became a guiding presence for the child. But the child must choose the path ahead.
Will the child grow into ten people or remain as one?
When the time comes, we shall have need of the link-maidens...
I see. That *is* inter-esting.
Indeed.
That child may have a vital role to play.
With that day in mind, I wanted to see what sort of person she is.

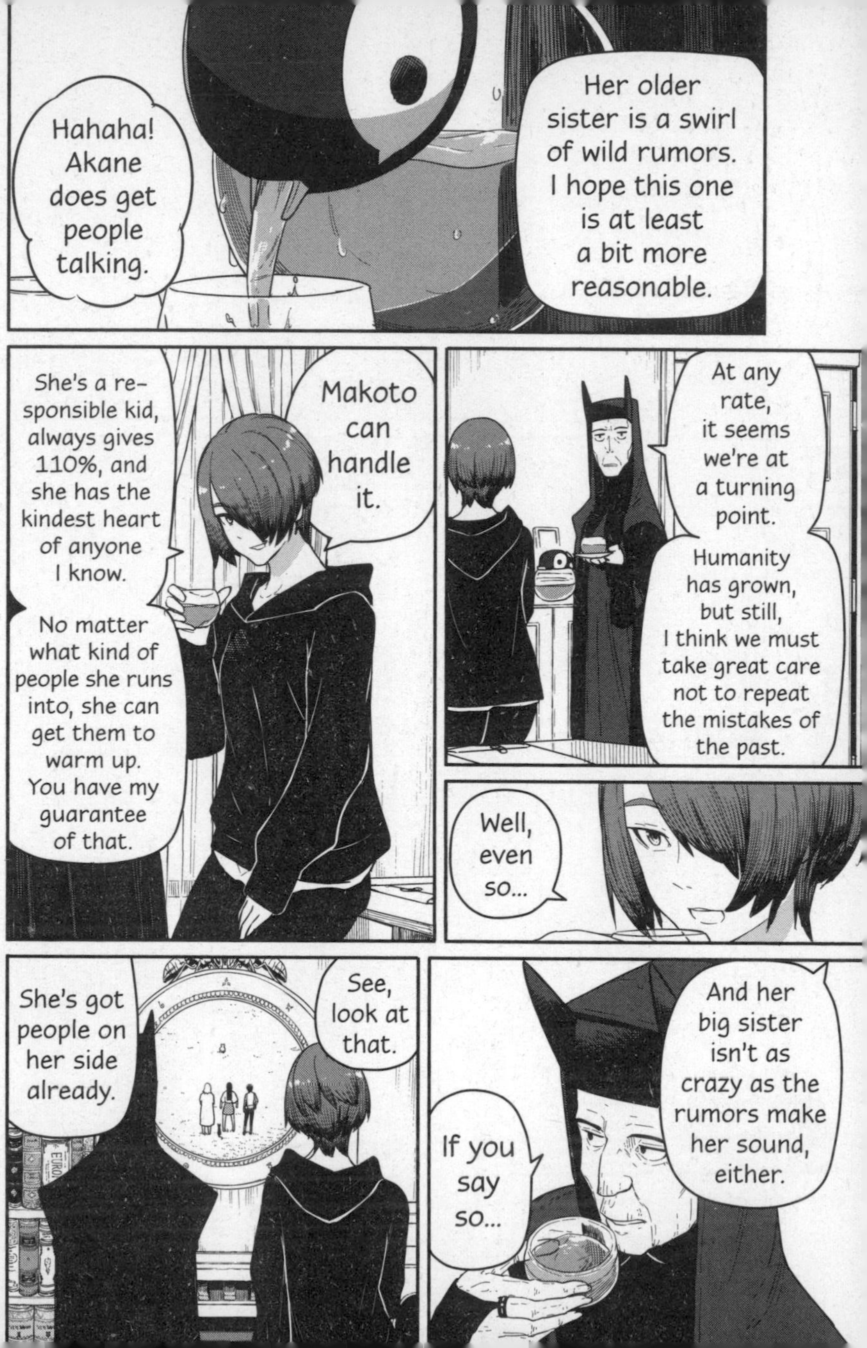
Her older sister is a swirl of wild rumors. I hope this one is at least a bit more reasonable.
Hahaha! Akane does get people talking.
At any rate, it seems we're at a turning point.
Humanity has grown, but still, I think we must take great care not to repeat the mistakes of the past.
Well, even so...
Makoto can handle it.
She's a re-sponsible kid, always gives 110%, and she has the kindest heart of anyone I know.
No matter what kind of people she runs into, she can get them to warm up. You have my guarantee of that.
And her big sister isn't as crazy as the rumors make her sound, either.
If you say so...
See, look at that.
She's got people on her side already.
EURO

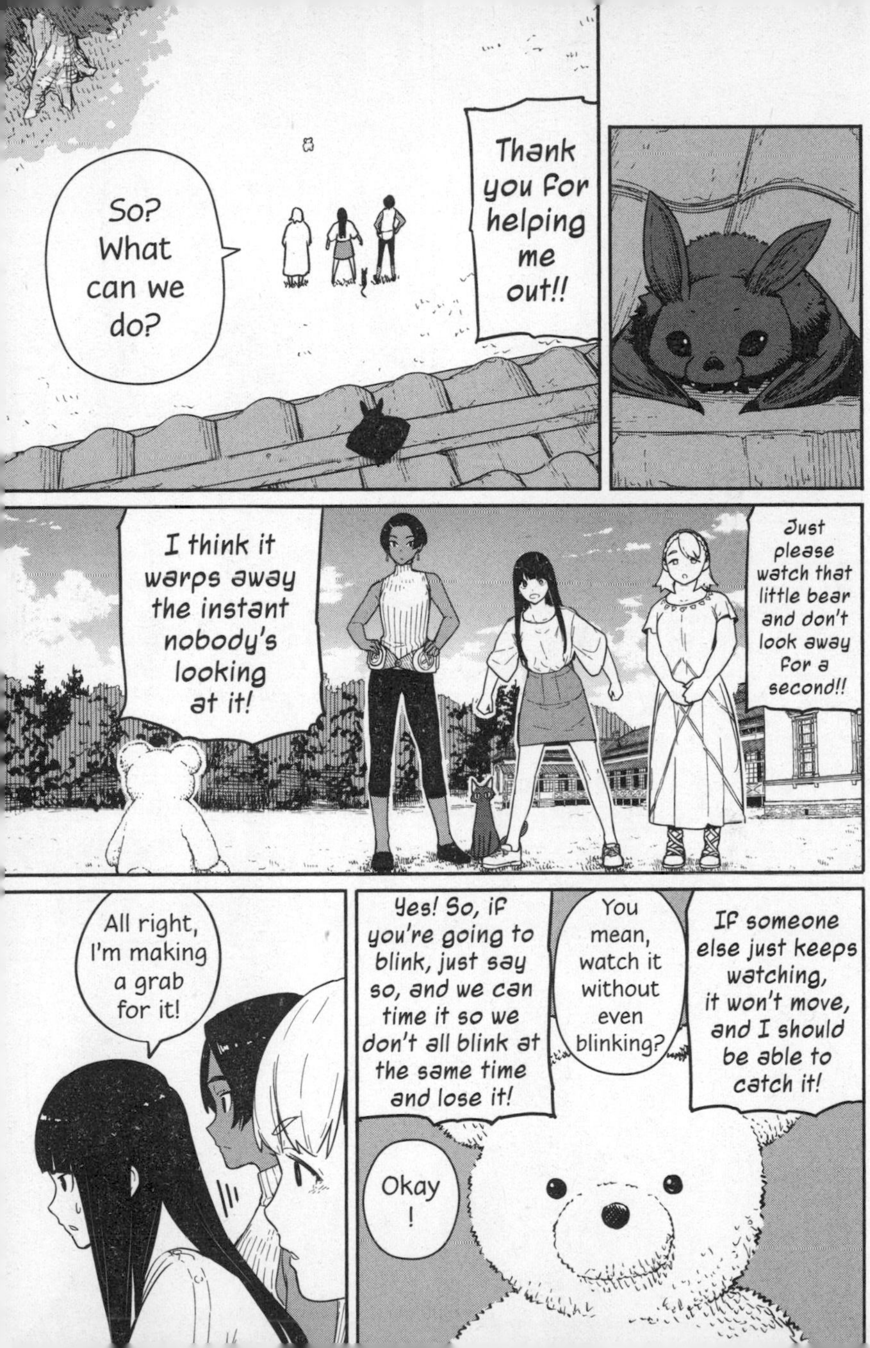
Thank you for helping me out!!
So? What can we do?
Just please watch that little bear and don't look away for a second!!
I think it warps away the instant nobody's looking at it!
If someone else just keeps watching, it won't move, and I should be able to catch it!
You mean, watch it without even blinking?
Yes! So, if you're going to blink, just say so, and we can time it so we don't all blink at the same time and lose it!
Okay!
All right, I'm making a grab for it!

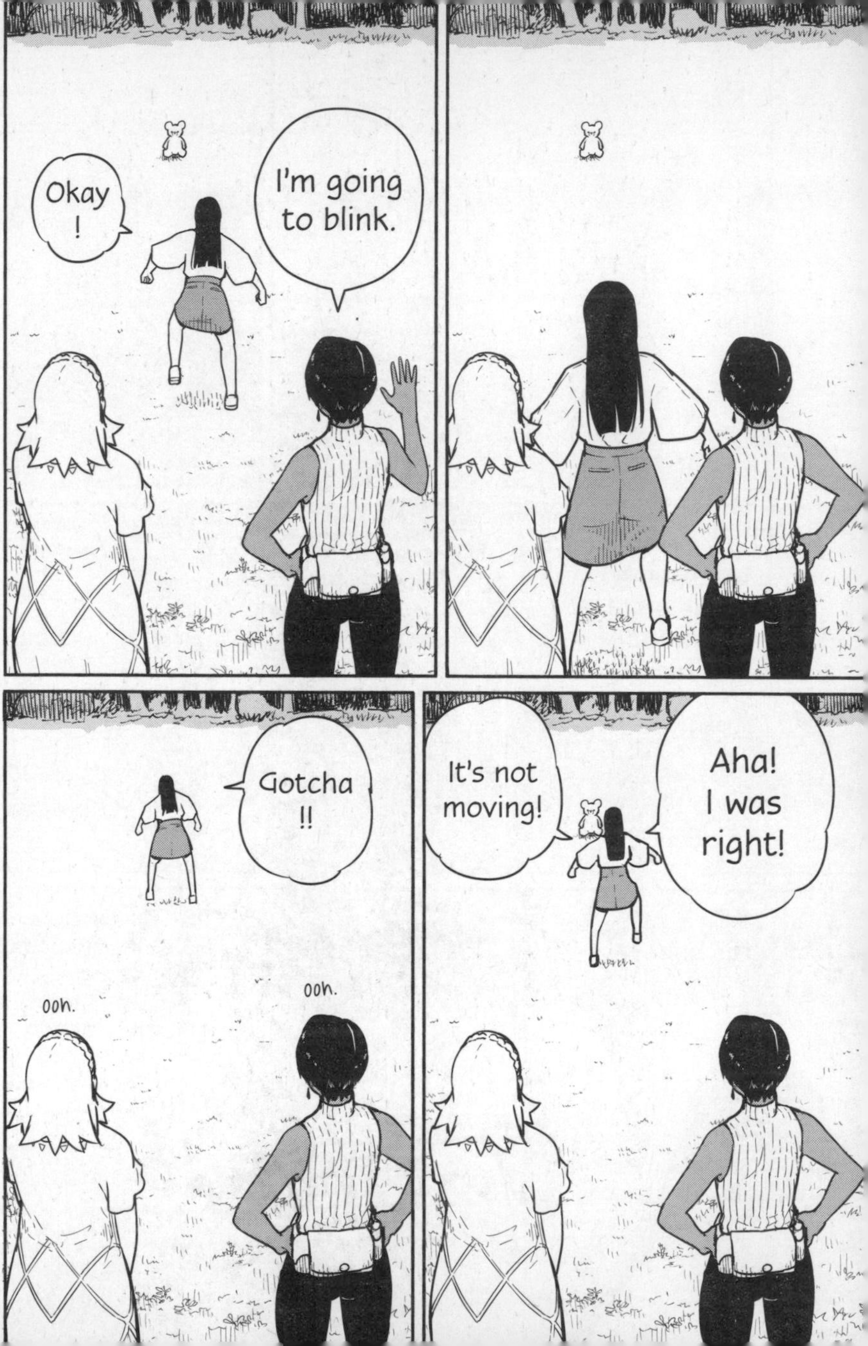
I'm going to blink.
Okay !
Aha! I was right!
It's not moving!
Gotcha !!
ooh.
ooh.

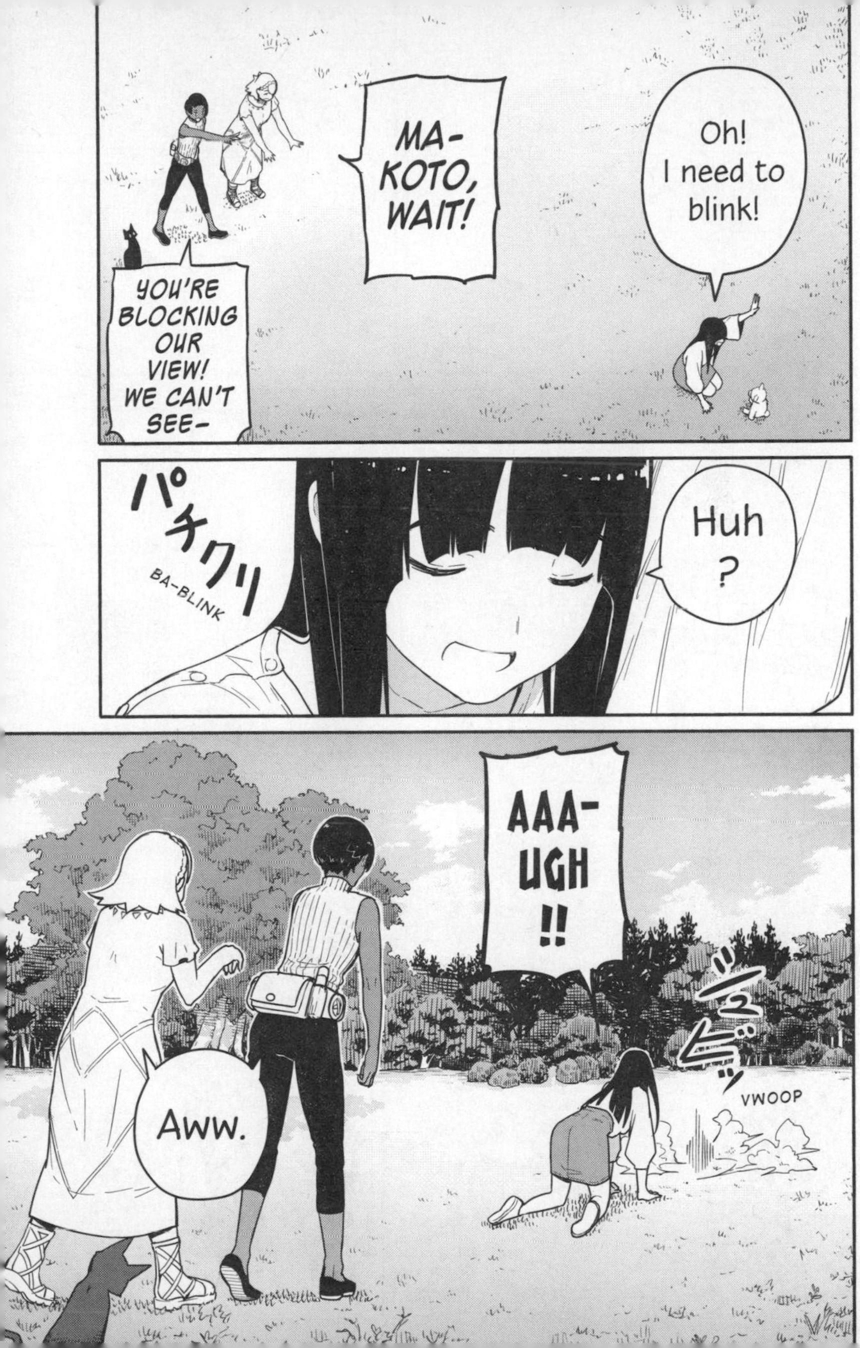
Oh! I need to blink!
MA-KOTO, WAIT!
YOU'RE BLOCKING OUR VIEW! WE CAN'T SEE-
Huh?
パチクリ
BA-BLINK
AAA-UGH!!
VWOOP
Aww.

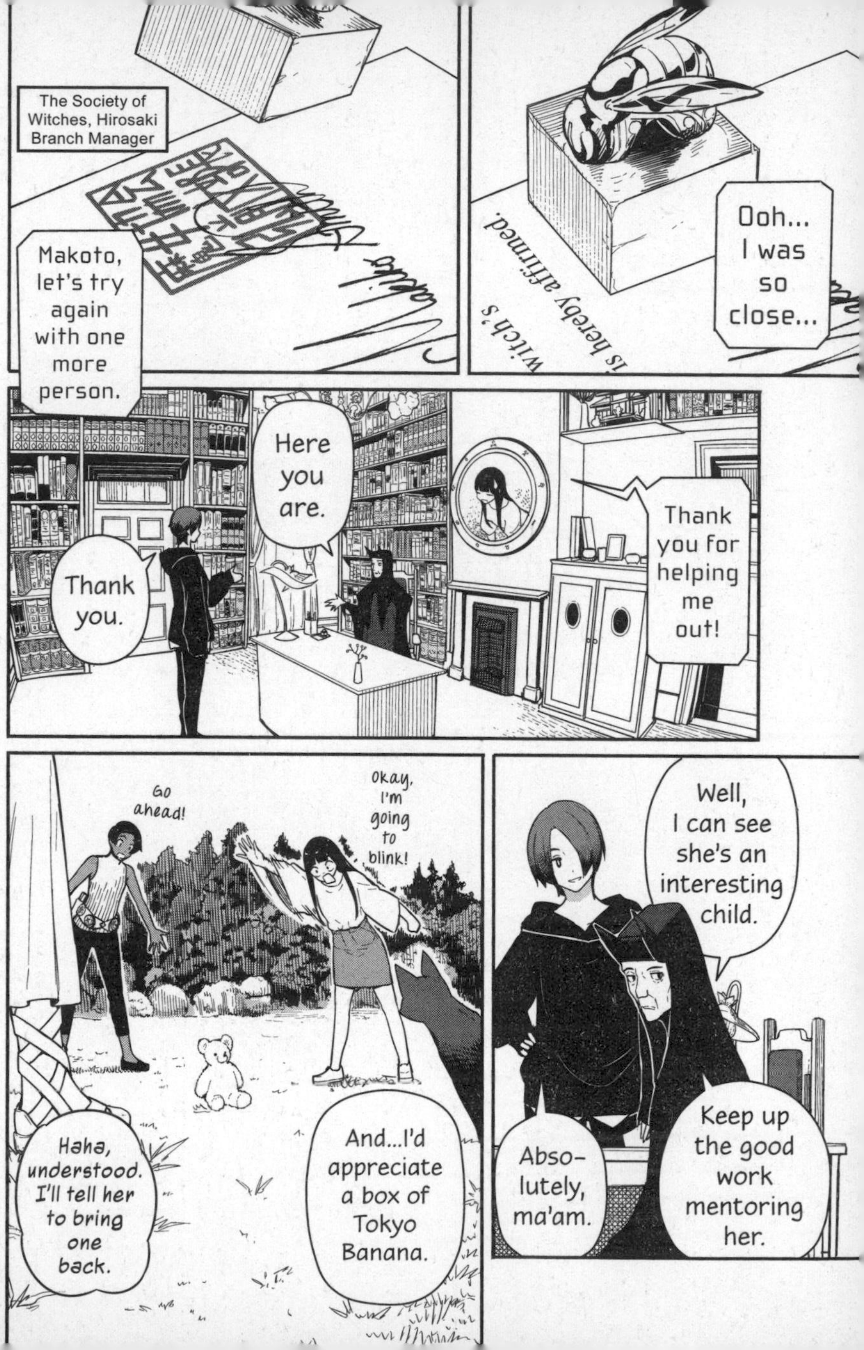
Ooh... I was so close...
The Society of Witches, Hirosaki Branch Manager
Makoto, let's try again with one more person.
Thank you for helping me out!
Here you are.
Thank you.
Well, I can see she's an interesting child.
Keep up the good work mentoring her.
Abso-lutely, ma'am.
Okay, I'm going to blink!
Go ahead!
And...I'd appreciate a box of Tokyo Banana.
Haha, understood. I'll tell her to bring one back.

Flying
Witch

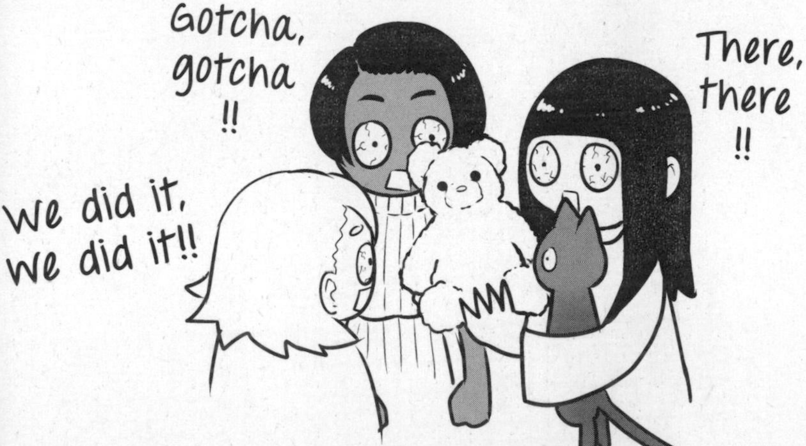
There, there!!
Gotcha, gotcha!!
We did it, we did it!!

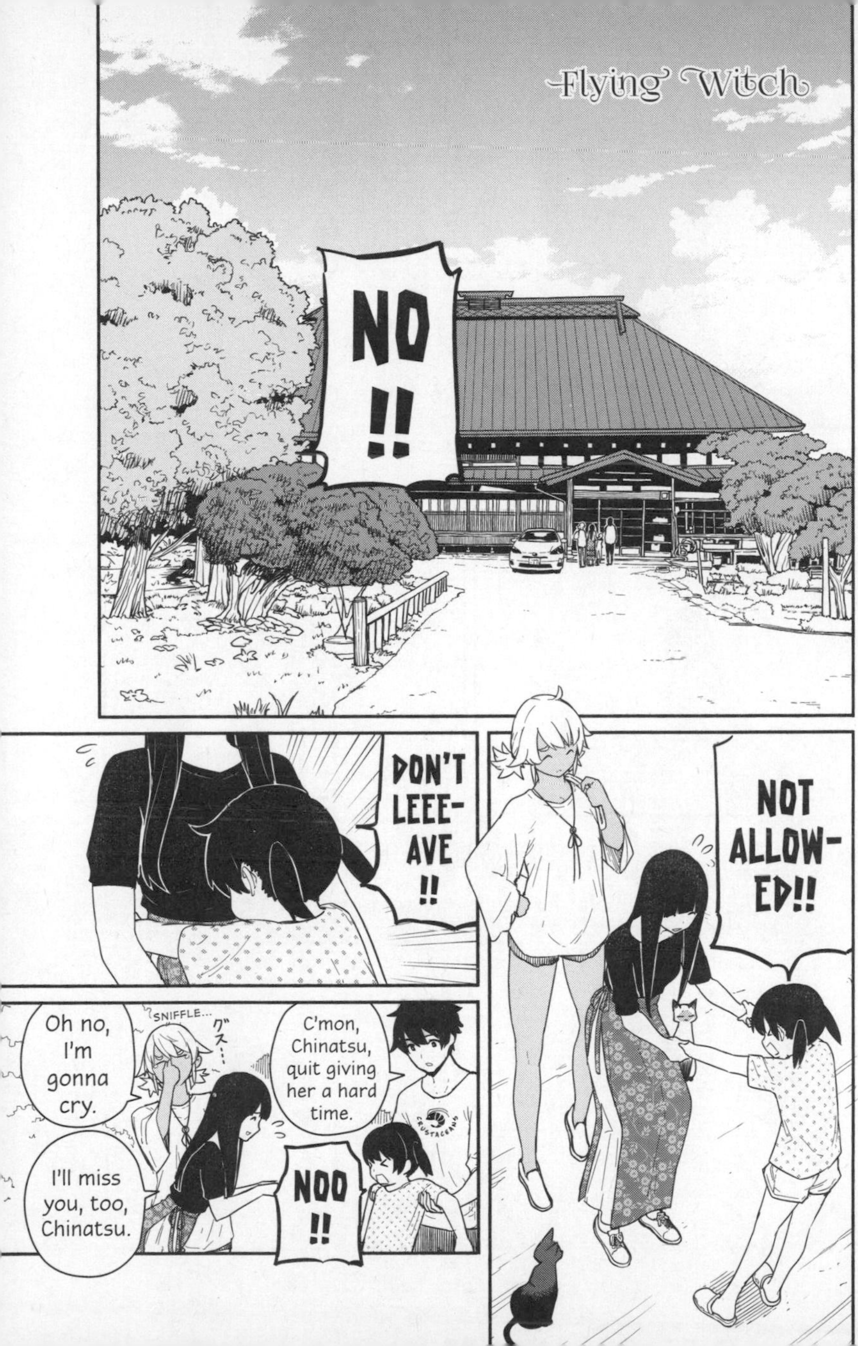
Flying Witch
NO!!
NOT ALLOWED!!
DON'T LEEE-AVE!!
C'mon, Chinatsu, quit giving her a hard time.
SNIFFLE... グス…
Oh no, I'm gonna cry.
NOO!!
I'll miss you, too, Chinatsu.

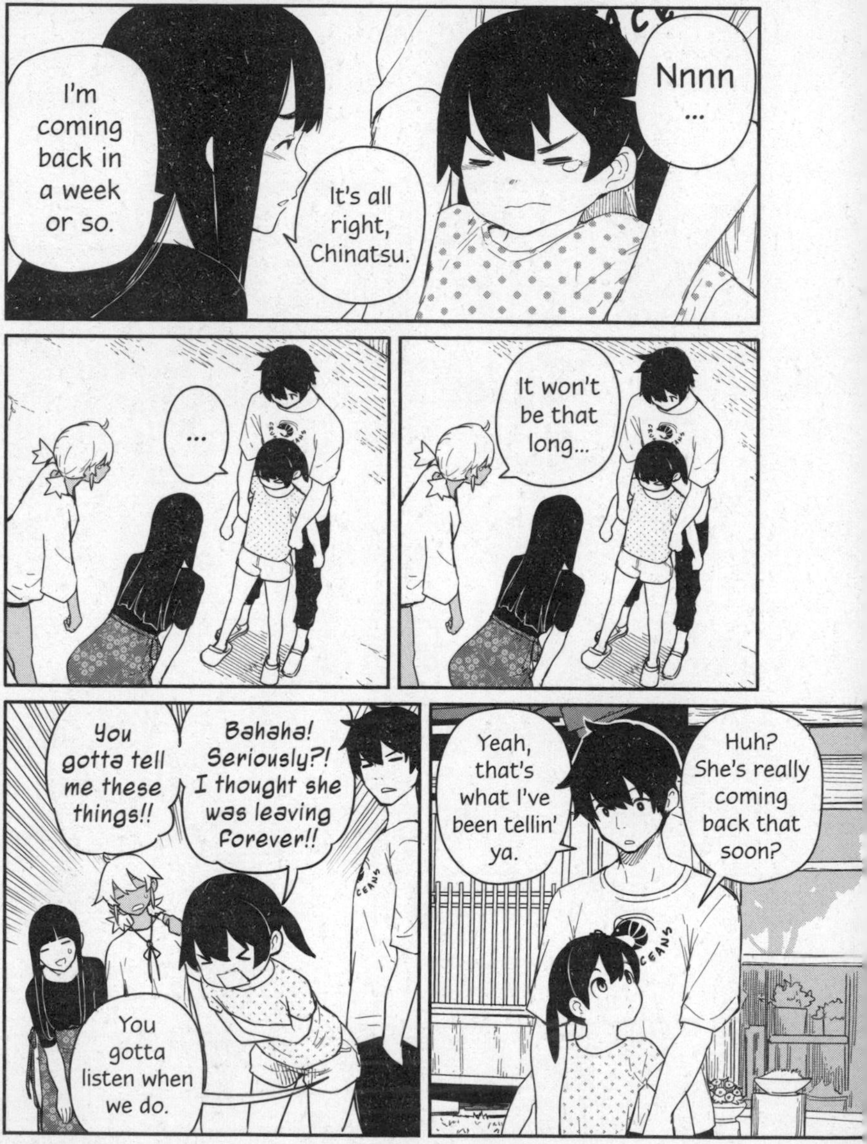

Nnnn ...
It's all right, Chinatsu.
I'm coming back in a week or so.
It won't be that long...
...
Huh? She's really coming back that soon?
Yeah, that's what I've been tellin' ya.
Bahaha! Seriously?! I thought she was leaving forever!!
You gotta tell me these things!!
You gotta listen when we do.

Chapter 57
Companionship on the Road, Kindness for Cats

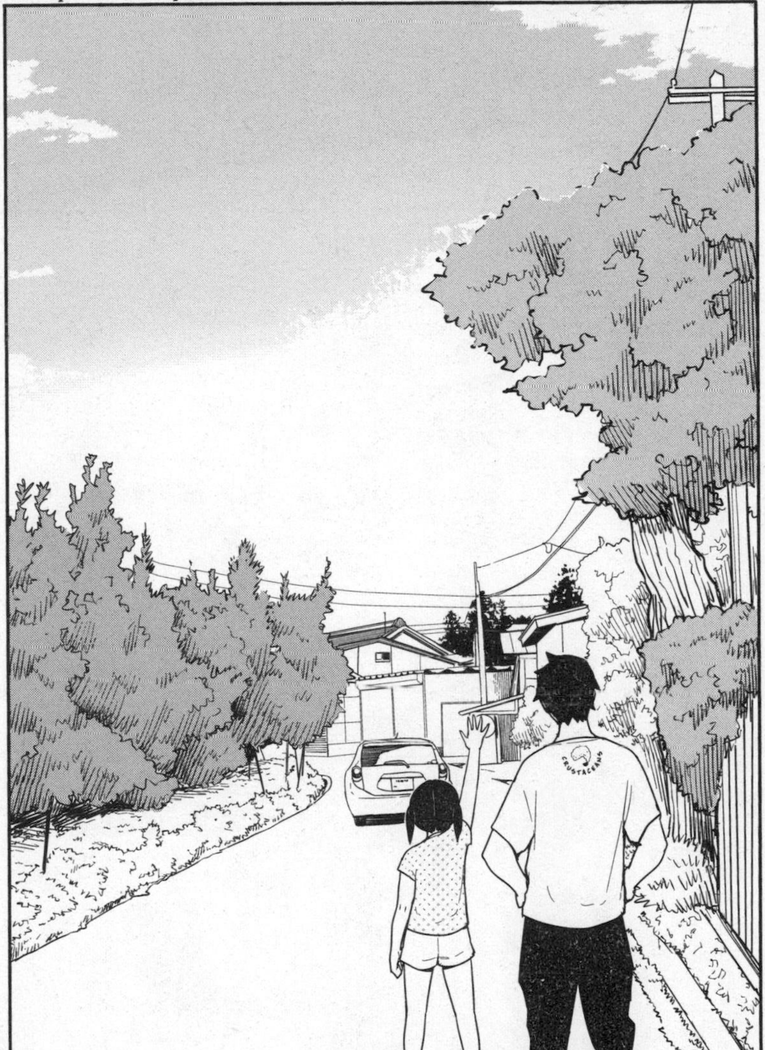
CRUSTACEANS

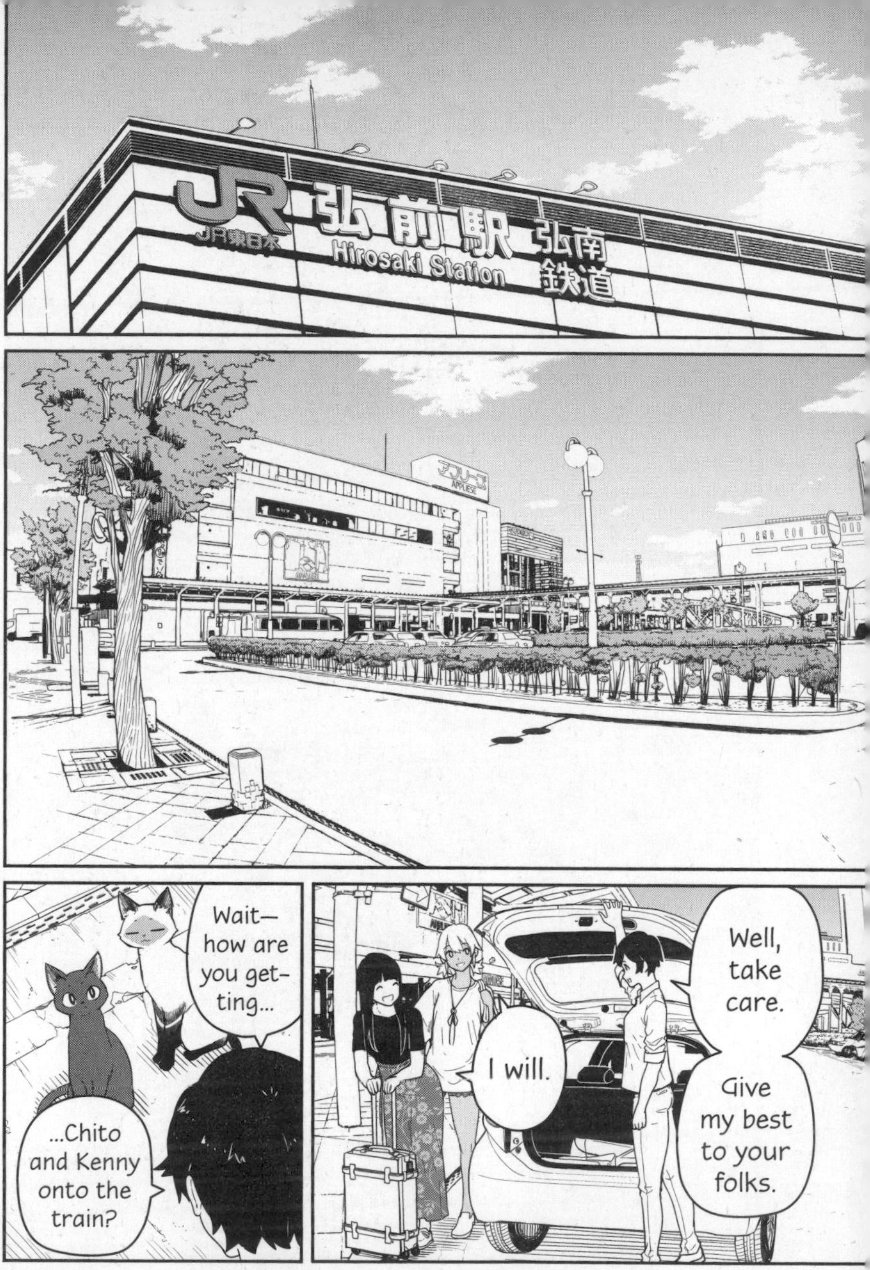
JR
JR東日本
弘前駅
Hirosaki Station
弘南鉄道
Well, take care.
Give my best to your folks.
I will.
Wait—how are you getting...
...Chito and Kenny onto the train?

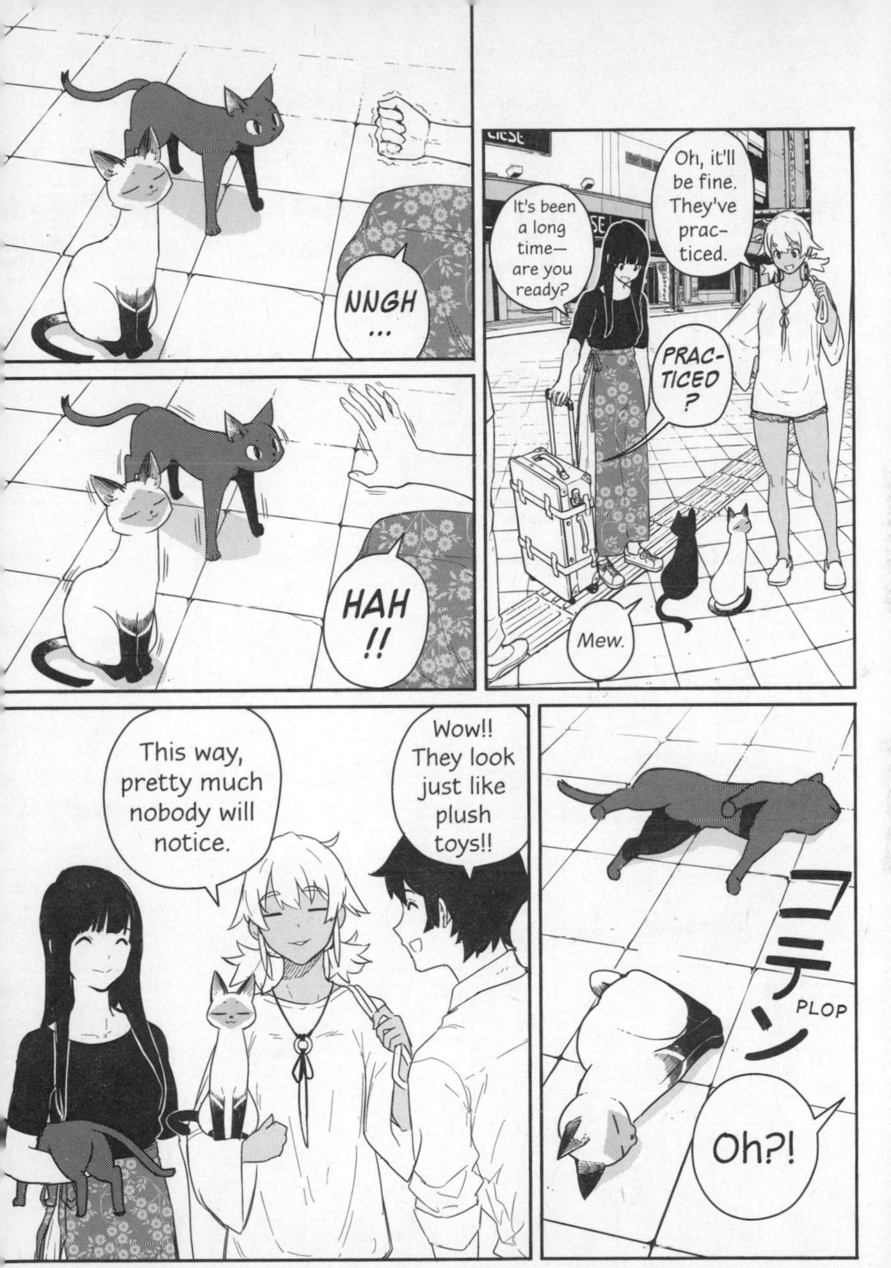

Oh, it'll be fine. They've prac- ticed.
It's been a long time— are you ready?
PRAC- TICED ?
Mew.
NNGH ...
HAH !!
コテン
PLOP
Oh?!
Wow!! They look just like plush toys!!
This way, pretty much nobody will notice.

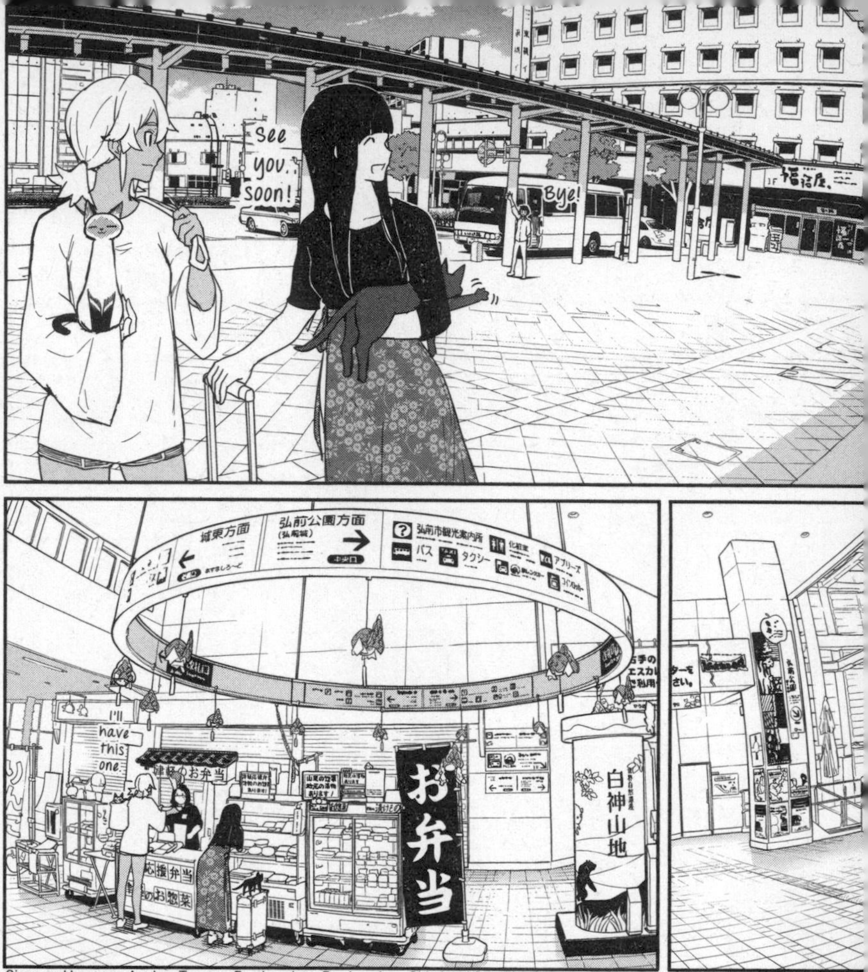
See you. soon!
Bye!
弘前公園方面
城東方面
お弁当
白神山地
I'll have this one.
Signs and banners: Apples, Tsugaru Box Lunches, Box Lunches, Shirakami Sanchi
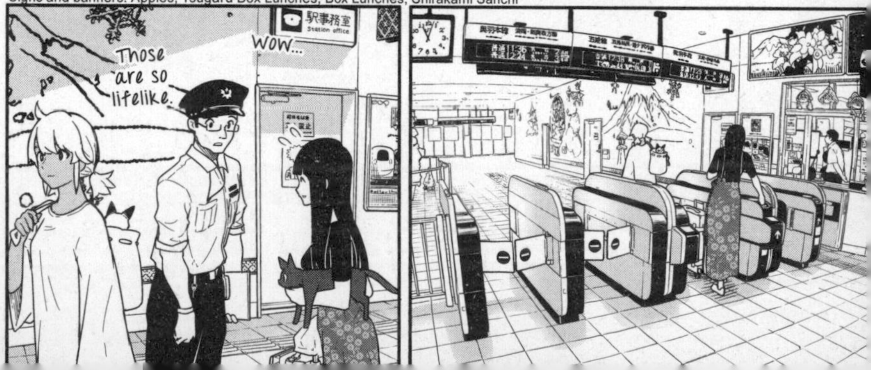
駅事務室
Station office
Wow...
Those are so lifelike.

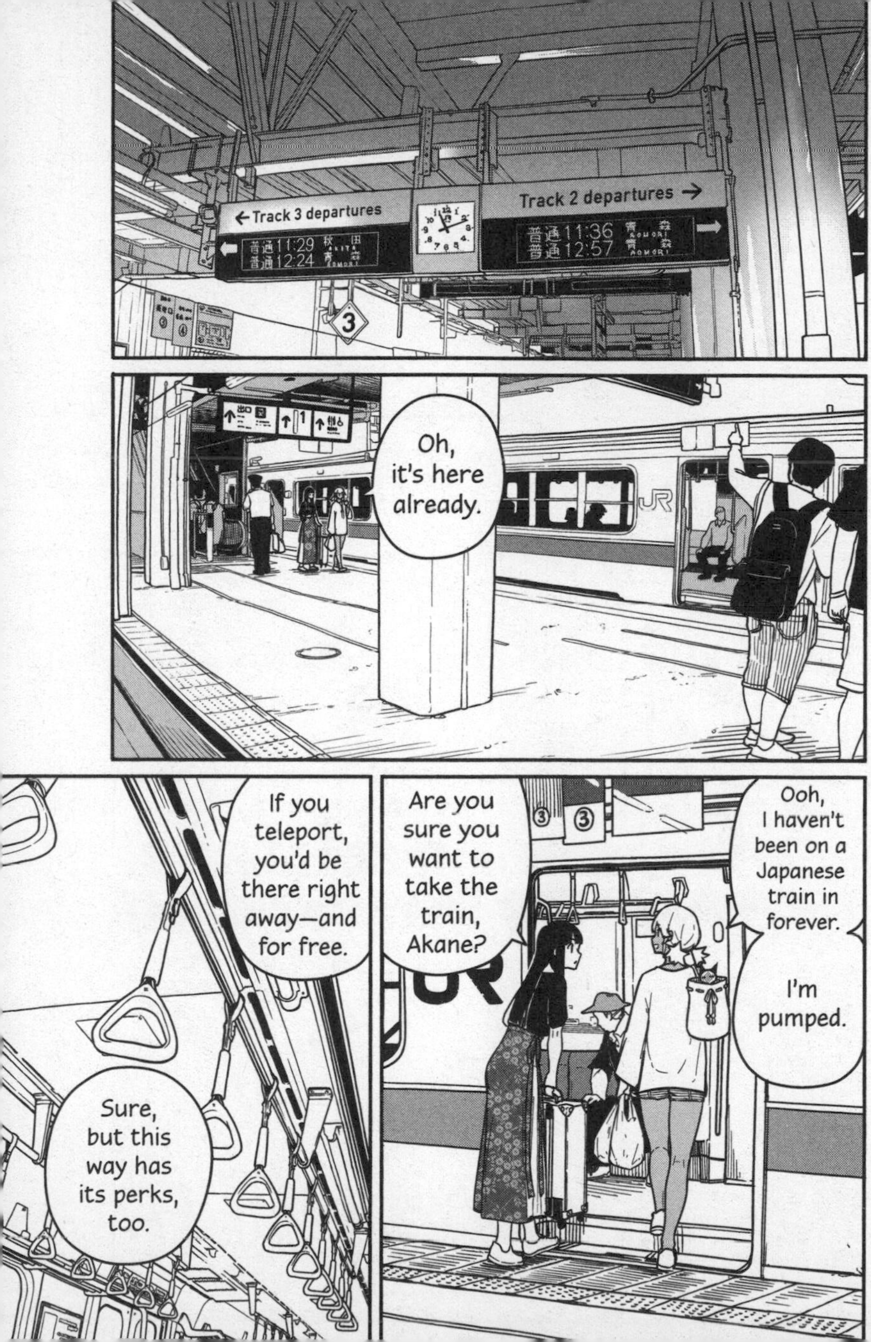
Track 2 departures
普通11:36 青森 AOMORI
普通12:57 青森 AOMORI
Track 3 departures
普通11:29 秋田 AKITA
普通12:24 青森 AOMORI
Oh, it's here already.
Ooh, I haven't been on a Japanese train in forever.
I'm pumped.
Are you sure you want to take the train, Akane?
If you teleport, you'd be there right away—and for free.
Sure, but this way has its perks, too.

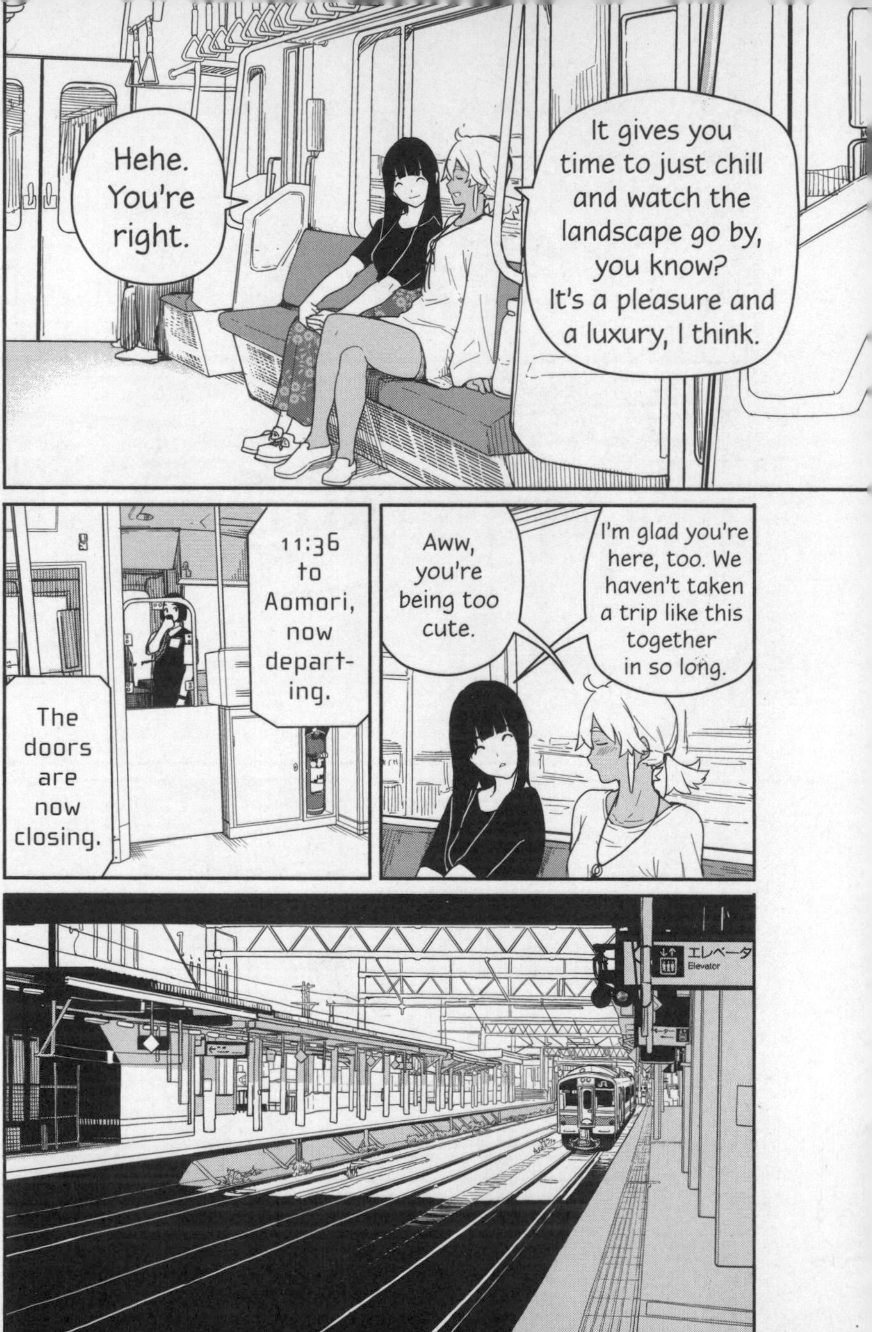
It gives you time to just chill and watch the landscape go by, you know? It's a pleasure and a luxury, I think.
Hehe. You're right.
I'm glad you're here, too. We haven't taken a trip like this together in so long.
Aww, you're being too cute.
11:36 to Aomori, now departing.
The doors are now closing.
エレベータ
Elevator

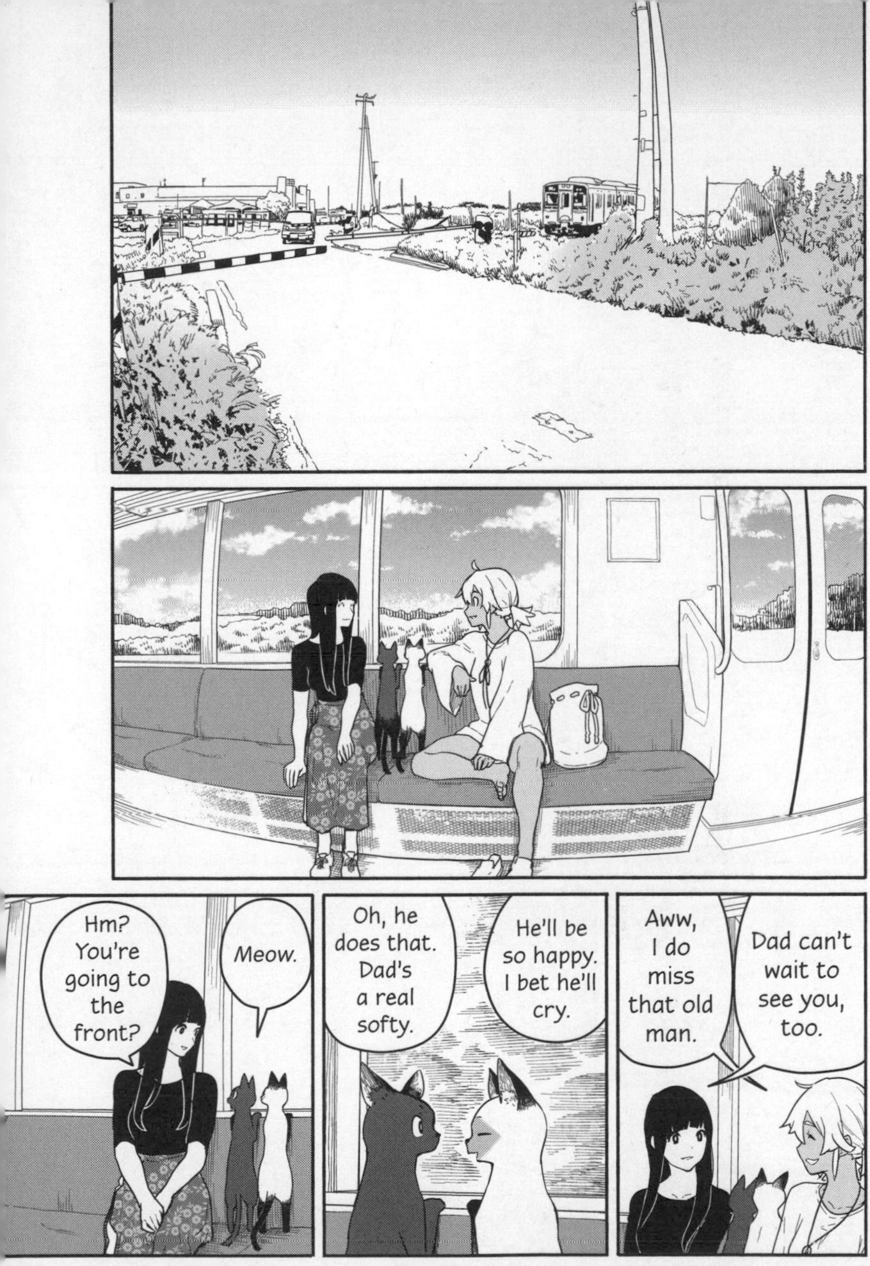
Dad can't wait to see you, too.
Aww, I do miss that old man.
He'll be so happy. I bet he'll cry.
Oh, he does that. Dad's a real softy.
Meow.
Hm? You're going to the front?

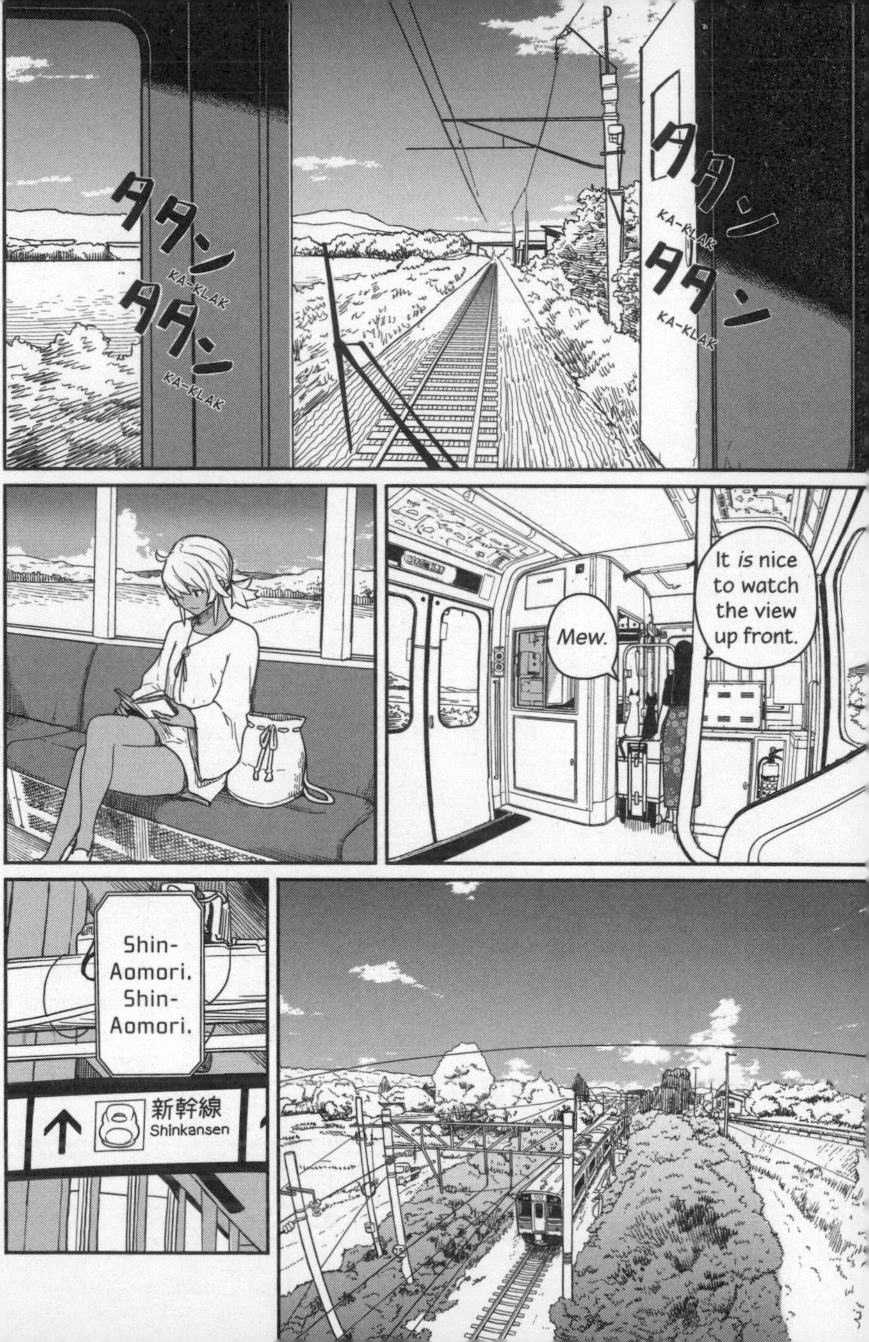
タタン
KA-KLAK
タタン
KA-KLAK
タタン
KA-KLAK
タタン
KA-KLAK
It *is* nice to watch the view up front.
Mew.
Shin-Aomori. Shin-Aomori.
新幹線
Shinkansen

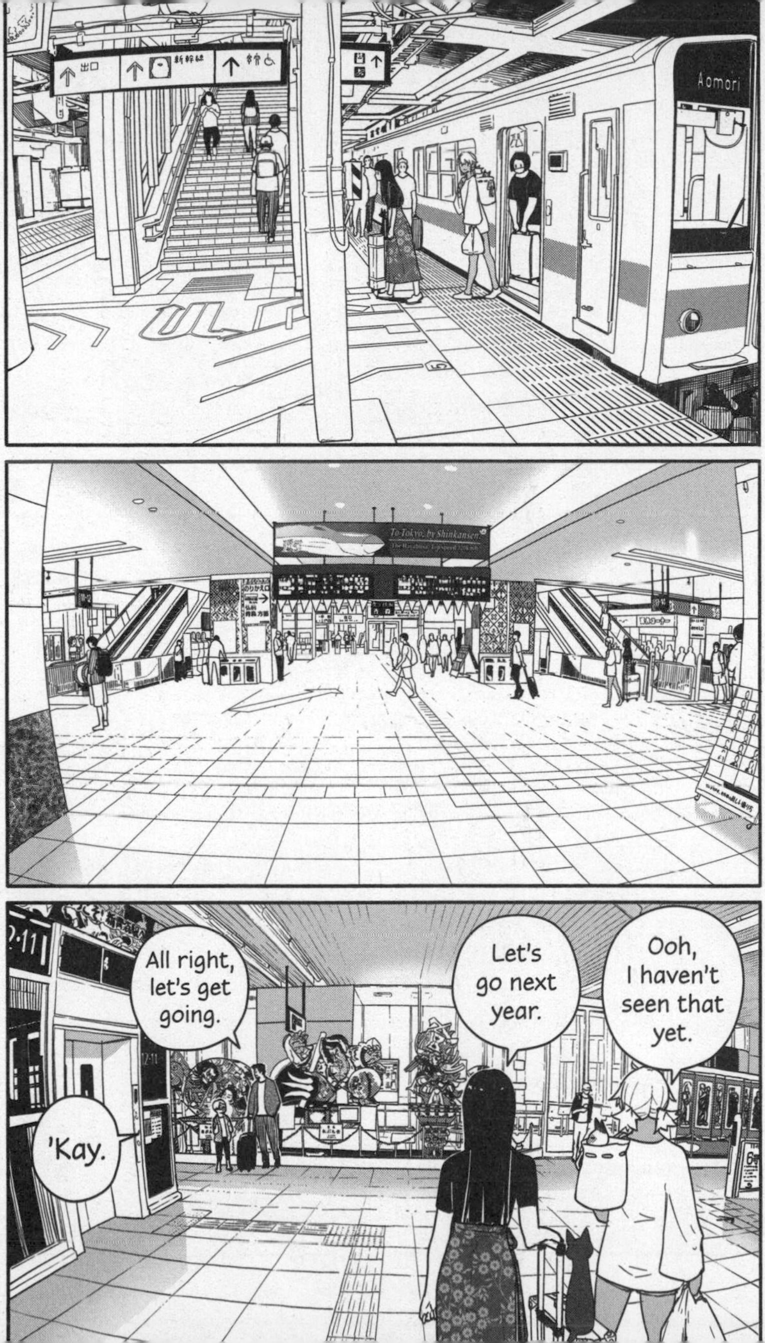
出口
新幹線
Aomori
To Tokyo, by Shinkansen.
Ooh, I haven't seen that yet.
Let's go next year.
All right, let's get going.
'Kay.

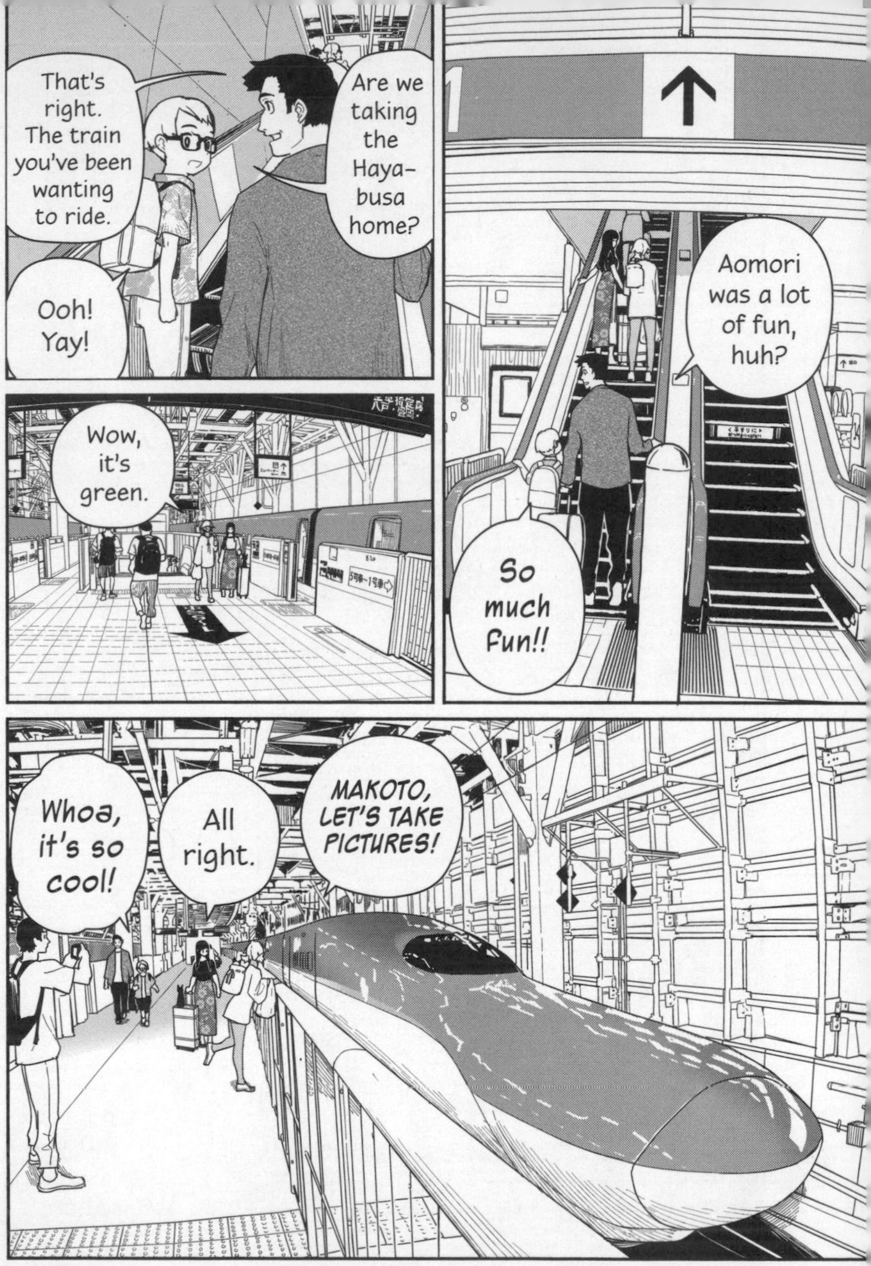
Aomori was a lot of fun, huh?
So much fun!!
Are we taking the Haya-busa home?
That's right. The train you've been wanting to ride.
Ooh! Yay!
Wow, it's green.
MAKOTO, LET'S TAKE PICTURES!
All right.
Whoa, it's so cool!

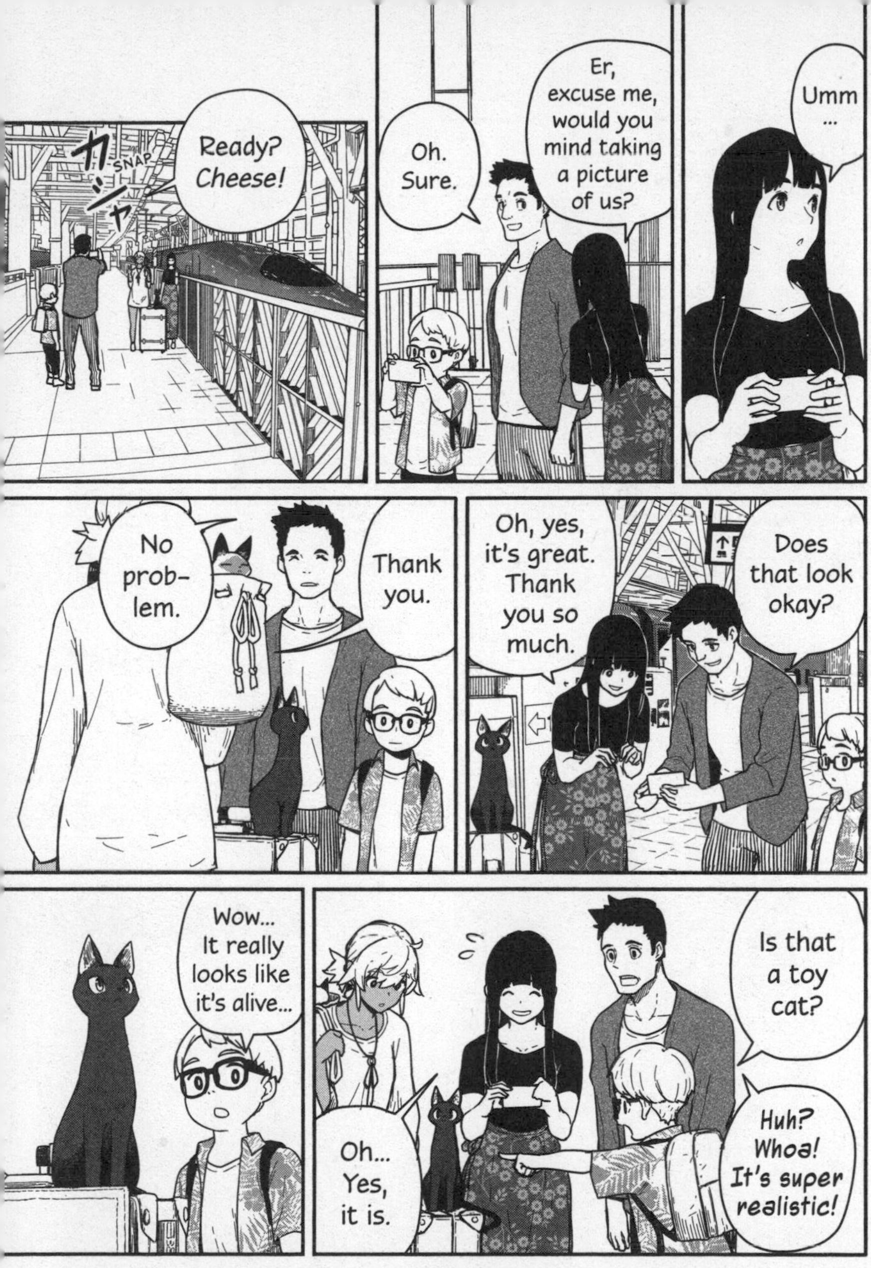
Umm ...
Er, excuse me, would you mind taking a picture of us?
Oh. Sure.
Ready? Cheese!
SNAP
Does that look okay?
Oh, yes, it's great. Thank you so much.
Thank you.
No prob-lem.
Is that a toy cat?
Huh? Whoa! It's super realistic!
Oh... Yes, it is.
Wow... It really looks like it's alive...

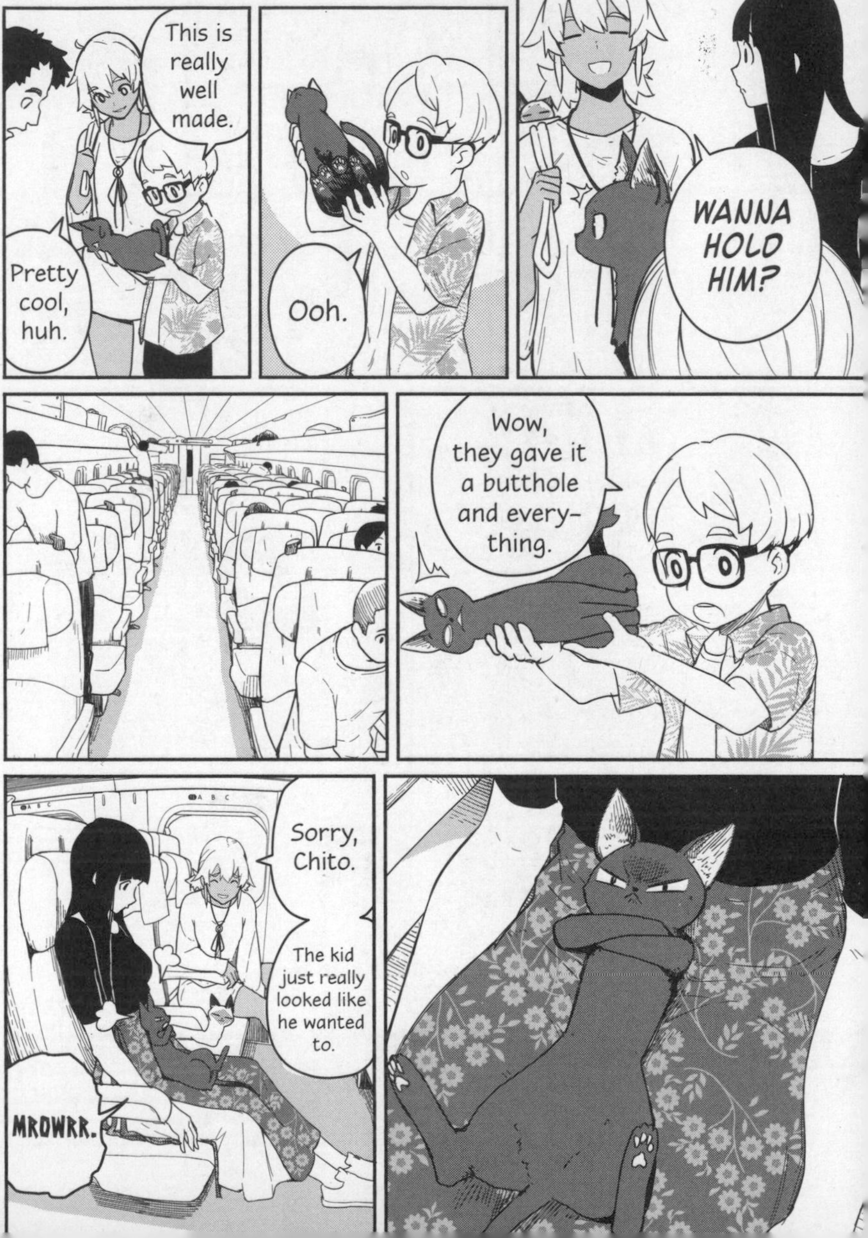
WANNA HOLD HIM?
Ooh.
This is really well made.
Pretty cool, huh.
Wow, they gave it a butthole and every-thing.
Sorry, Chito.
The kid just really looked like he wanted to.
MROWRR.

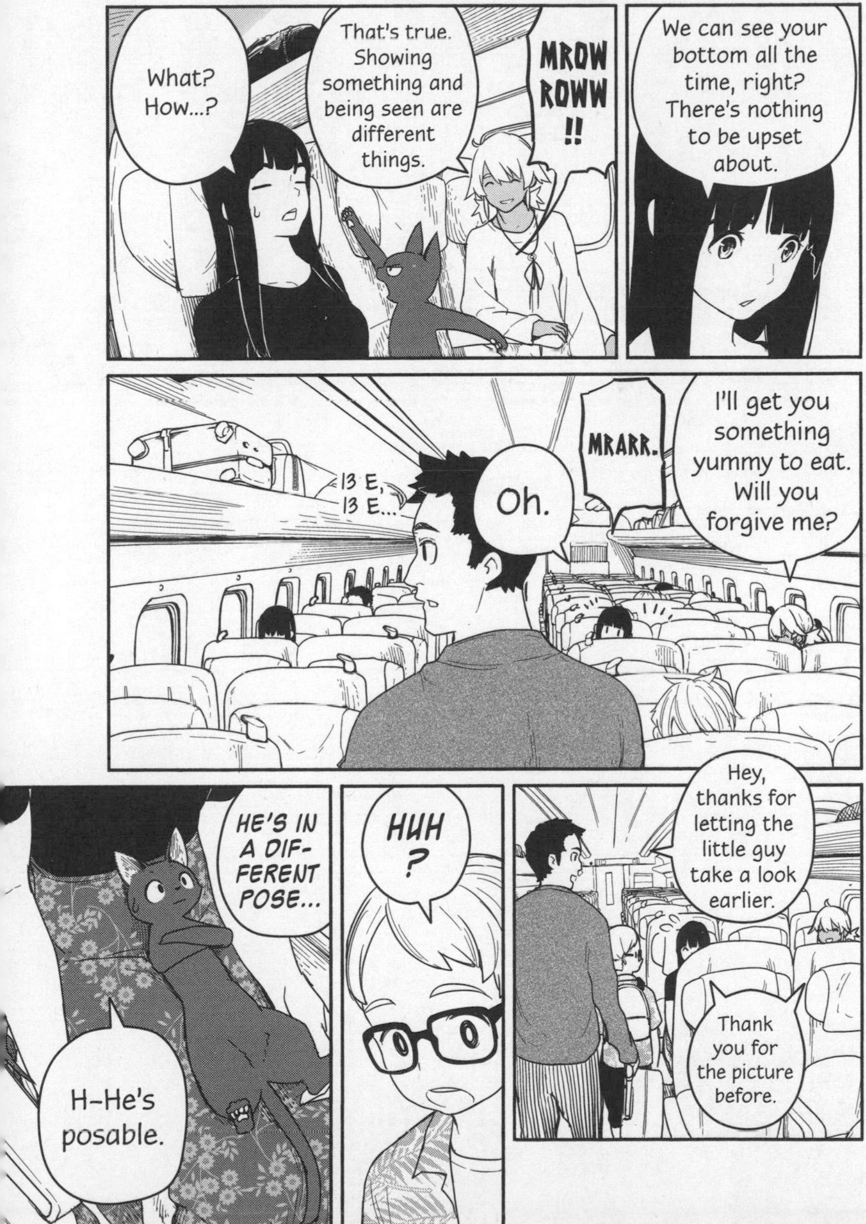
We can see your bottom all the time, right? There's nothing to be upset about.
MROW ROWW !!
That's true. Showing something and being seen are different things.
What? How...?
I'll get you something yummy to eat. Will you forgive me?
MRARR.
Oh.
13 E, 13 E...
Hey, thanks for letting the little guy take a look earlier.
Thank you for the picture before.
HUH ?
HE'S IN A DIF-FERENT POSE...
H-He's posable.

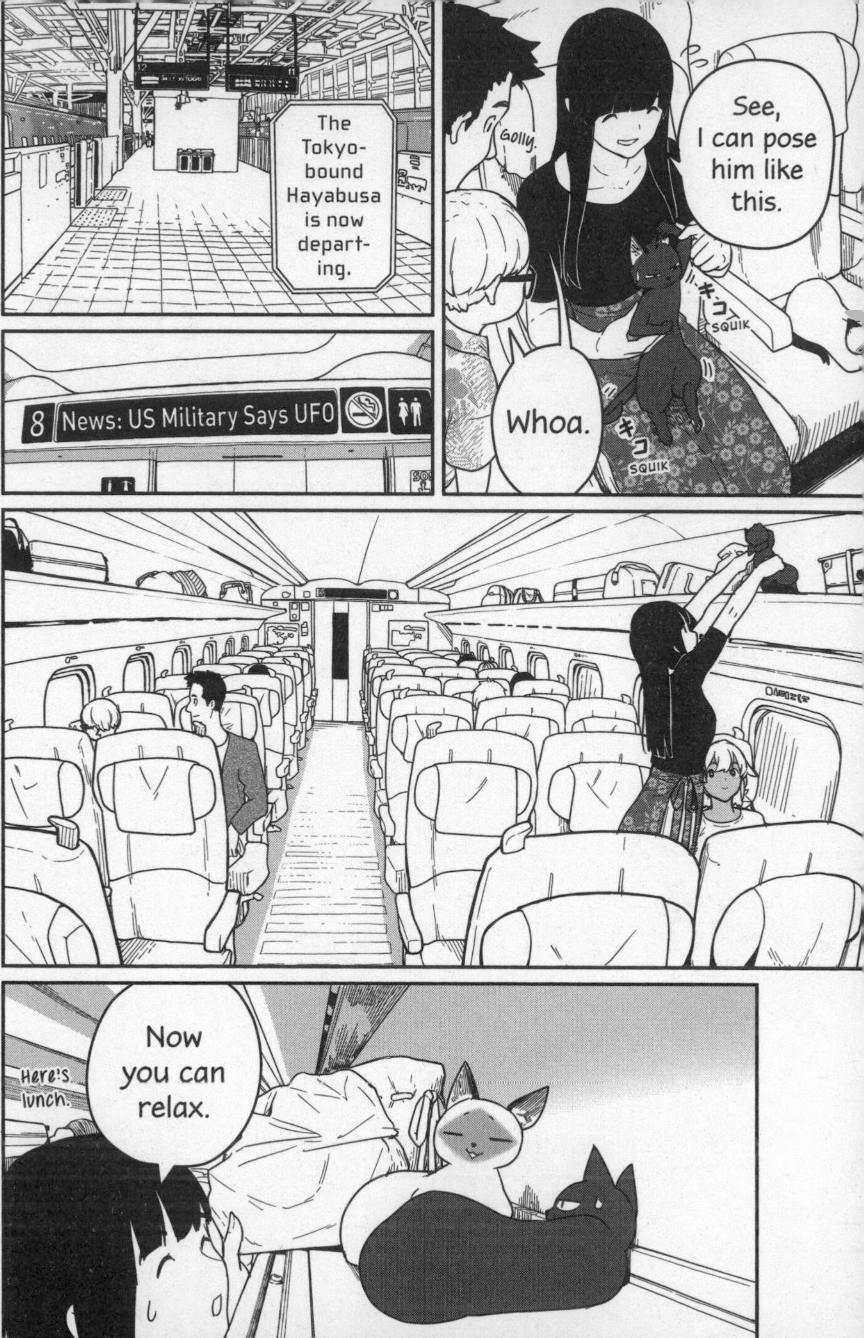
See, I can pose him like this.
Golly.
キコ SQUIK
Whoa.
キコ SQUIK
The Tokyo-bound Hayabusa is now departing.
8 News: US Military Says UFO
Now you can relax.
Here's lunch.

(Nah, I'm good)
Kaki-no-pii

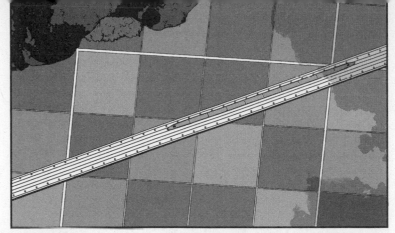

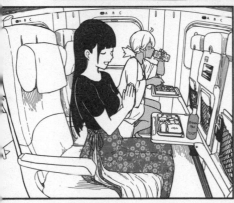

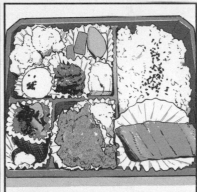

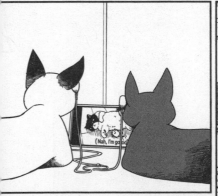

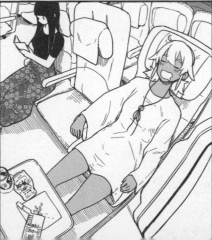

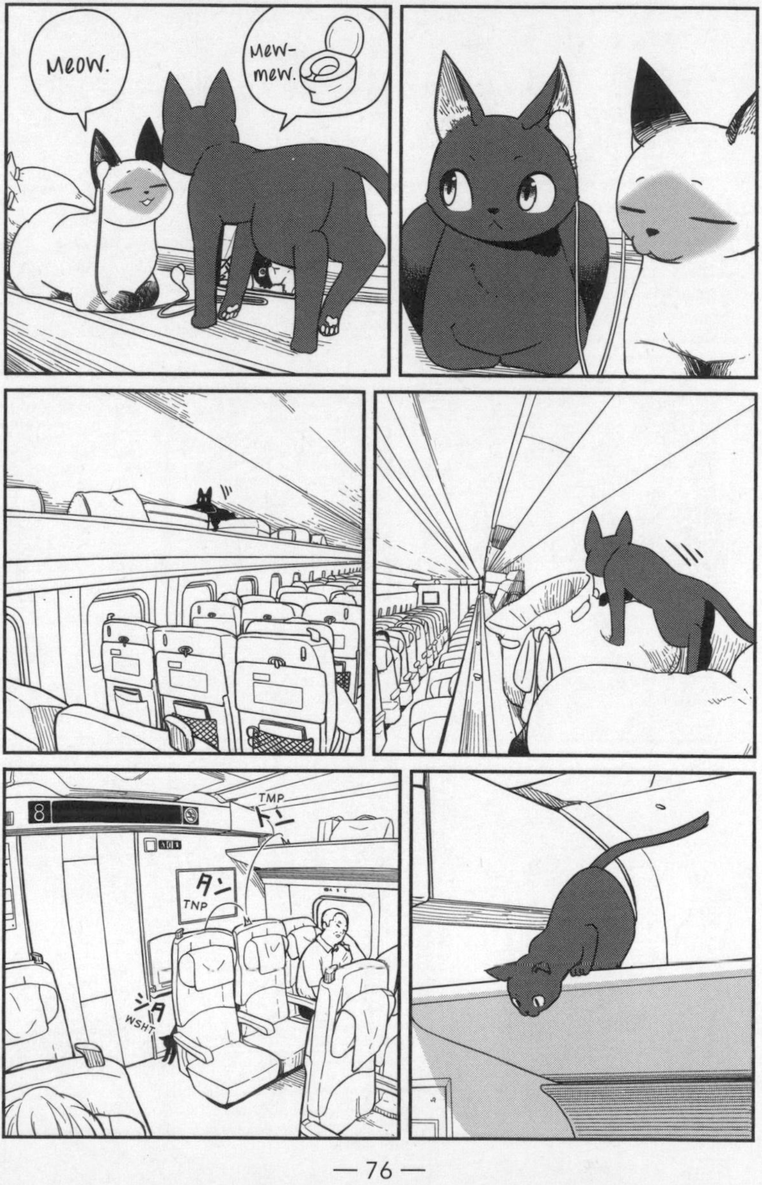
Mew-mew.
Meow.
TMP トン
タン TNP
シタ WSHT

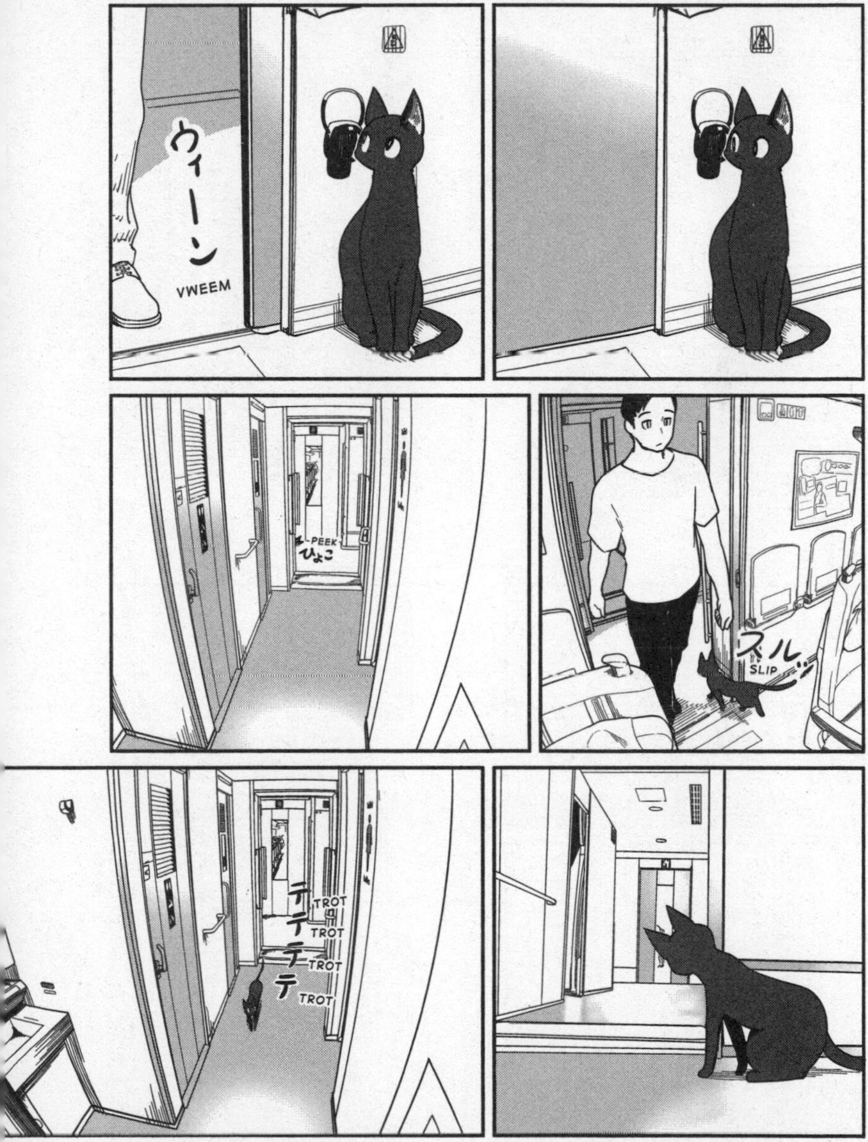
ウィーン
VWEEM
ズル
SLIP
ぴょこ
PEEK
テ
TROT
テ
TROT
テ
TROT
テ
TROT

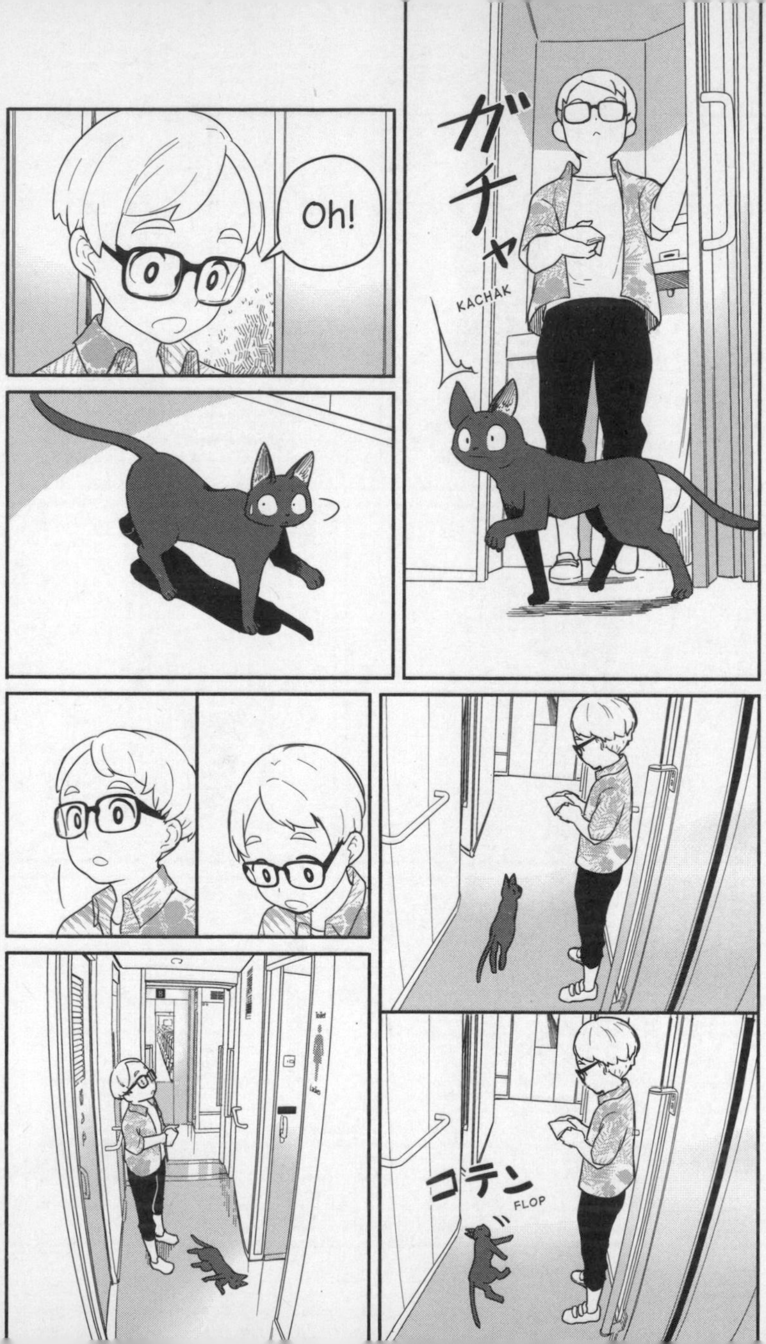
ガチャ
KACHAK
Oh!
コテン
FLOP

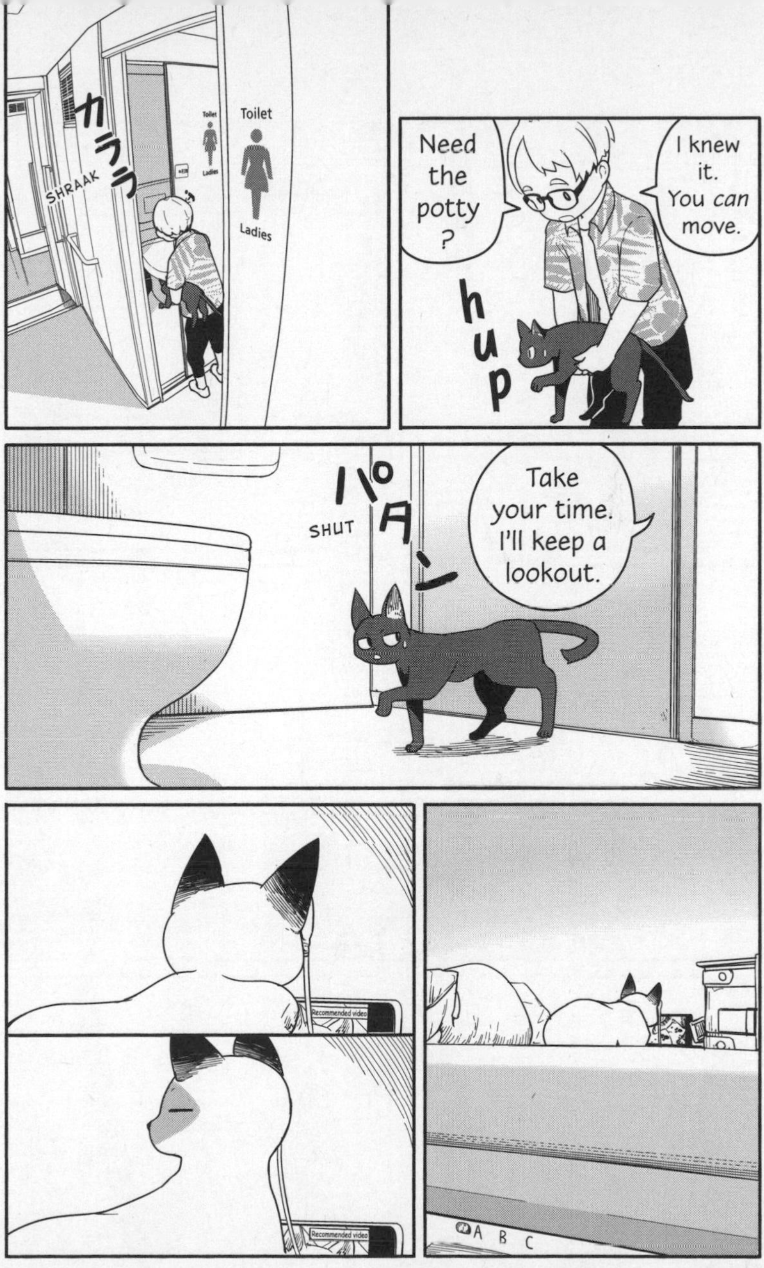
I knew it. You *can* move.
Need the potty?
hup
Toilet
Ladies
Toilet
Ladies
カララ
SHRAAK
Take your time. I'll keep a lookout.
パタン
SHUT
A B C
Recommended video
Recommended video

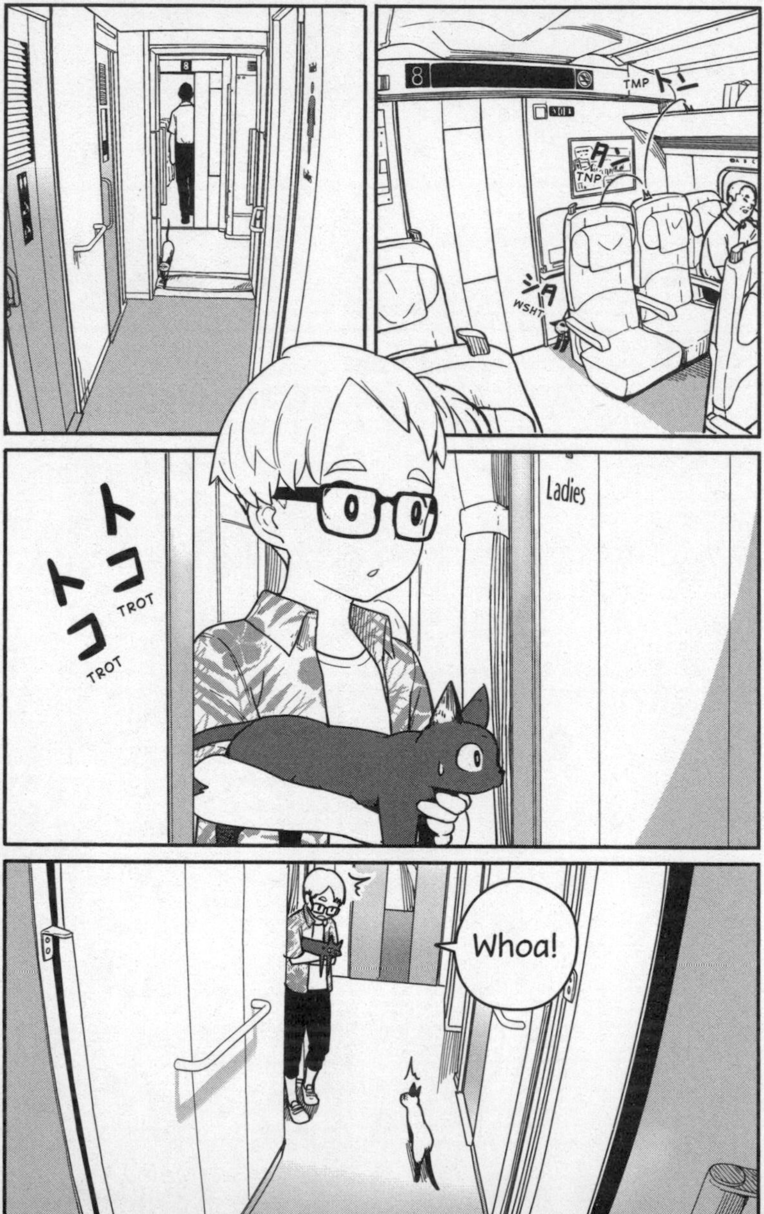
8
TMP
トン
タン
TNP
シタ
WSHT
トコトコ
TROT TROT
Ladies
Whoa!

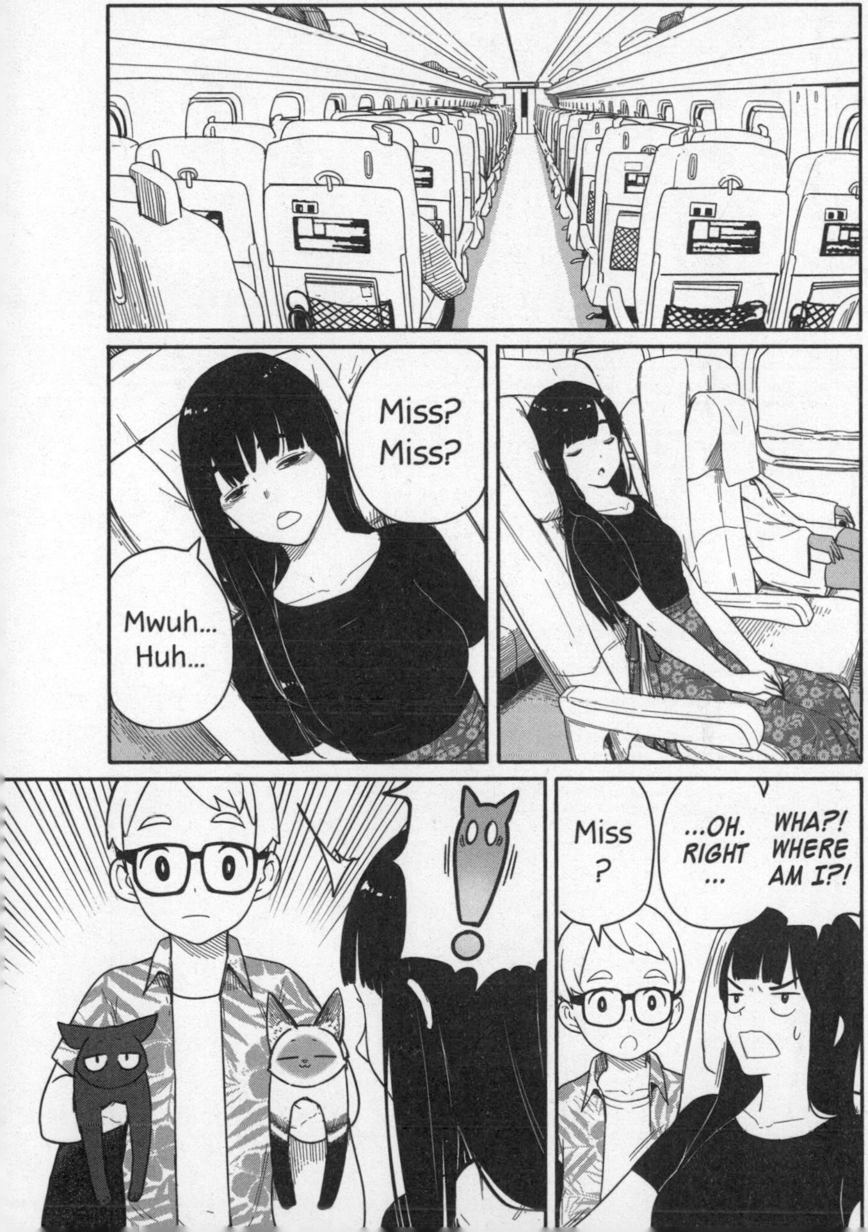
Miss? Miss?
Mwuh... Huh...
WHA?! WHERE AM I?!
...OH. RIGHT ...
Miss ?

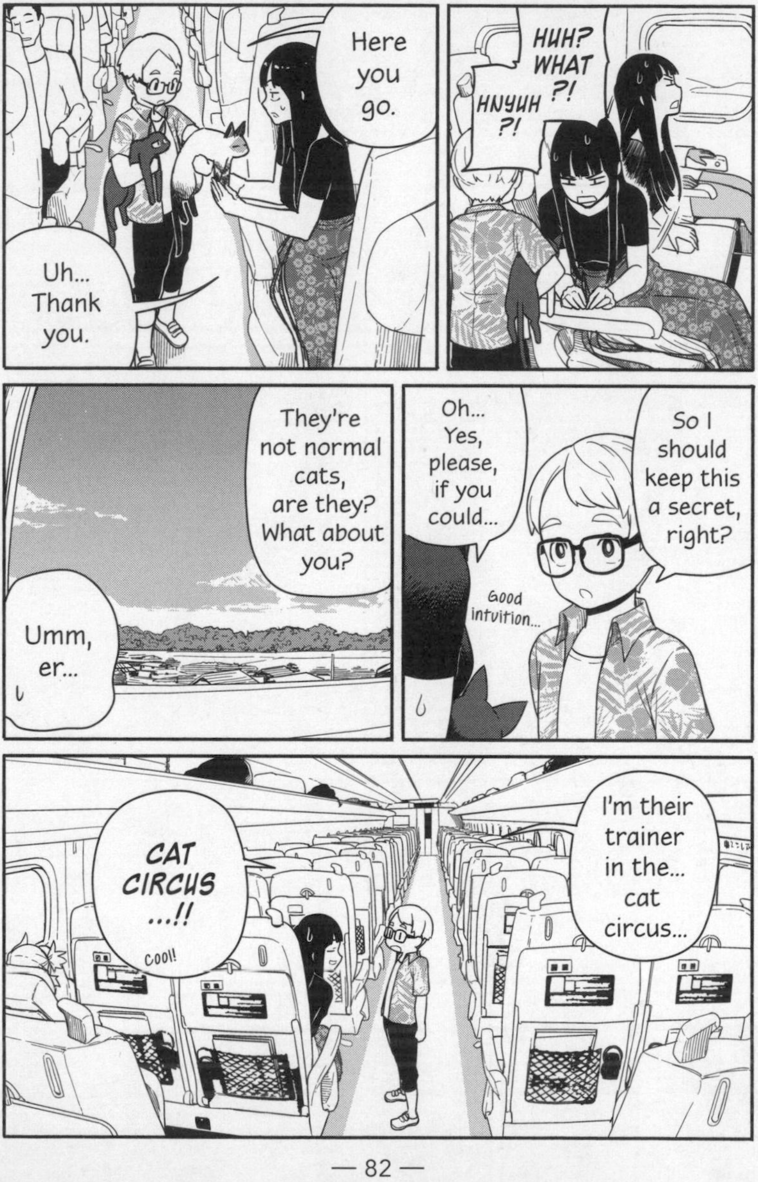
HUH? WHAT ?!
HNYUH ?!
Here you go.
Uh... Thank you.
So I should keep this a secret, right?
Oh... Yes, please, if you could...
Good intuition...
They're not normal cats, are they? What about you?
Umm, er...
I'm their trainer in the... cat circus...
CAT CIRCUS ...!!
Cool!

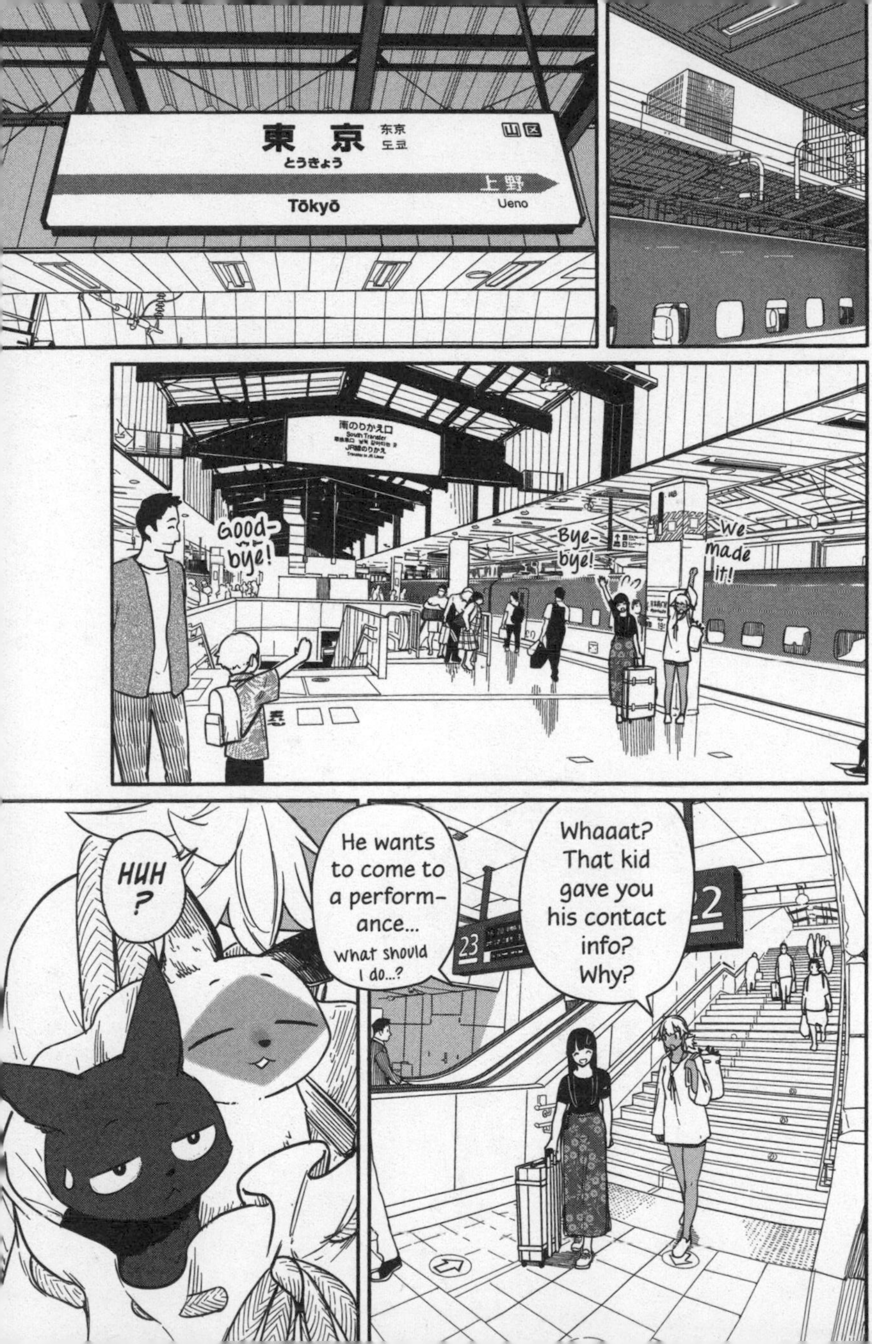
東京
东京
도쿄
とうきょう
Tōkyō
山区
上野
Ueno
南のりかえ口
South Transfer
JR線のりかえ
We made it!
Bye-bye!
Good-bye!
Whaaat? That kid gave you his contact info? Why?
23
22
He wants to come to a performance... what should I do...?
HUH?

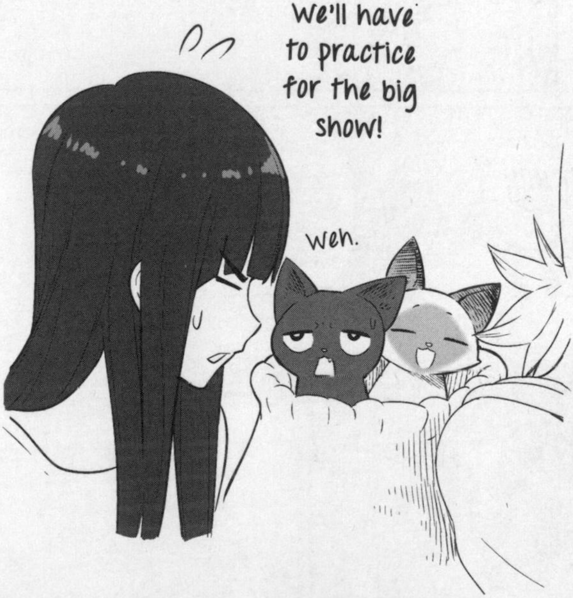
We'll have to practice for the big show!
weh.

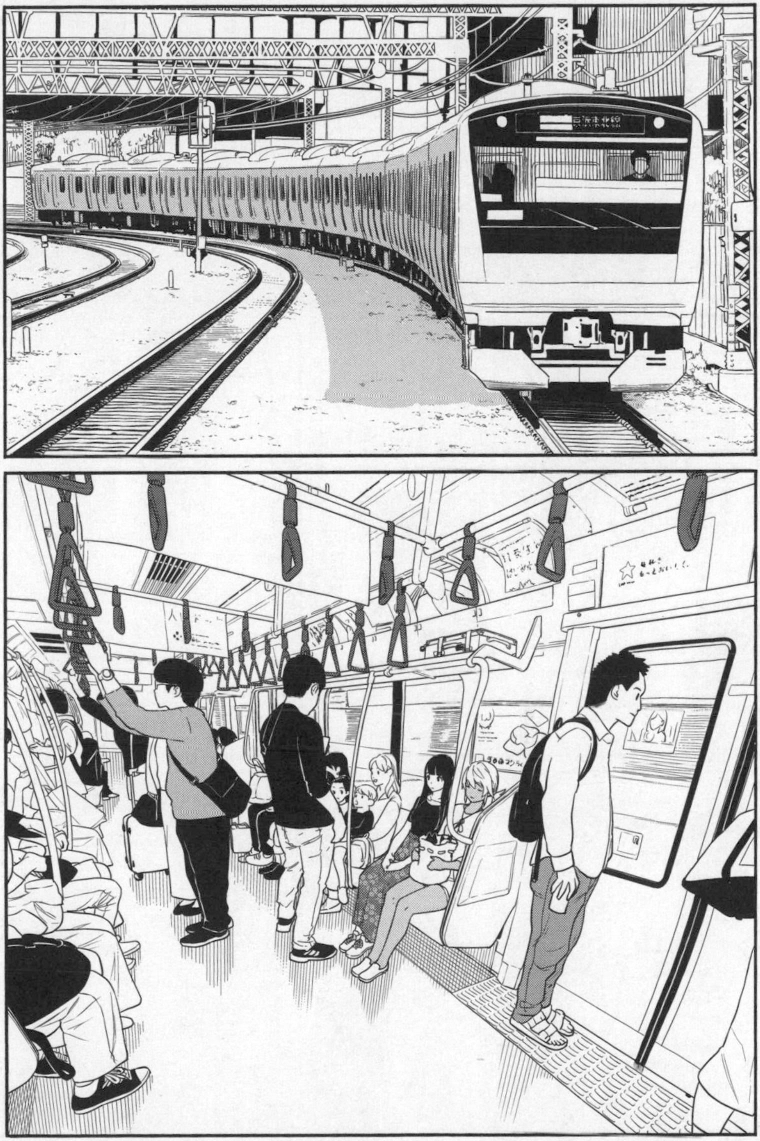

When boarding, please move toward the middle of the train car.

Please be careful when stepping off the train.

This is Kawasaki.

Yamate. Yamate.

JK 06	山手	山手 야마테	浜
石川町 Ishikawachō		Yamate	根岸 Negishi

やまて

Crowd sickness... We're too used to places with few people around...

I feel kind of... exhausted being around so many people...

Chapter 58 Four Months' Absence (from Family) Makes the Heart Grow Fonder (of Friends)

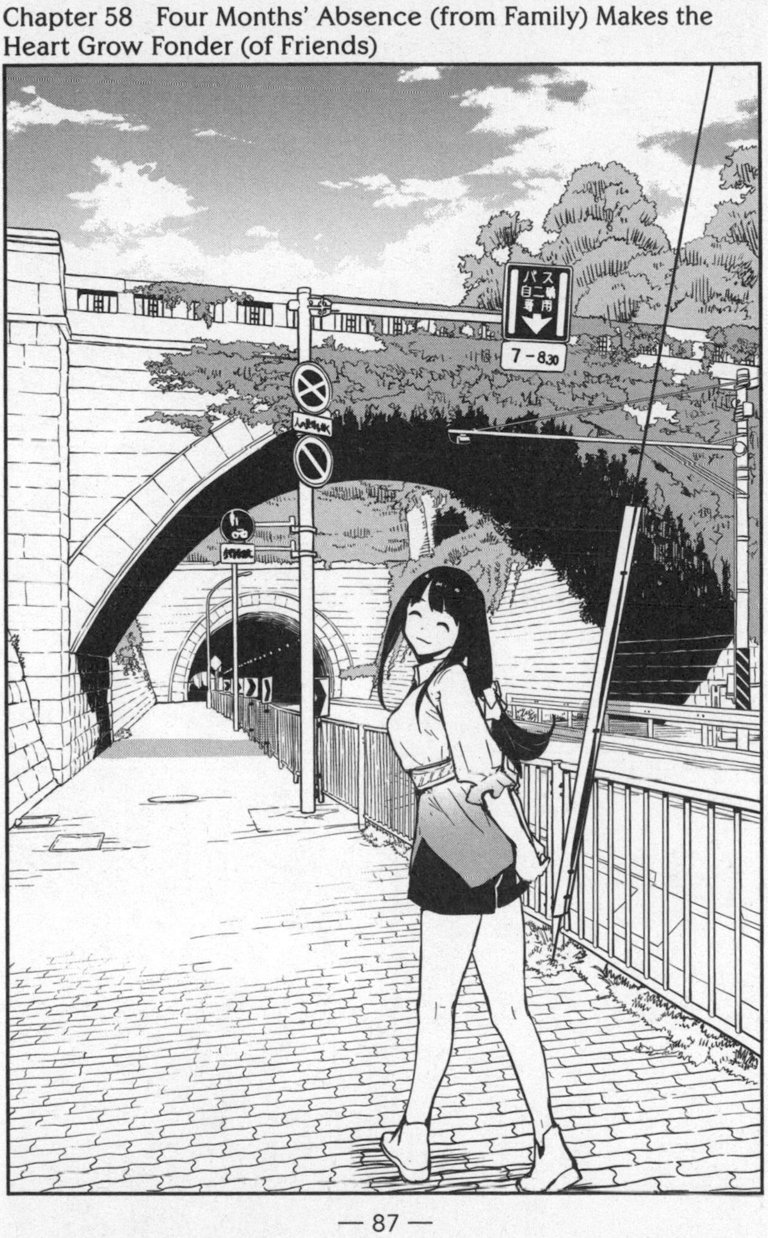
バス
自二輪
専用
7 - 8.30

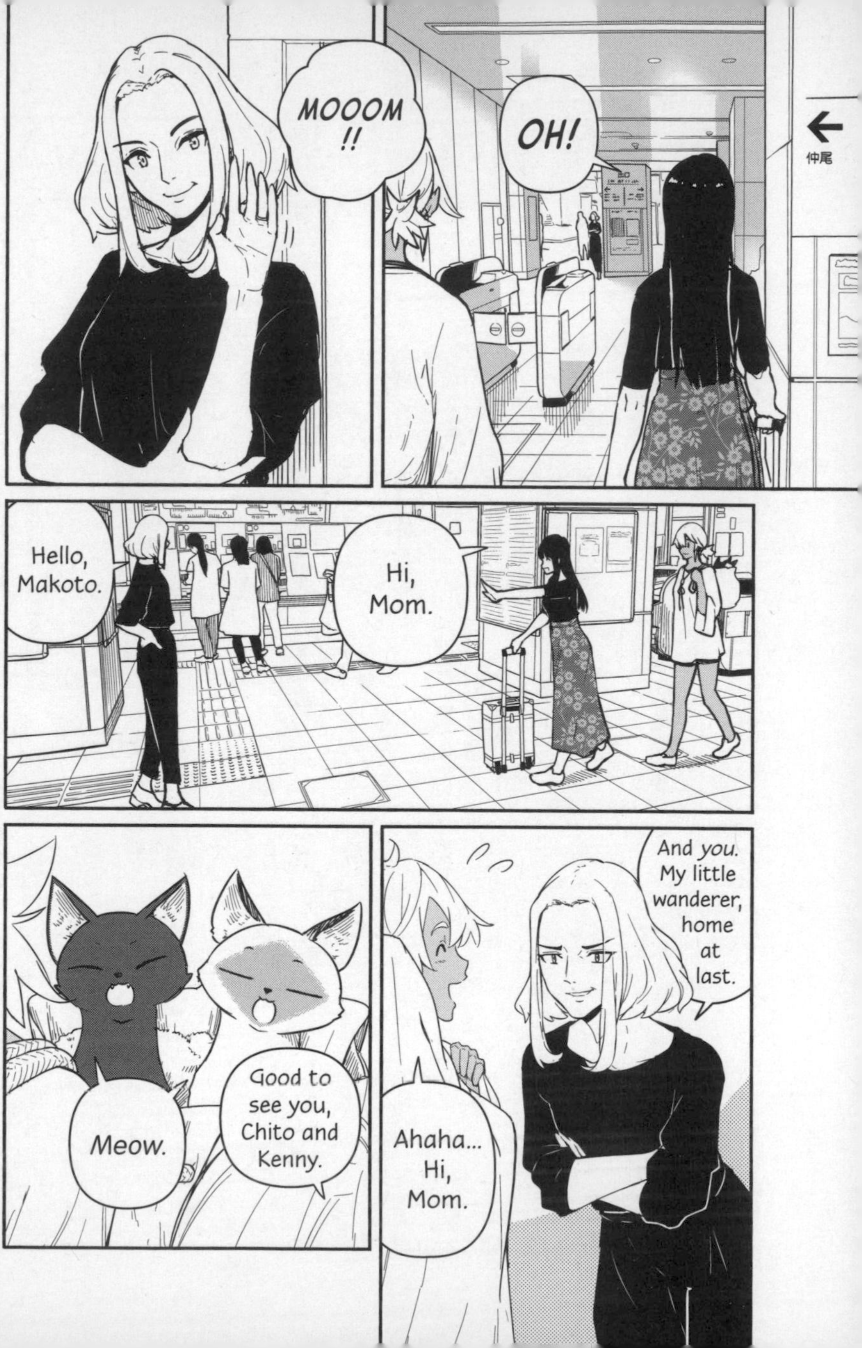

OH!
仲尾
MOOOM !!
Hi, Mom.
Hello, Makoto.
And you. My little wanderer, home at last.
Ahaha... Hi, Mom.
Good to see you, Chito and Kenny.
Meow.

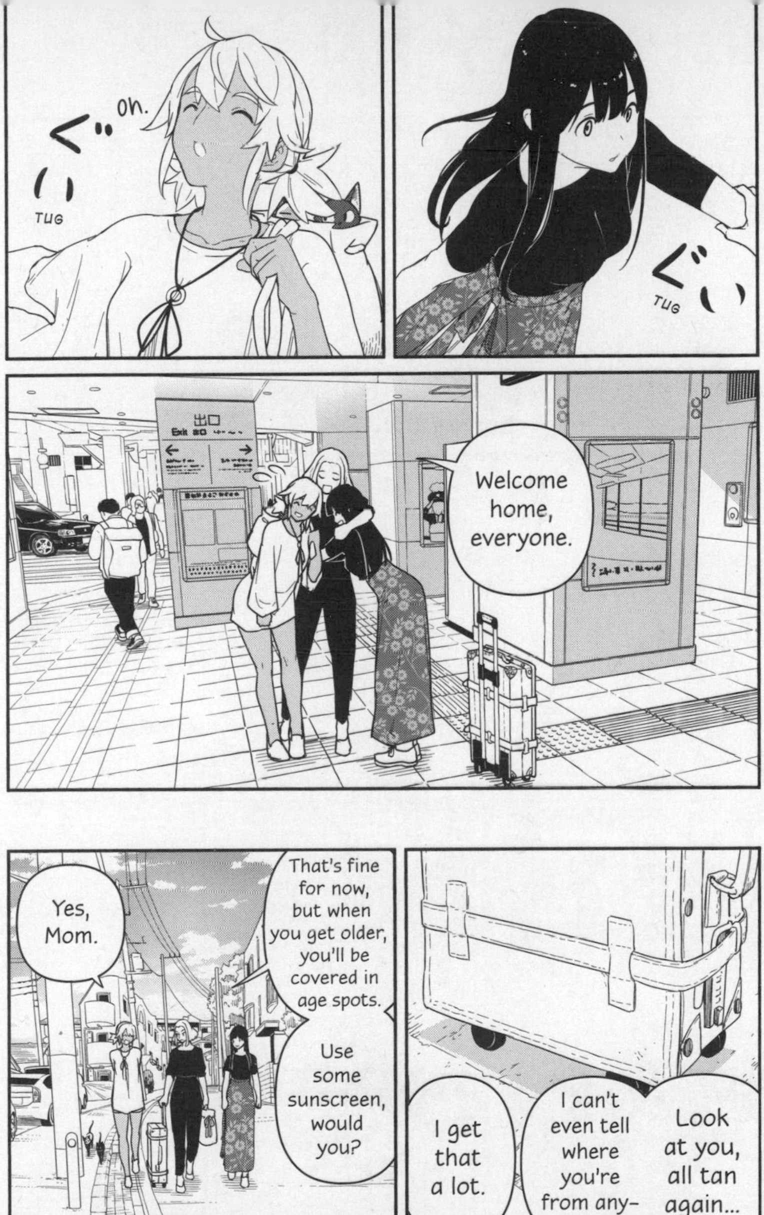
ぐい
TUG
oh.
ぐい
TUG
Welcome home, everyone.
Look at you, all tan again...
I can't even tell where you're from any-more.
I get that a lot.
That's fine for now, but when you get older, you'll be covered in age spots.
Use some sunscreen, would you?
Yes, Mom.

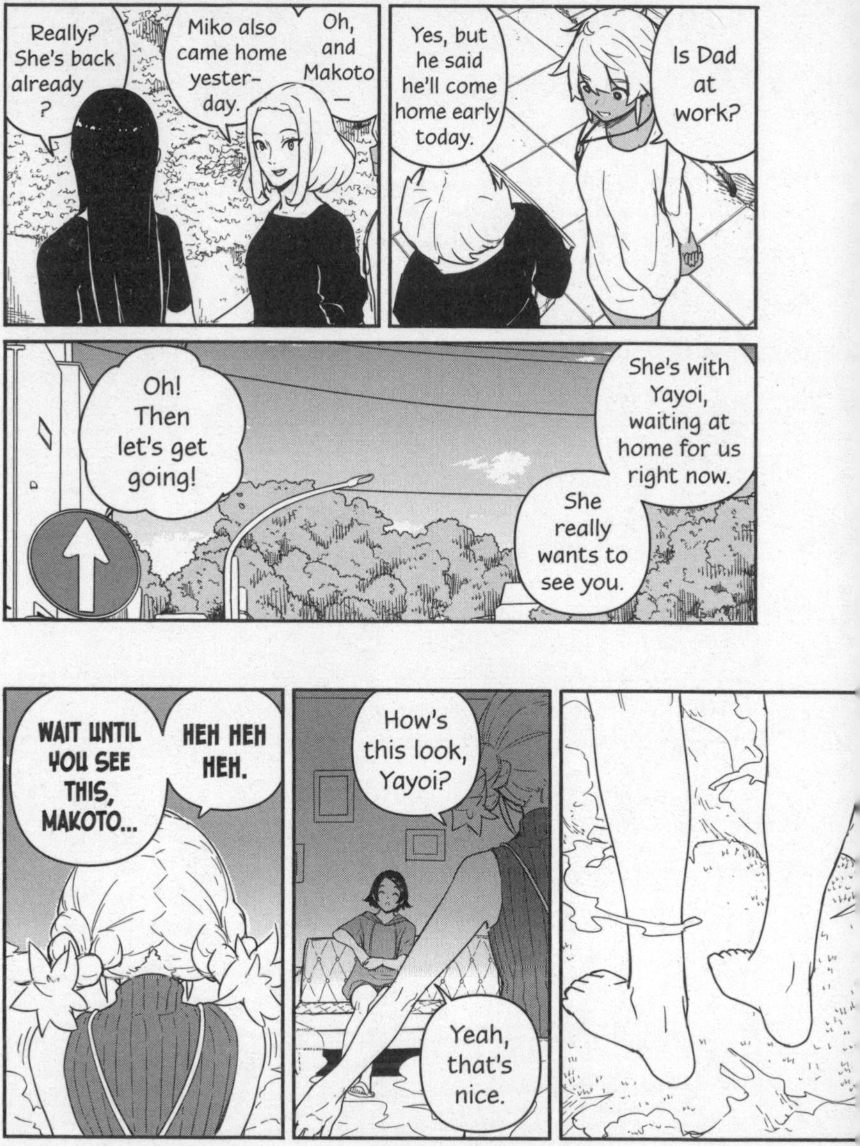
Is Dad at work?
Yes, but he said he'll come home early today.
Oh, and Makoto—
Miko also came home yester-day.
Really? She's back already?
She's with Yayoi, waiting at home for us right now.
She really wants to see you.
Oh! Then let's get going!
How's this look, Yayoi?
Yeah, that's nice.
HEH HEH HEH.
WAIT UNTIL YOU SEE THIS, MAKOTO...

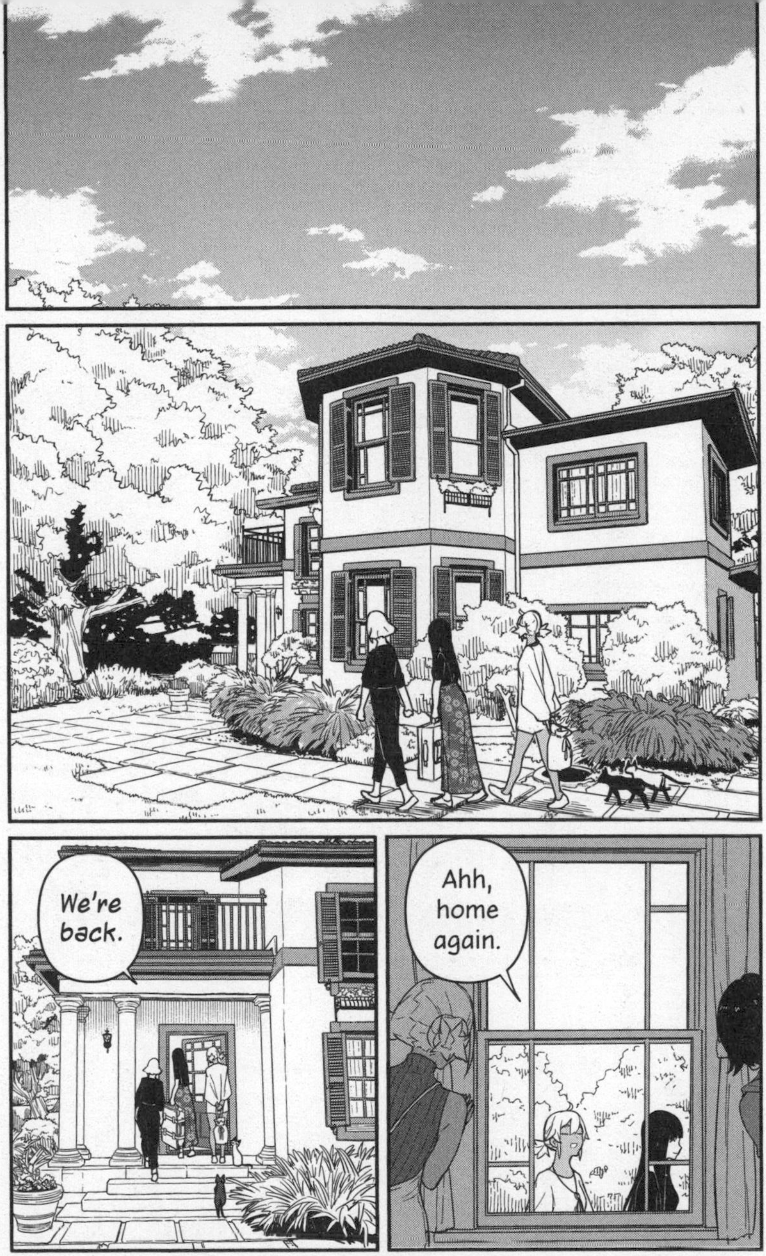
Ahh, home again.
We're back.

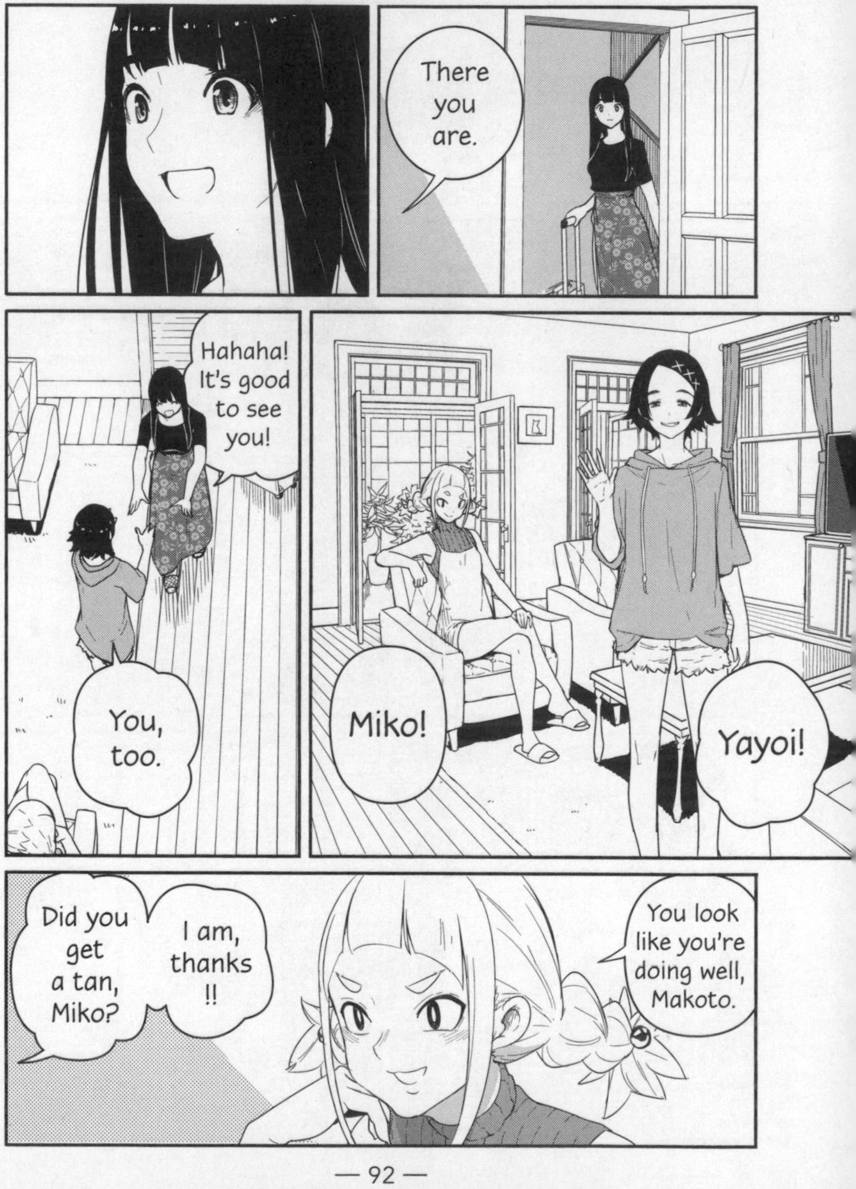
There you are.
Yayoi!
Miko!
Hahaha! It's good to see you!
You, too.
You look like you're doing well, Makoto.
I am, thanks !!
Did you get a tan, Miko?

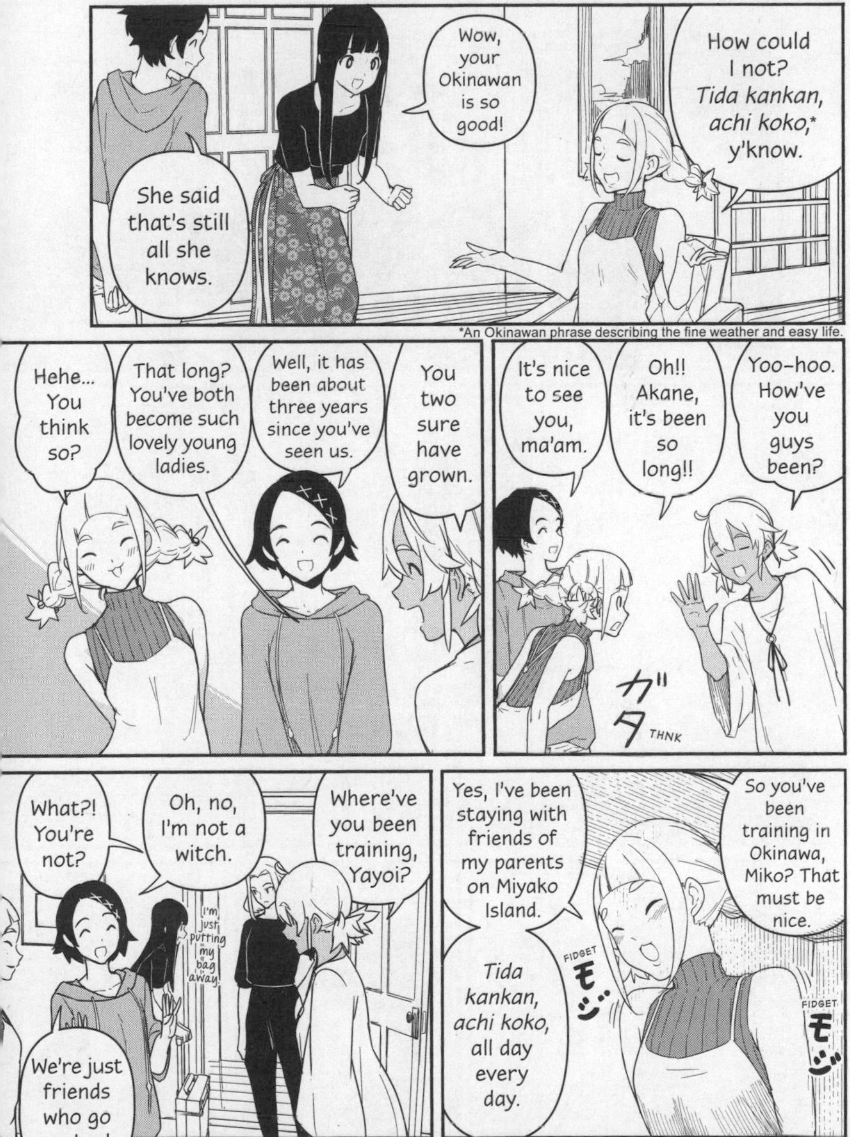
How could I not? Tida kankan, achi koko,* y'know.
Wow, your Okinawan is so good!
She said that's still all she knows.
Yoo-hoo. How've you guys been?
Oh!! Akane, it's been so long!!
It's nice to see you, ma'am.
ガタ
THNK
You two sure have grown.
Well, it has been about three years since you've seen us.
That long? You've both become such lovely young ladies.
Hehe... You think so?
So you've been training in Okinawa, Miko? That must be nice.
Yes, I've been staying with friends of my parents on Miyako Island.
Tida kankan, achi koko, all day every day.
FIDGET
モジ
FIDGET
モジ
Where've you been training, Yayoi?
Oh, no, I'm not a witch.
What?! You're not?
I'm just putting my bag away.
We're just friends who go way back.

*An Okinawan phrase describing the fine weather and easy life.

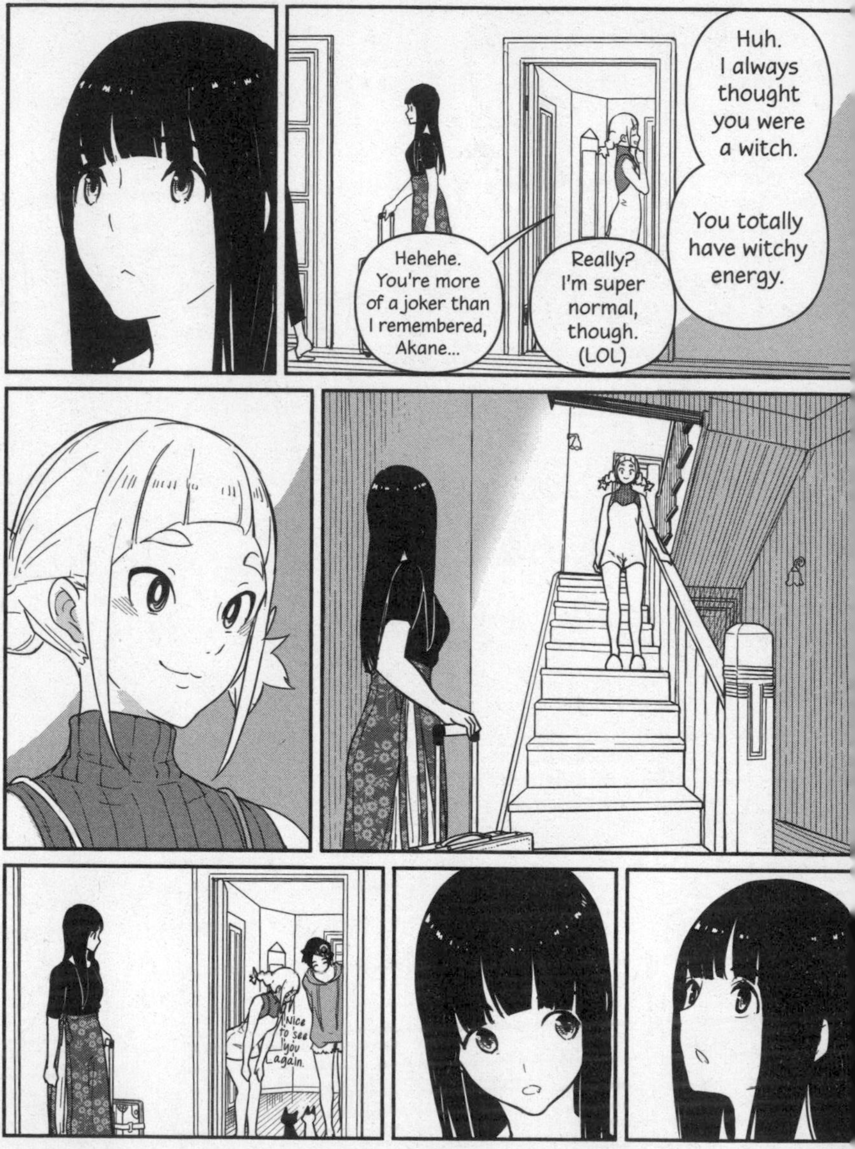
Huh. I always thought you were a witch.
You totally have witchy energy.
Really? I'm super normal, though. (LOL)
Hehehe. You're more of a joker than I remembered, Akane...
Nice to see you again.

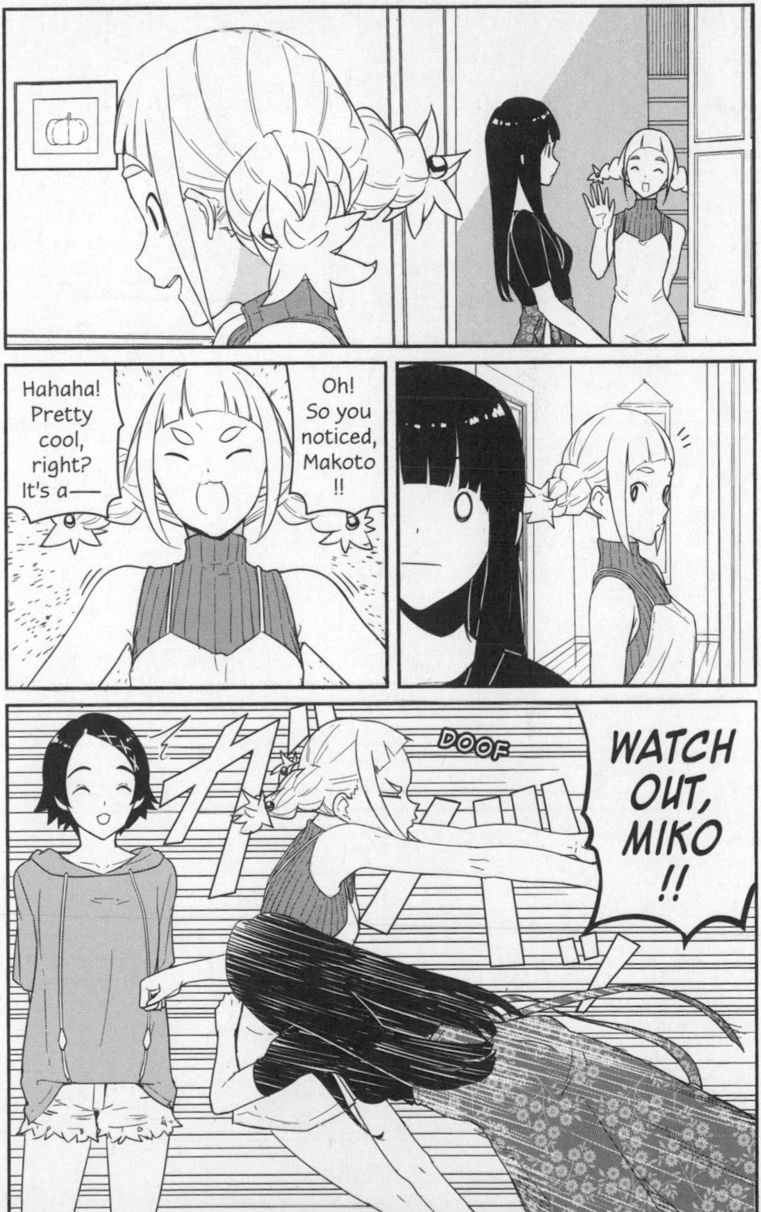
Oh! So you noticed, Makoto!!
Hahaha! Pretty cool, right? It's a——
WATCH OUT, MIKO!!
DOOF

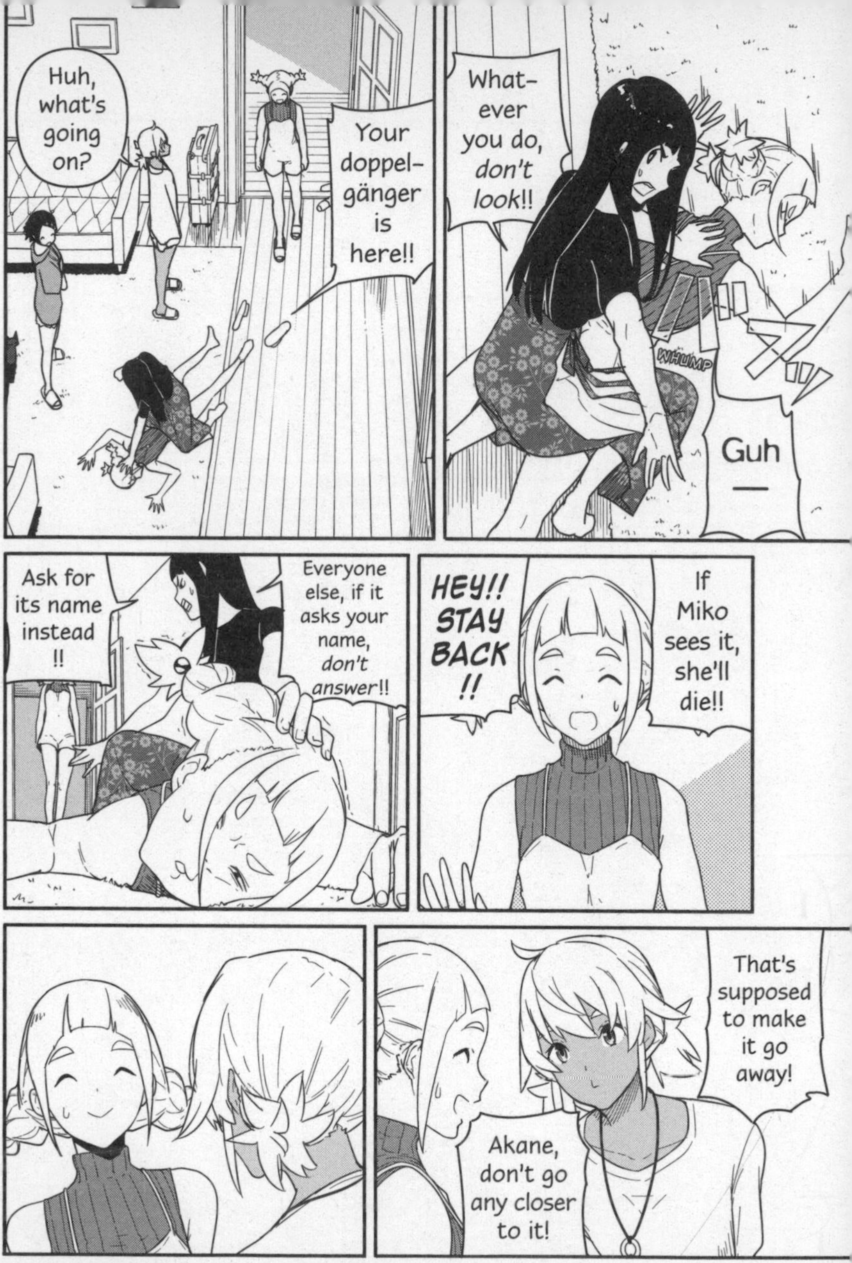
What-ever you do, don't look!!
WHUMP
Guh —
Your doppel-gänger is here!!
Huh, what's going on?
If Miko sees it, she'll die!!
HEY!! STAY BACK !!
Everyone else, if it asks your name, don't answer!!
Ask for its name instead !!
That's supposed to make it go away!
Akane, don't go any closer to it!

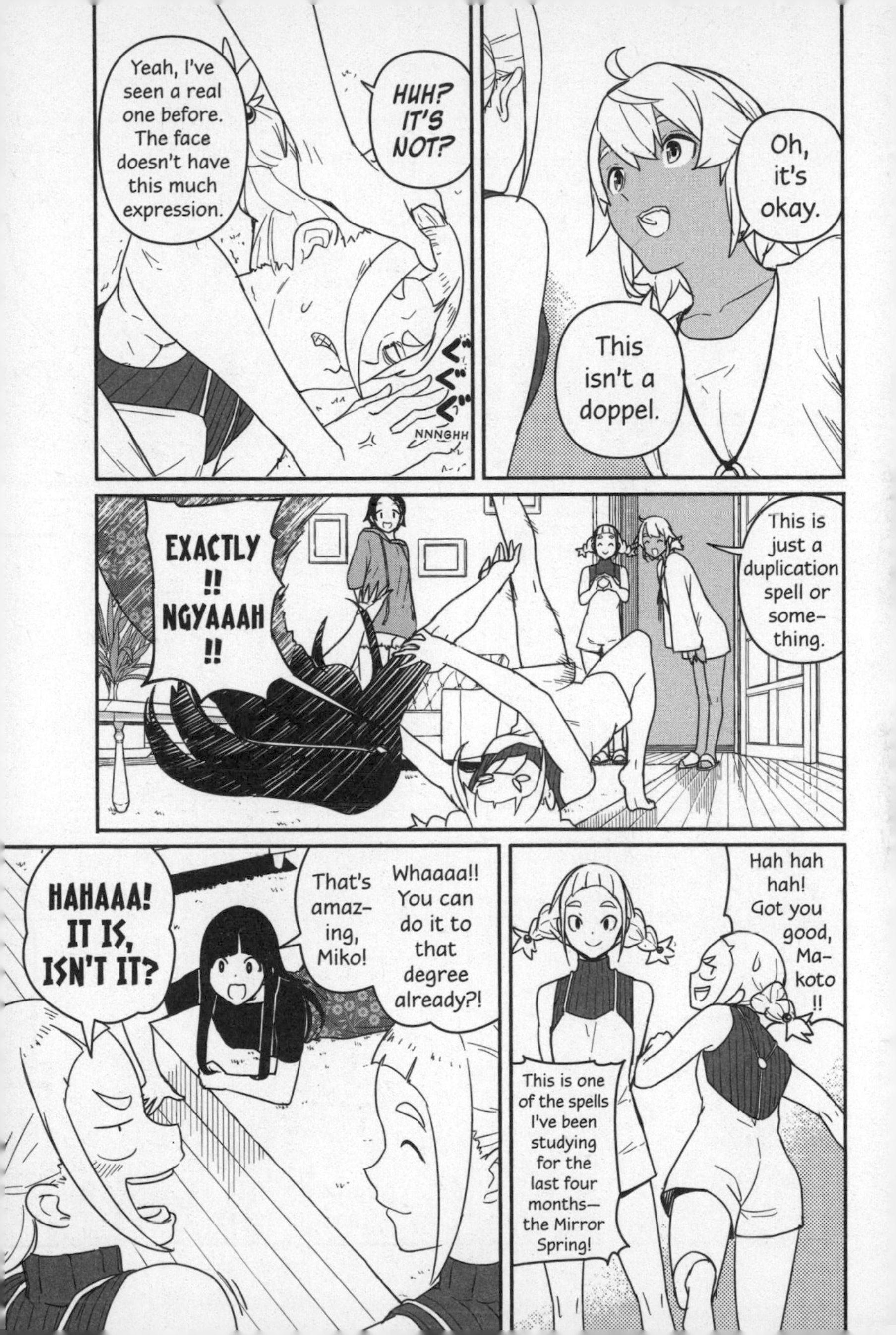
Oh, it's okay.
This isn't a doppel.
HUH? IT'S NOT?
Yeah, I've seen a real one before. The face doesn't have this much expression.
NNNGHH
This is just a duplication spell or some-thing.
EXACTLY !! NGYAAAH !!
Hah hah hah! Got you good, Ma-koto !!
This is one of the spells I've been studying for the last four months— the Mirror Spring!
Whaaaa!! You can do it to that degree already?!
That's amaz-ing, Miko!
HAHAAA! IT IS, ISN'T IT?

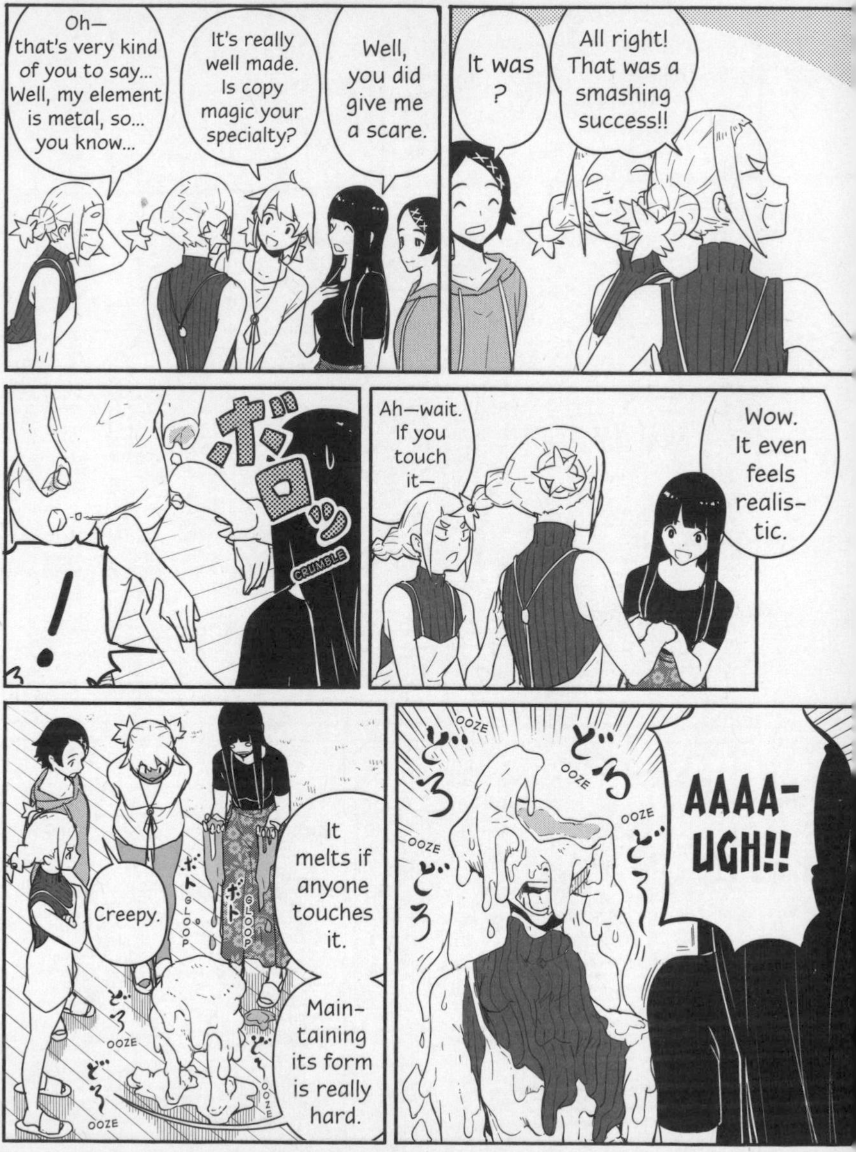
All right! That was a smashing success!!
It was ?
Well, you did give me a scare.
It's really well made. Is copy magic your specialty?
Oh— that's very kind of you to say... Well, my element is metal, so... you know...
Wow. It even feels realis-tic.
Ah—wait. If you touch it—
CRUMBLE
!
OOZE
OOZE
OOZE
OOZE
AAAA-UGH!!
It melts if anyone touches it.
Main-taining its form is really hard.
GLOOP
GLOOP
Creepy.
OOZE
OOZE
OOZE

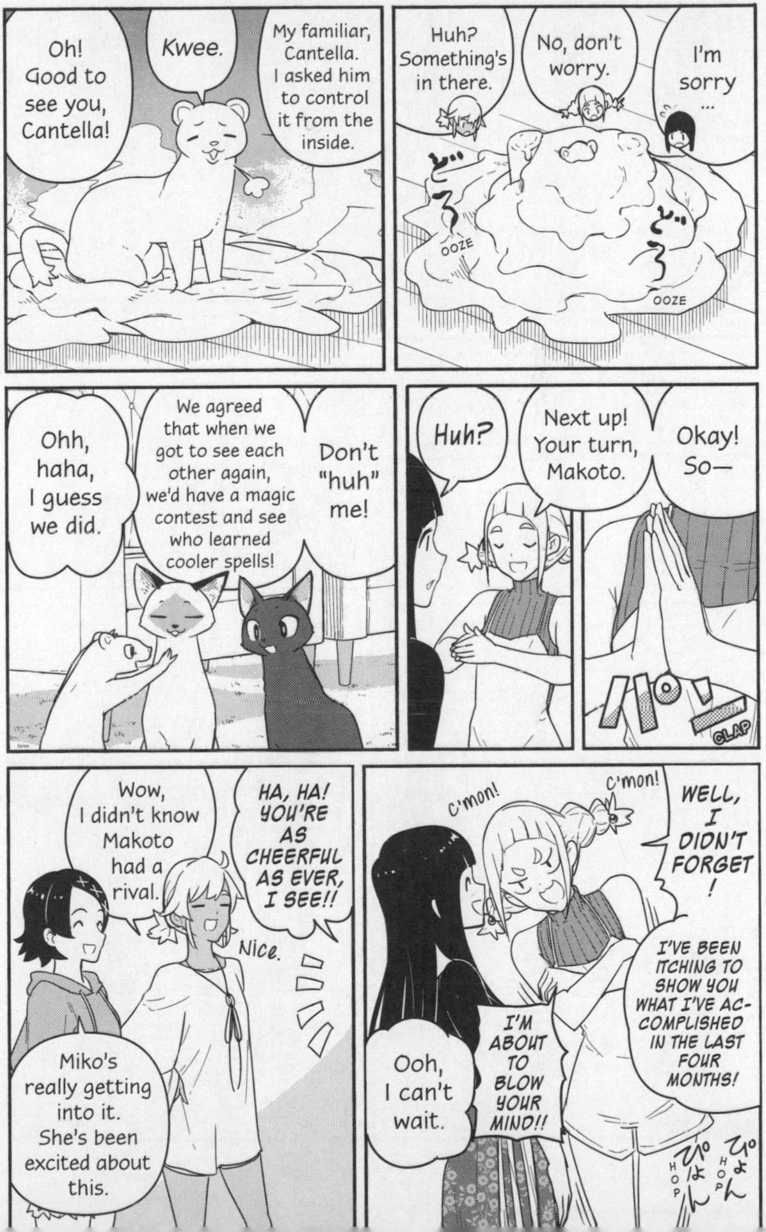

I'm sorry ...
No, don't worry.
Huh? Something's in there.
OOZE
OOZE
My familiar, Cantella. I asked him to control it from the inside.
Kwee.
Oh! Good to see you, Cantella!
Okay! So—
CLAP
Next up! Your turn, Makoto.
Huh?
Don't "huh" me!
We agreed that when we got to see each other again, we'd have a magic contest and see who learned cooler spells!
Ohh, haha, I guess we did.
WELL, I DIDN'T FORGET!
C'mon!
C'mon!
I'VE BEEN ITCHING TO SHOW YOU WHAT I'VE ACCOMPLISHED IN THE LAST FOUR MONTHS!
I'M ABOUT TO BLOW YOUR MIND!!
Ooh, I can't wait.
HOP
HOP
HA, HA! YOU'RE AS CHEERFUL AS EVER, I SEE!!
Wow, I didn't know Makoto had a rival.
Nice.
Miko's really getting into it. She's been excited about this.

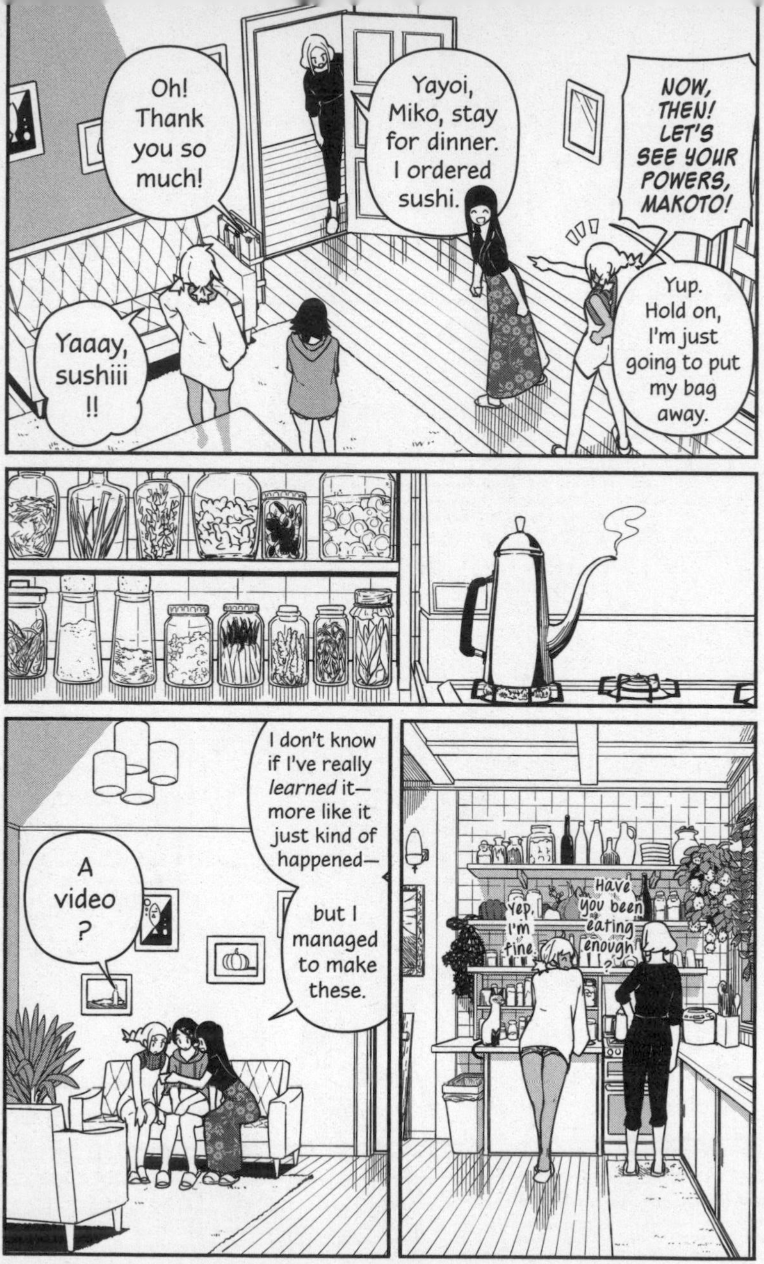
NOW, THEN! LET'S SEE YOUR POWERS, MAKOTO!
Yup. Hold on, I'm just going to put my bag away.
Yayoi, Miko, stay for dinner. I ordered sushi.
Oh! Thank you so much!
Yaaay, sushiii !!
Have you been eating enough?
Yep, I'm fine.
I don't know if I've really *learned* it— more like it just kind of happened—
but I managed to make these.
A video ?

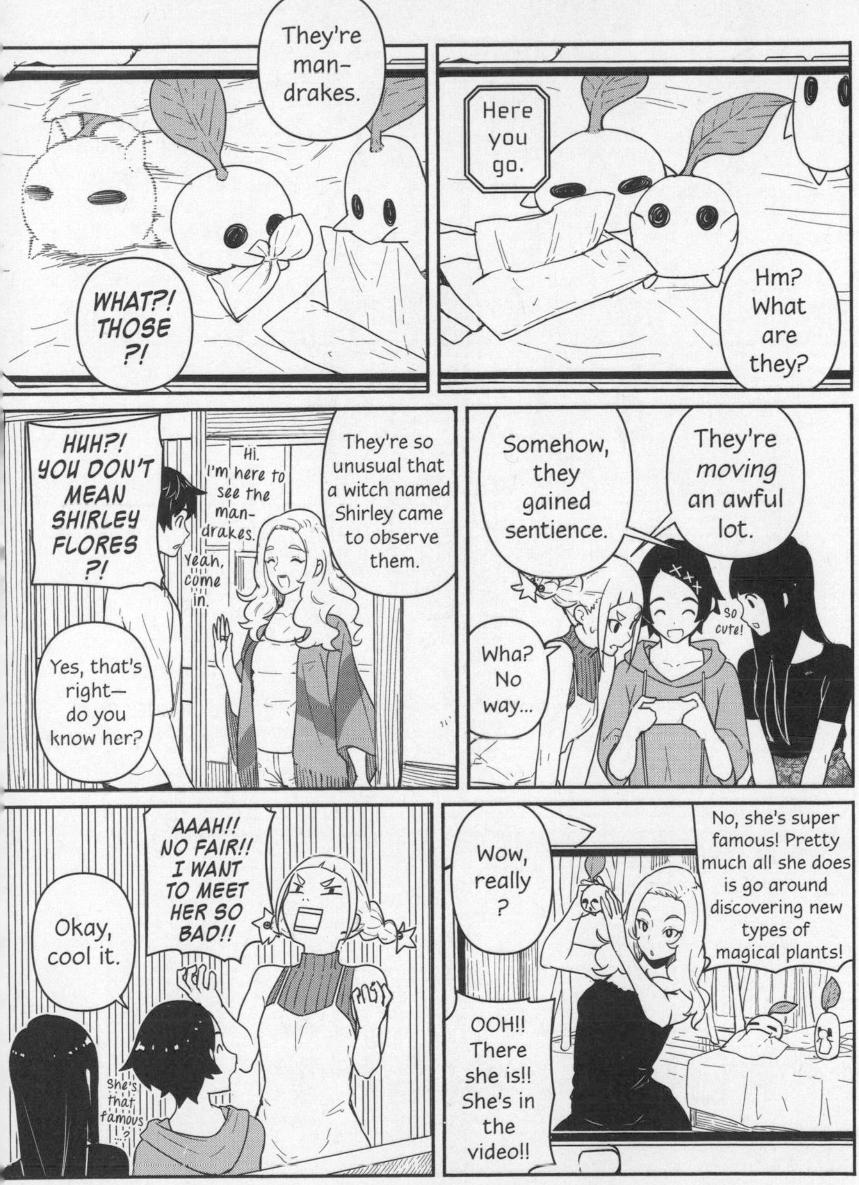
Here you go.
Hm? What are they?
They're man-drakes.
WHAT?! THOSE ?!
They're moving an awful lot.
Somehow, they gained sentience.
So cute!
Wha? No way...
They're so unusual that a witch named Shirley came to observe them.
Hi. I'm here to see the man-drakes.
Yeah, come in.
HUH?! YOU DON'T MEAN SHIRLEY FLORES ?!
Yes, that's right—do you know her?
No, she's super famous! Pretty much all she does is go around discovering new types of magical plants!
Wow, really ?
OOH!! There she is!! She's in the video!!
AAAH!! NO FAIR!! I WANT TO MEET HER SO BAD!!
Okay, cool it.
She's that famous ...?

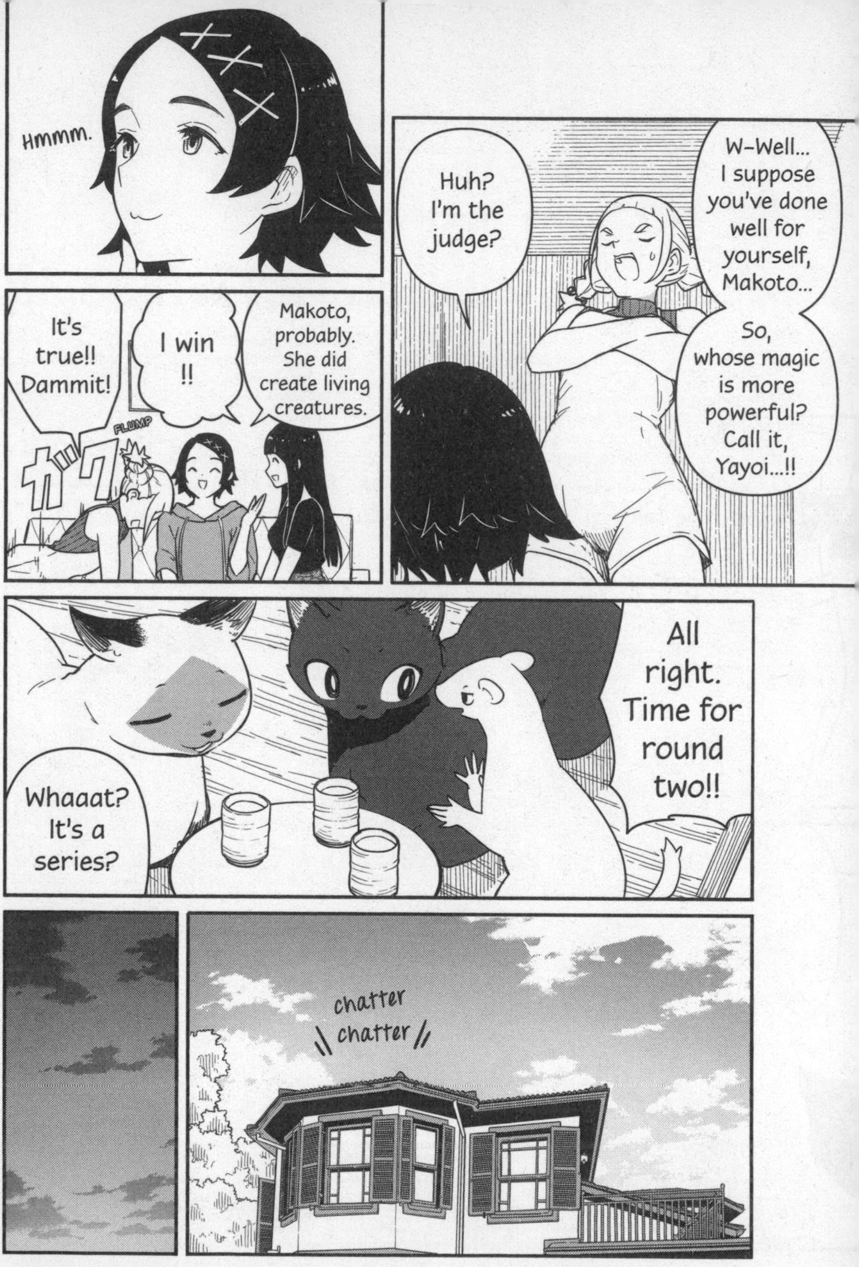
W-Well... I suppose you've done well for yourself, Makoto...
So, whose magic is more powerful? Call it, Yayoi...!!
Huh? I'm the judge?
Hmmm.
Makoto, probably. She did create living creatures.
I win !!
It's true!! Dammit!
FLUMP
ガク
All right. Time for round two!!
Whaaat? It's a series?
chatter chatter

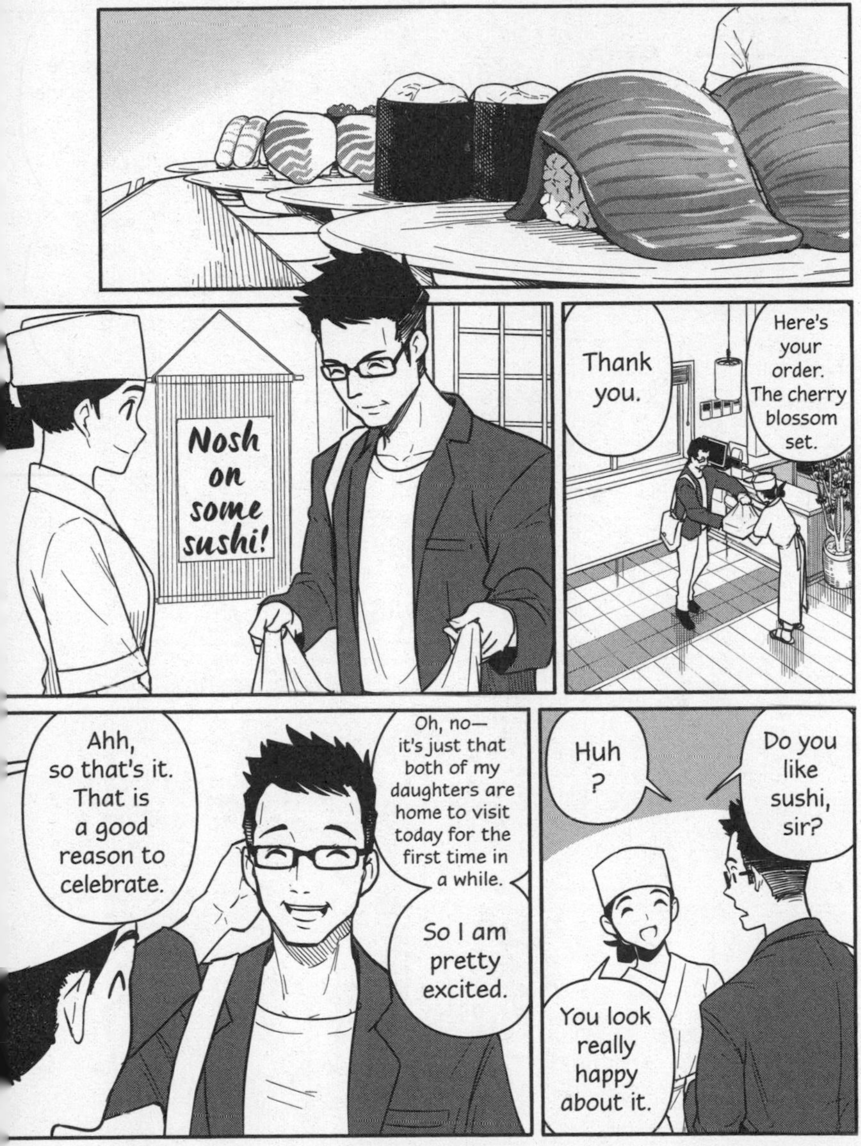
Here's your order. The cherry blossom set.
Thank you.
Nosh on some sushi!
Do you like sushi, sir?
Huh?
You look really happy about it.
Oh, no— it's just that both of my daughters are home to visit today for the first time in a while.
So I am pretty excited.
Ahh, so that's it. That is a good reason to celebrate.

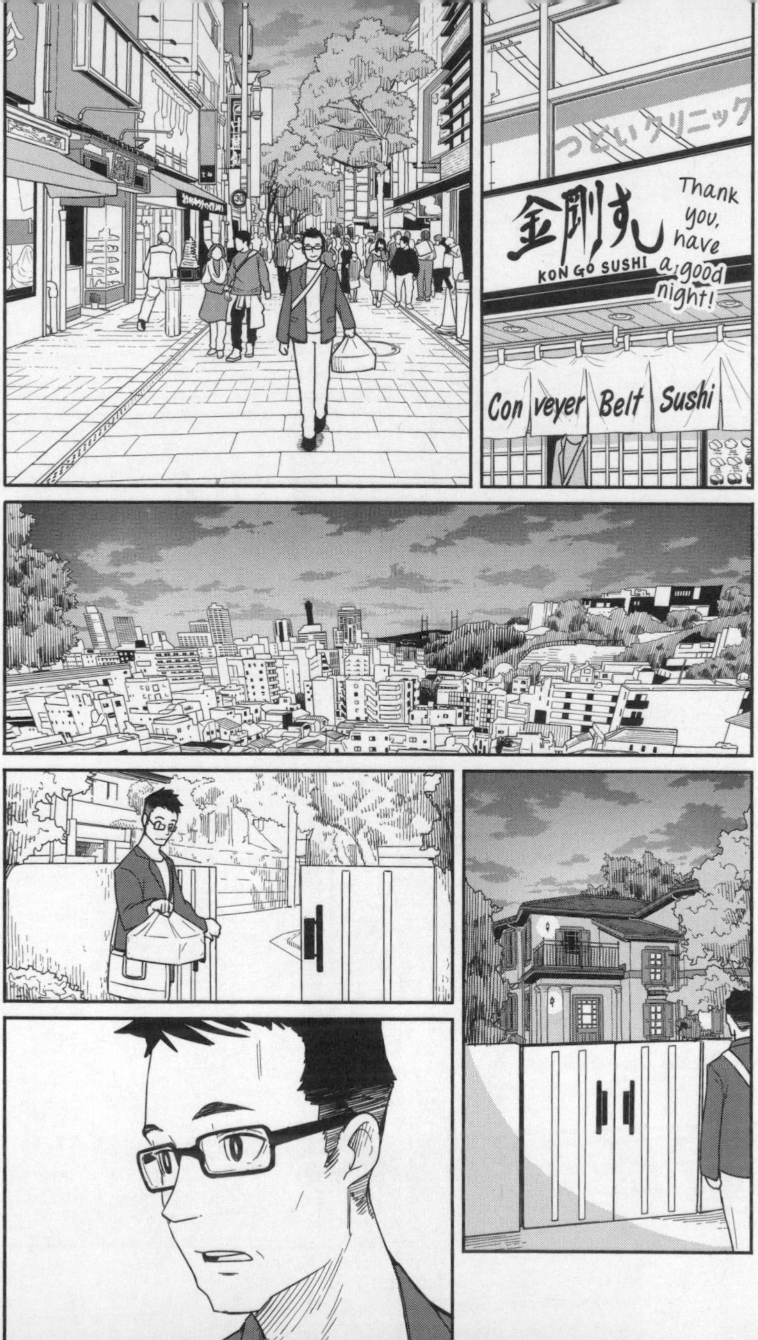
つどいクリニック
金剛すし
KON GO SUSHI
Thank you, have a good night!
Con veyer Belt Sushi

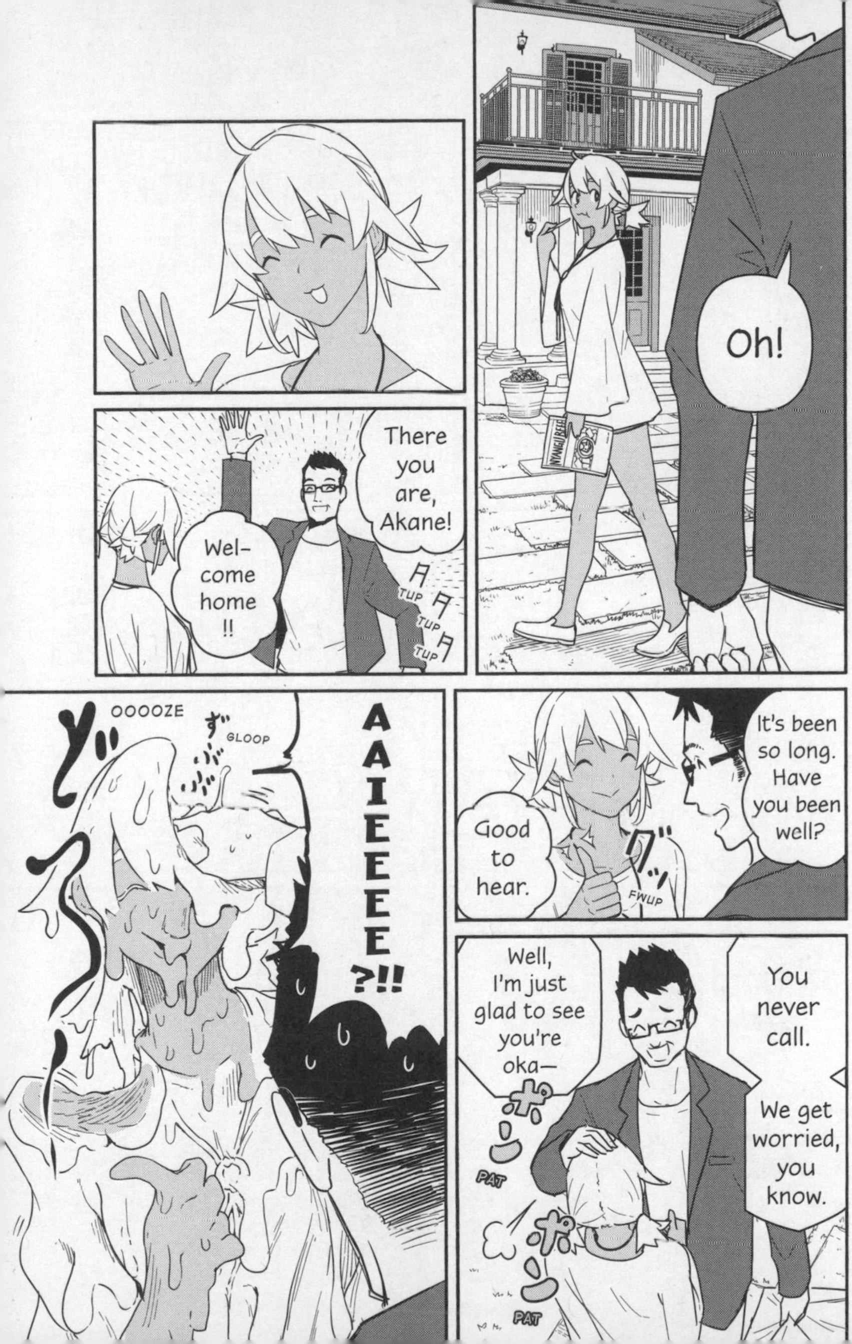
Oh!
There you are, Akane!
Wel-come home!!
TUP
TUP
TUP
It's been so long. Have you been well?
Good to hear.
FWUP
You never call.
We get worried, you know.
Well, I'm just glad to see you're oka—
PAT
PAT
AAIEEEEE?!!
OOOOZE
GLOOP

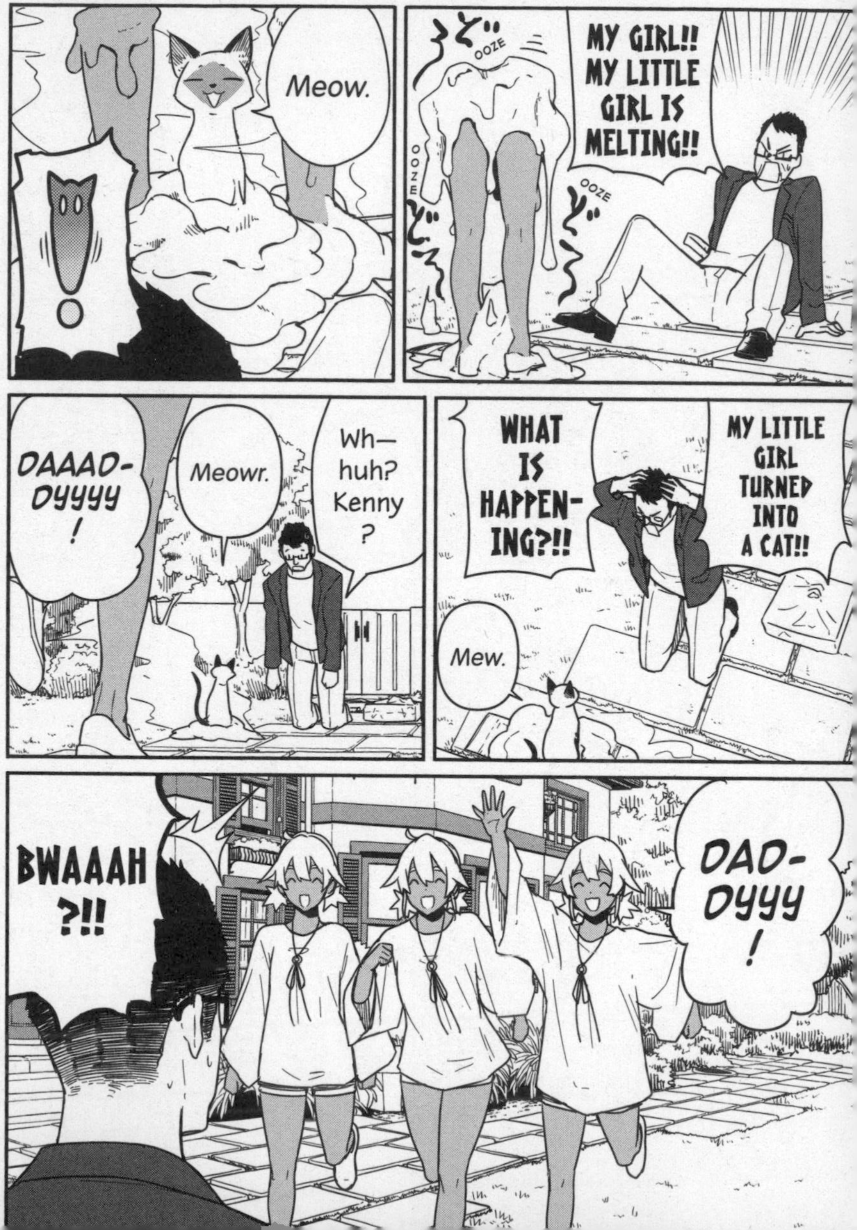
MY GIRL!! MY LITTLE GIRL IS MELTING!!
OOZE
OOZE
OOZE
Meow.
MY LITTLE GIRL TURNED INTO A CAT!!
WHAT IS HAPPEN-ING?!!
Mew.
Wh— huh? Kenny ?
Meowr.
DAAAD-Dyyyy !
DAD-Dyyy !
BWAAAH ?!!

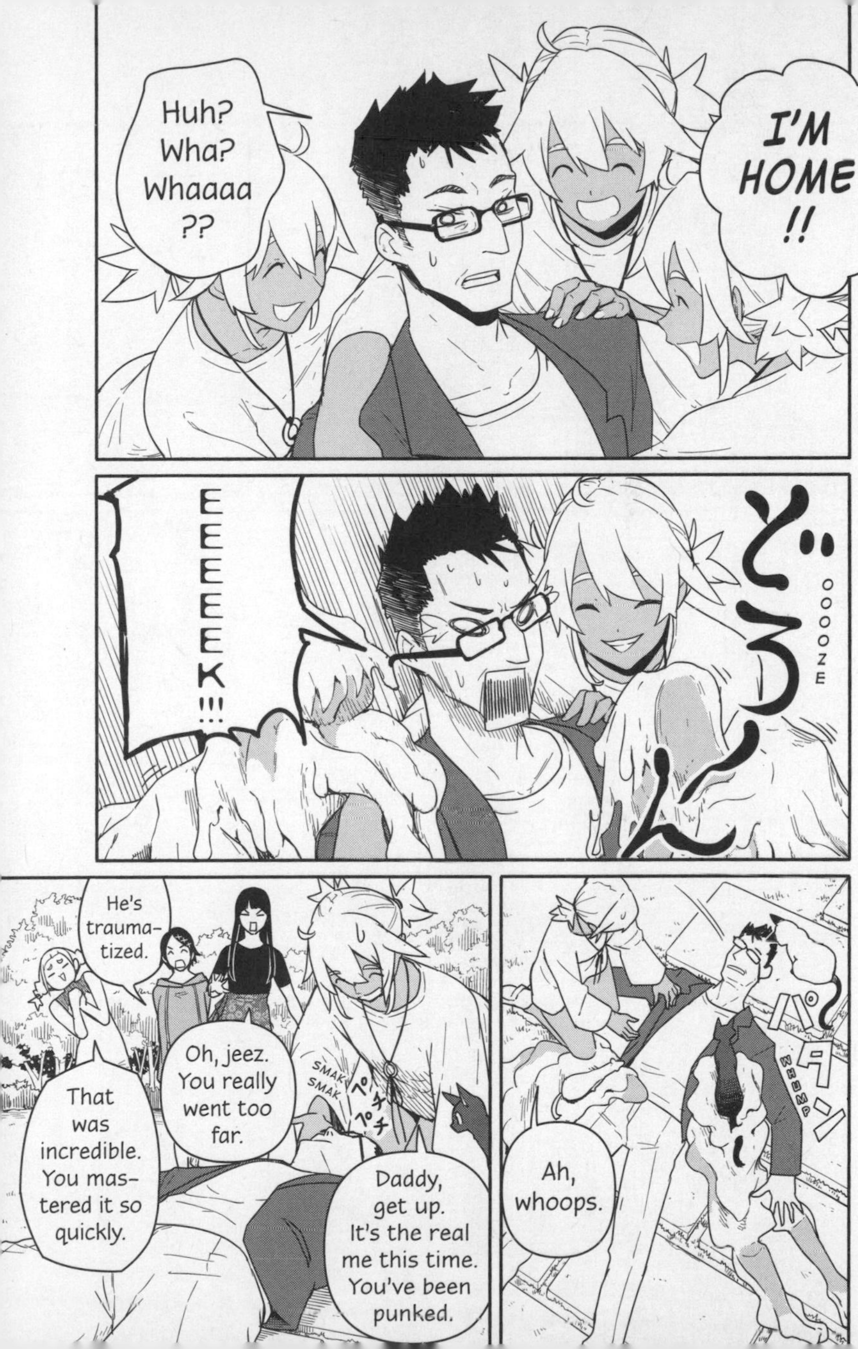
I'M HOME!!
Huh? Wha? Whaaaa??
どろ～ん
OOOOZE
EEEEEK!!!
パタ～ン
WHUMP
Ah, whoops.
SMAK SMAK
ペチペチ
Daddy, get up. It's the real me this time. You've been punked.
Oh, jeez. You really went too far.
He's traumatized.
That was incredible. You mastered it so quickly.

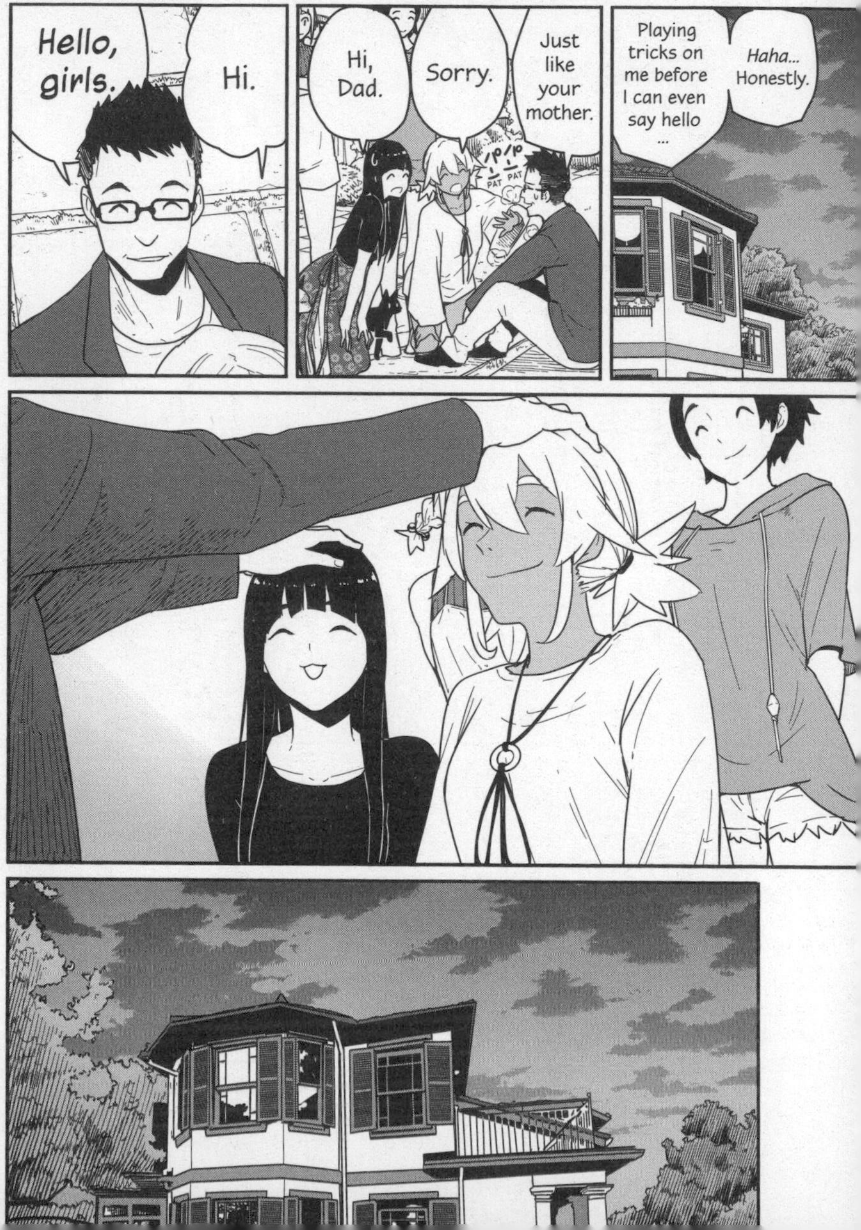
Haha... Honestly.
Playing tricks on me before I can even say hello ...
Just like your mother.
PAT PAT
Sorry.
Hi, Dad.
Hi.
Hello, girls.

Flying
Witch

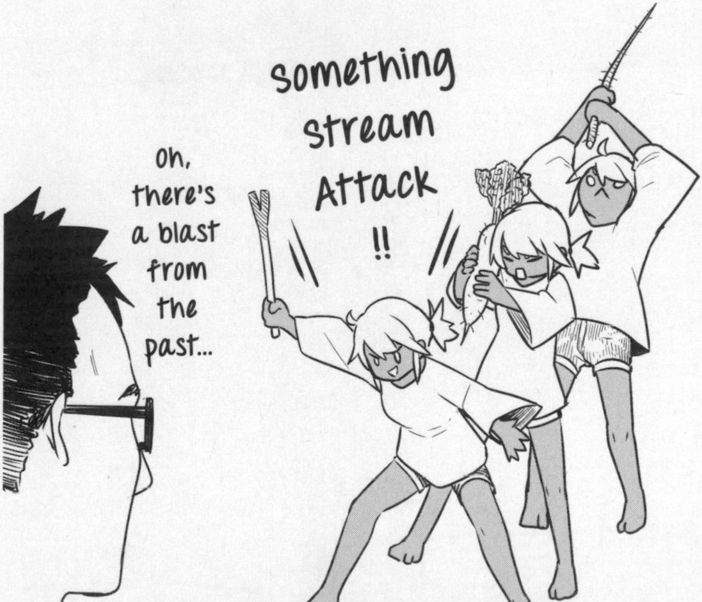
Something Stream Attack !!
Oh, there's a blast from the past...

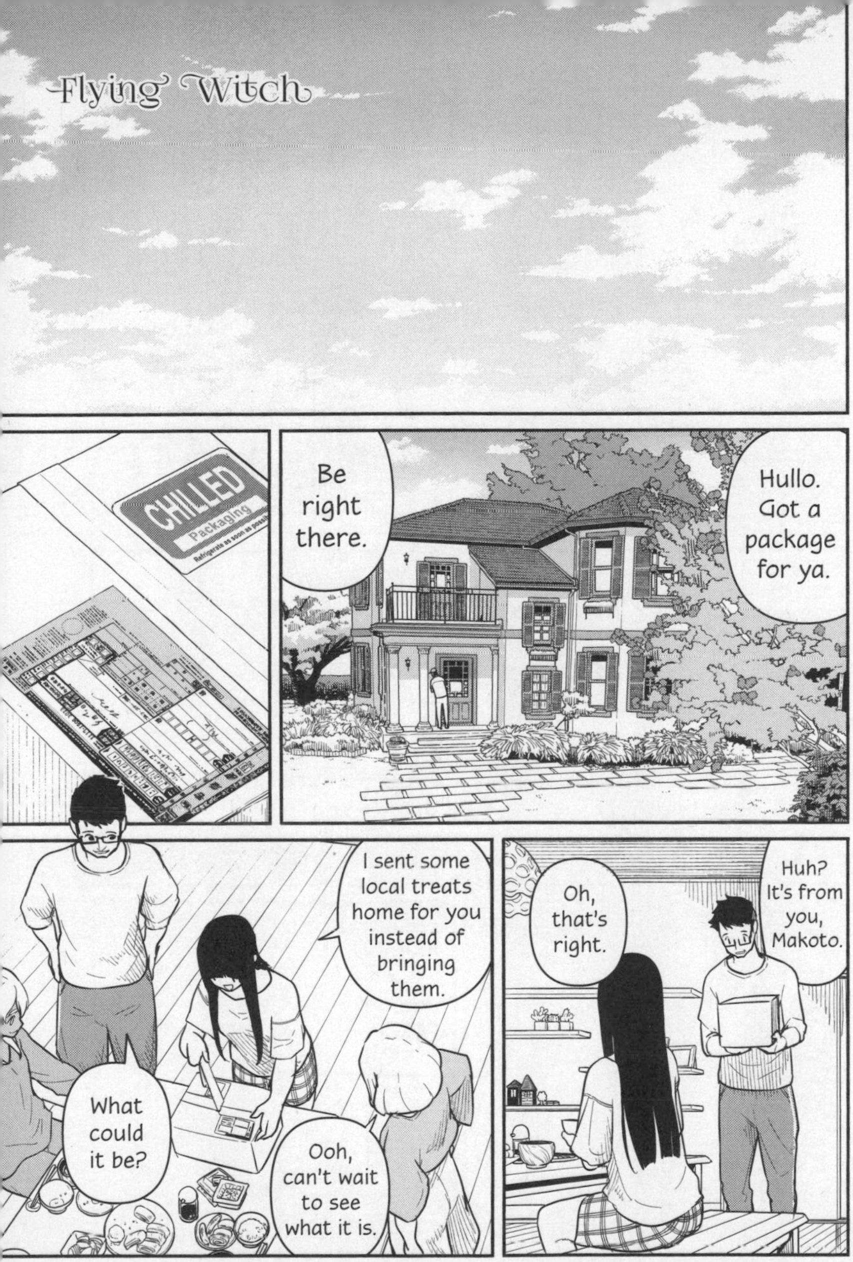
Flying Witch
Hullo. Got a package for ya.
Be right there.
CHILLED
Packaging
Huh? It's from you, Makoto.
Oh, that's right.
I sent some local treats home for you instead of bringing them.
What could it be?
Ooh, can't wait to see what it is.

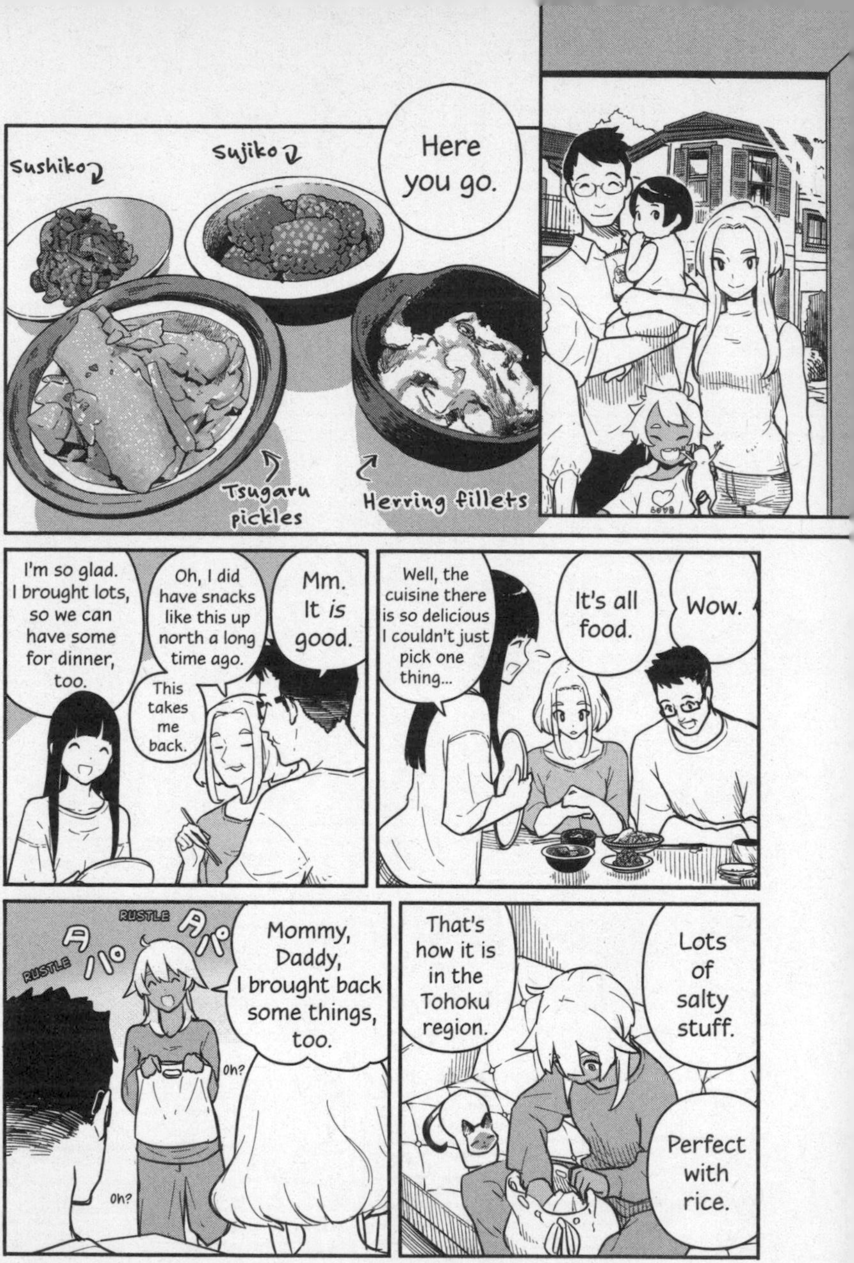
Here you go.
Sujiko
Sushiko
Herring fillets
Tsugaru pickles
Wow.
It's all food.
Well, the cuisine there is so delicious I couldn't just pick one thing...
Mm. It *is* good.
Oh, I did have snacks like this up north a long time ago.
This takes me back.
I'm so glad. I brought lots, so we can have some for dinner, too.
Lots of salty stuff.
That's how it is in the Tohoku region.
Perfect with rice.
Mommy, Daddy, I brought back some things, too.
Oh?
RUSTLE
RUSTLE
Oh?

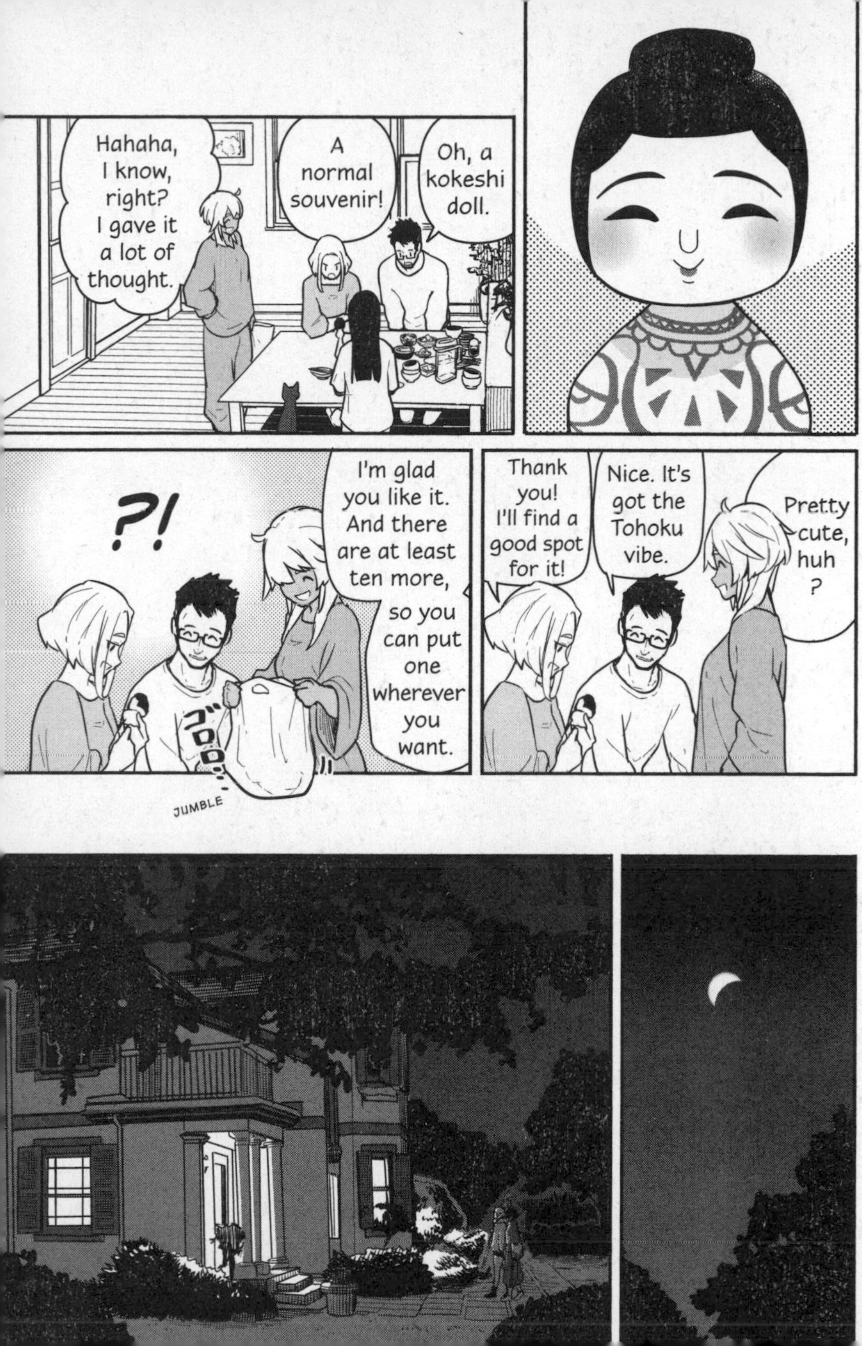
Oh, a kokeshi doll.
A normal souvenir!
Hahaha, I know, right? I gave it a lot of thought.
Pretty cute, huh?
Nice. It's got the Tohoku vibe.
Thank you! I'll find a good spot for it!
I'm glad you like it. And there are at least ten more,
so you can put one wherever you want.
?!
ゴロロ
JUMBLE

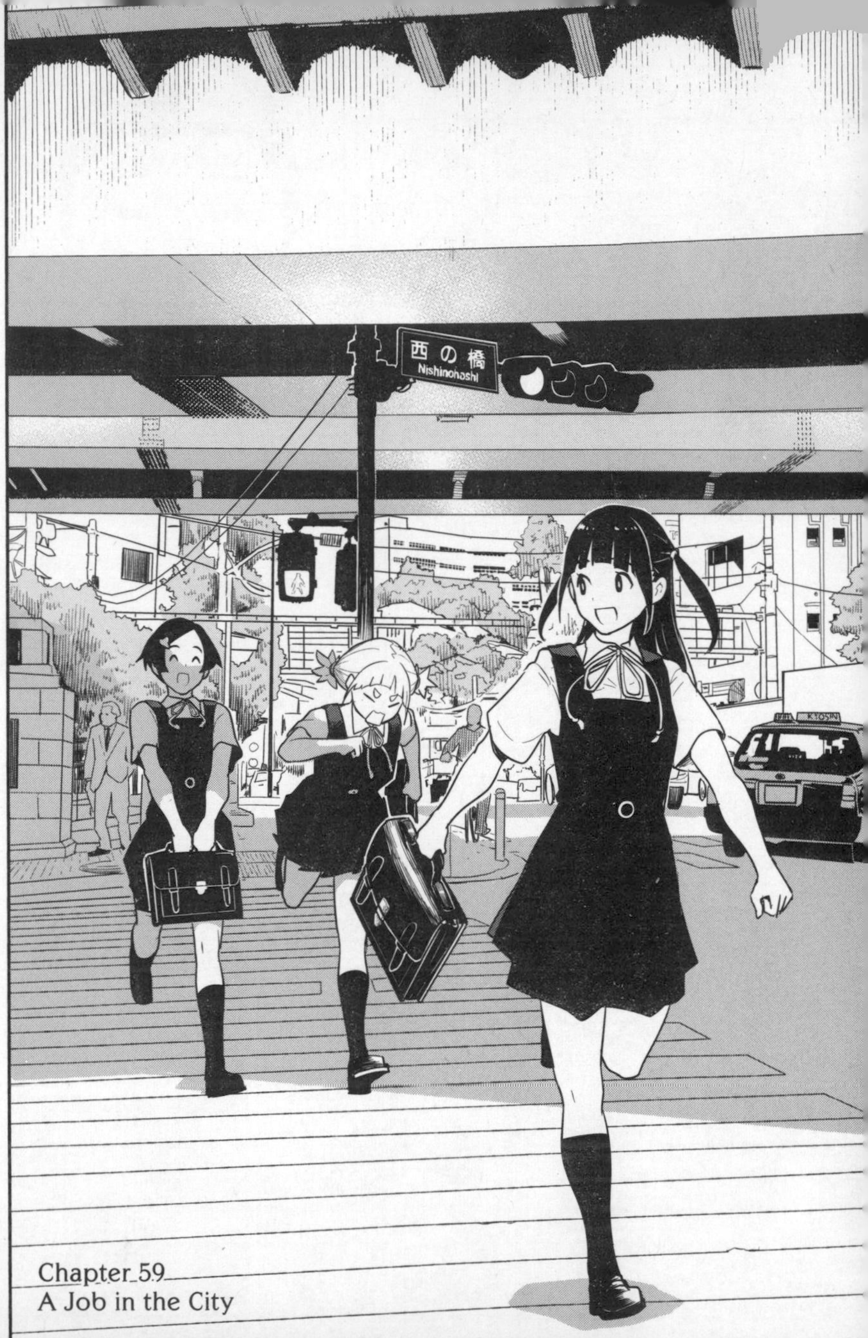
西の橋
Nishinohashi

Chapter 59
A Job in the City

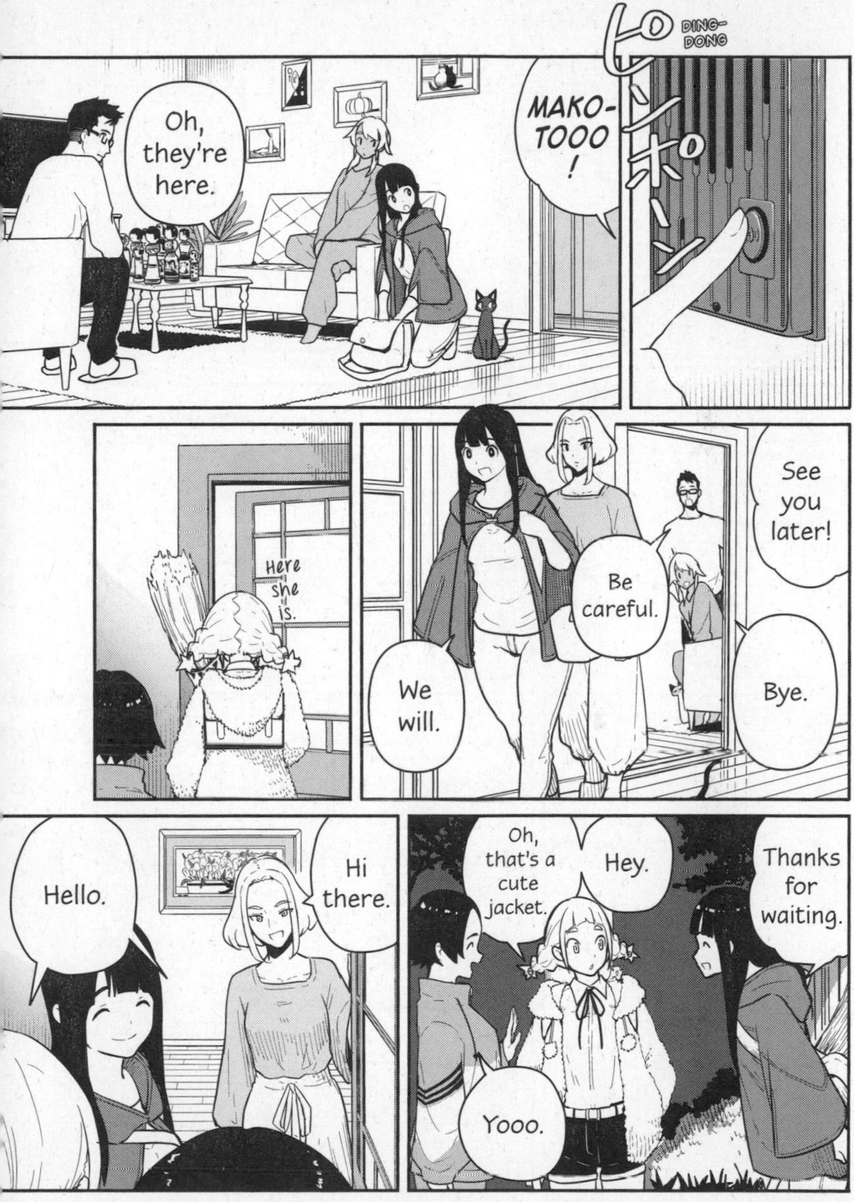
DING-DONG
MAKO-TOOO!
Oh, they're here.
See you later!
Be careful.
Bye.
We will.
Here she is.
Thanks for waiting.
Hey.
Oh, that's a cute jacket.
Yooo.
Hi there.
Hello.

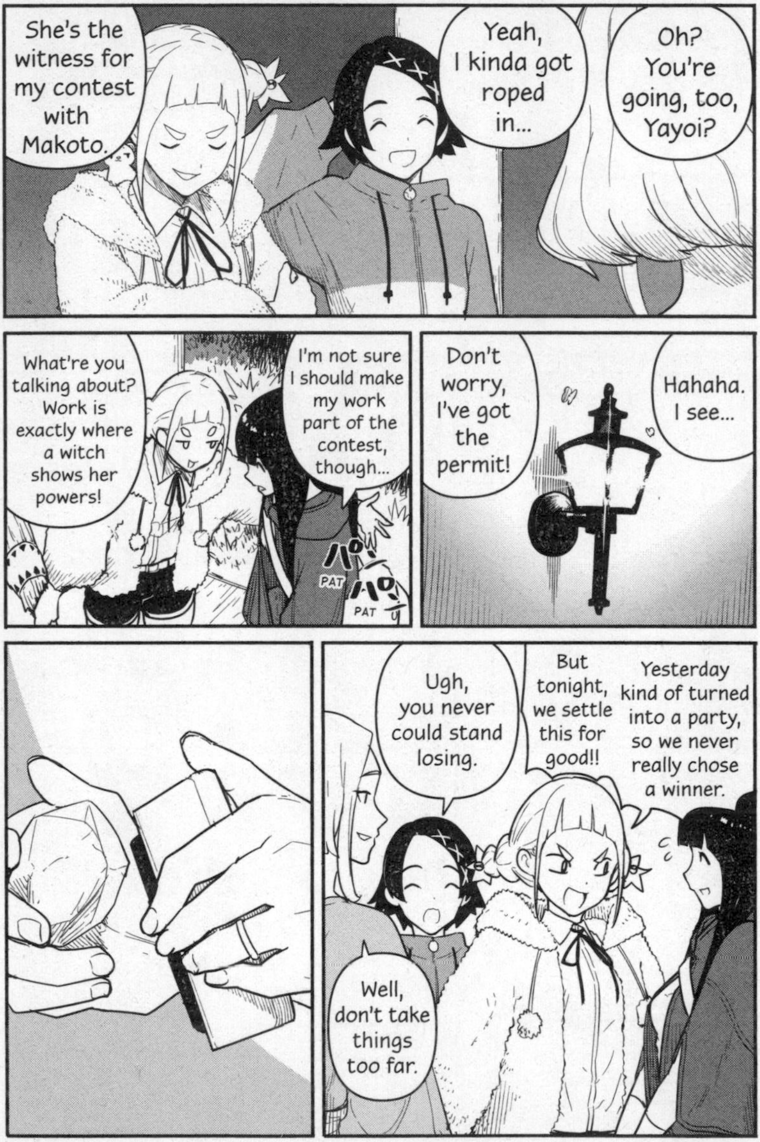
Oh? You're going, too, Yayoi?
Yeah, I kinda got roped in...
She's the witness for my contest with Makoto.
Hahaha. I see...
Don't worry, I've got the permit!
I'm not sure I should make my work part of the contest, though...
What're you talking about? Work is exactly where a witch shows her powers!
PAT
PAT
Yesterday kind of turned into a party, so we never really chose a winner.
But tonight, we settle this for good!!
Ugh, you never could stand losing.
Well, don't take things too far.

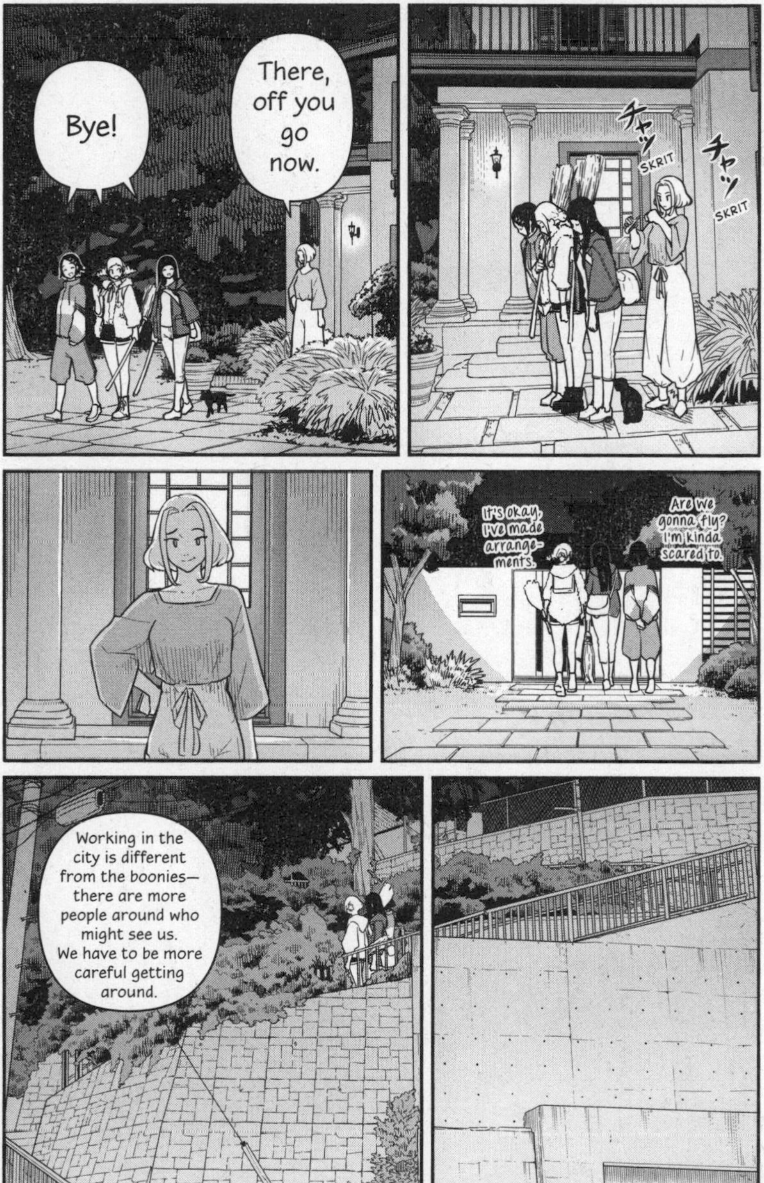
チャッ
SKRIT
チャッ
SKRIT
There, off you go now.
Bye!
Are we gonna fly? I'm kinda scared to.
It's okay, I've made arrangements.
Working in the city is different from the boonies—there are more people around who might see us. We have to be more careful getting around.

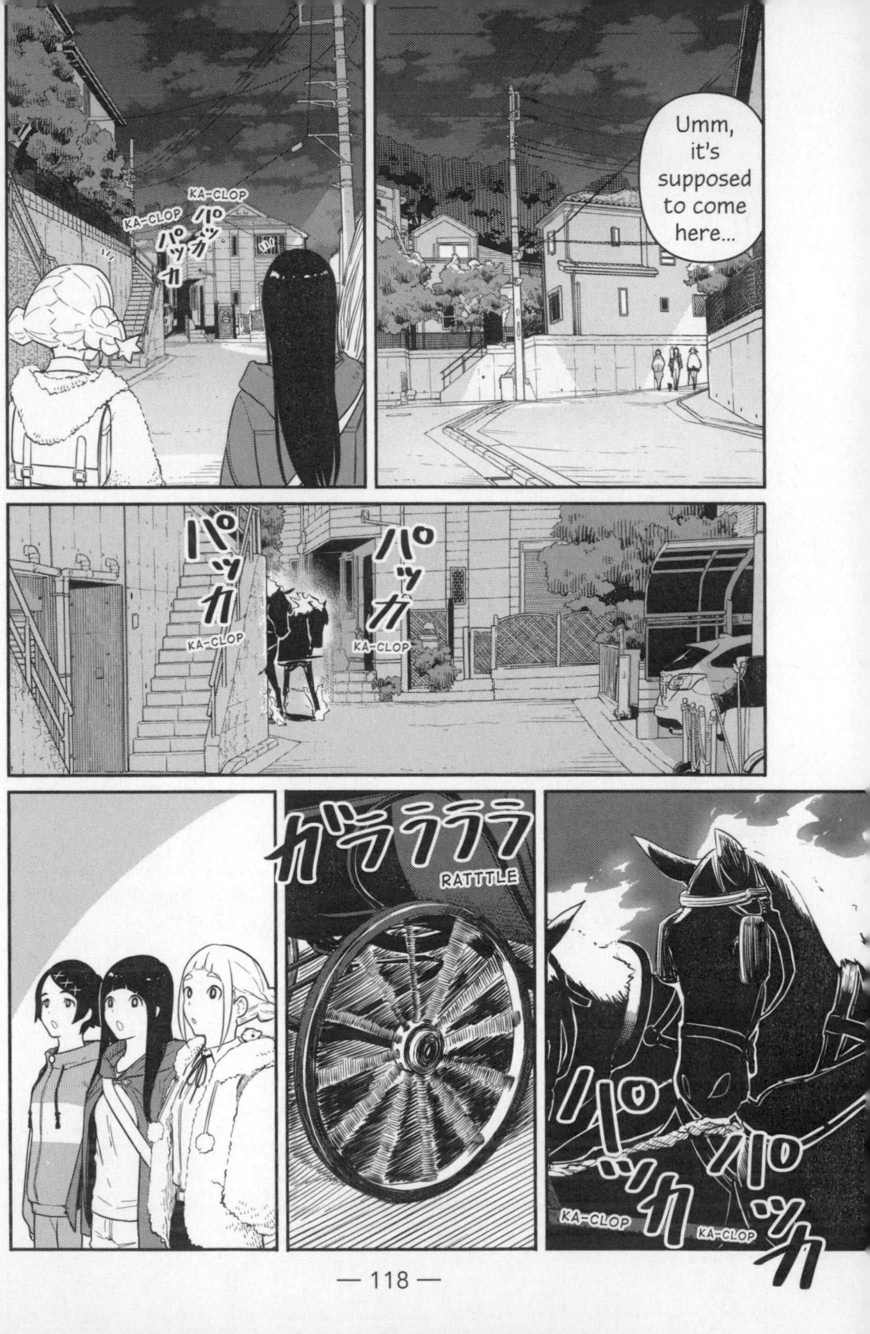
Umm, it's supposed to come here...
パッカ
KA-CLOP
パッカ
KA-CLOP
パッカ
KA-CLOP
パッカ
KA-CLOP
パッカ
KA-CLOP
パッカ
KA-CLOP
ガラララララ
RATTTLE

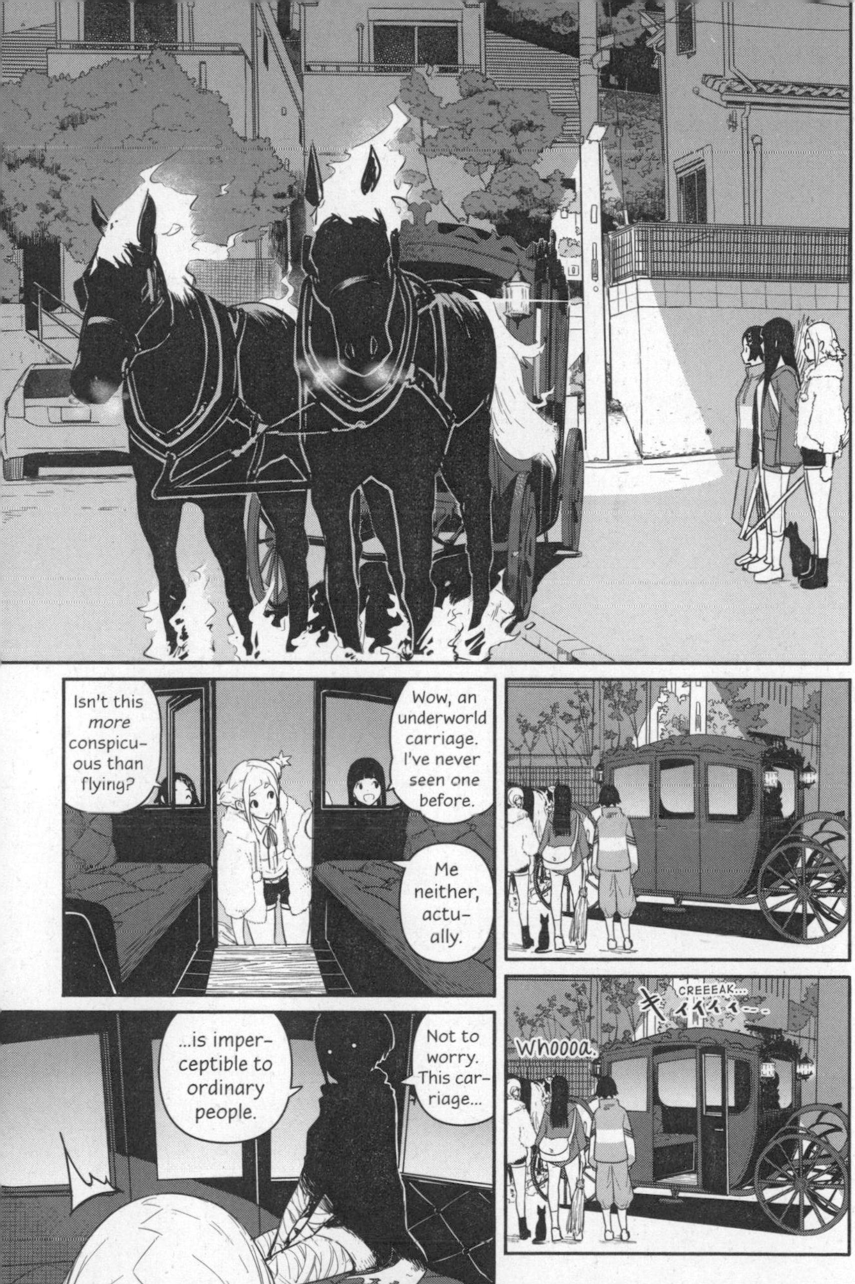
CREEEAK...
Whoooa.
Wow, an underworld carriage. I've never seen one before.
Me neither, actually.
Isn't this *more* conspicuous than flying?
Not to worry. This carriage...
...is imperceptible to ordinary people.

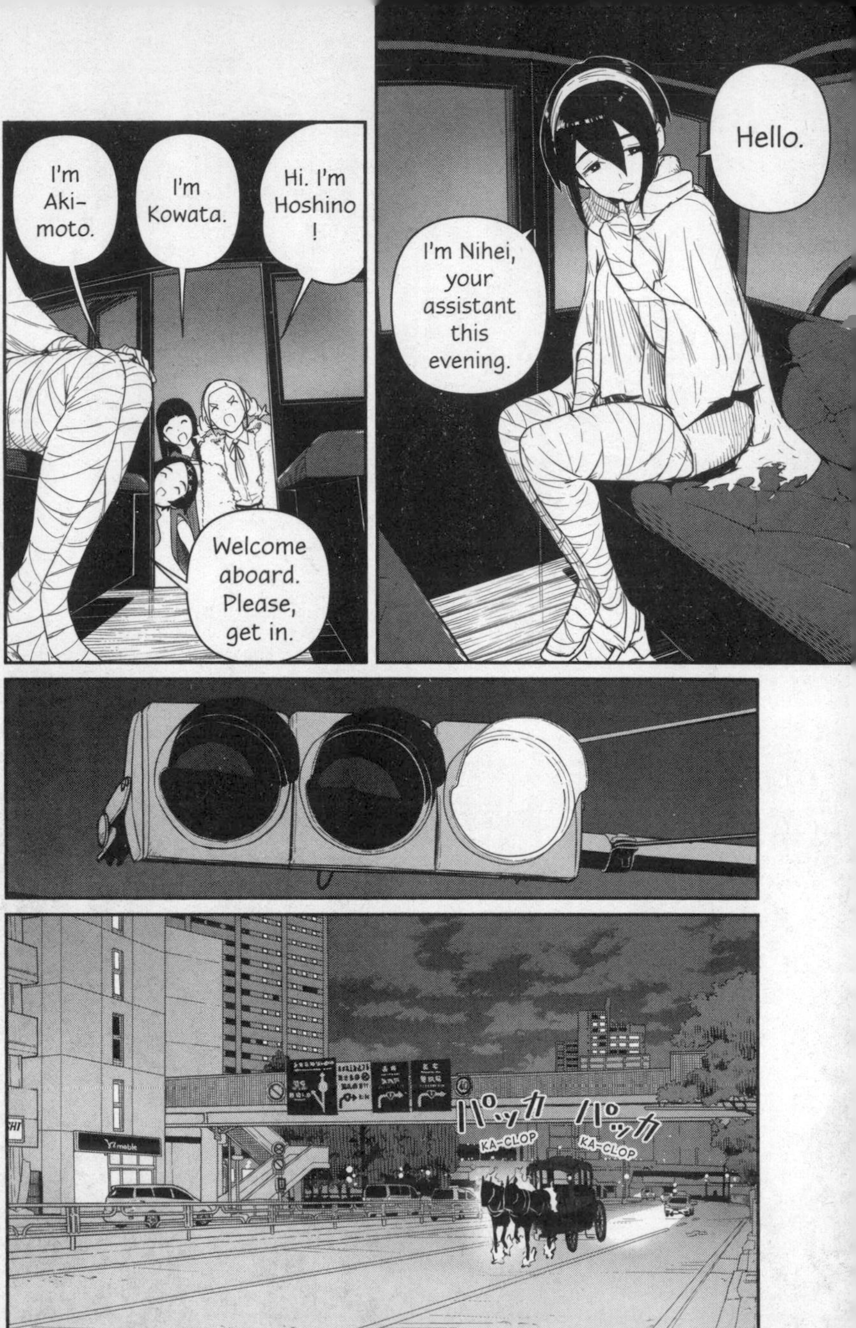
Hello.
I'm Nihei, your assistant this evening.
Hi. I'm Hoshino!
I'm Kowata.
I'm Aki-moto.
Welcome aboard. Please, get in.
パッカ
KA-CLOP
パッカ
KA-CLOP

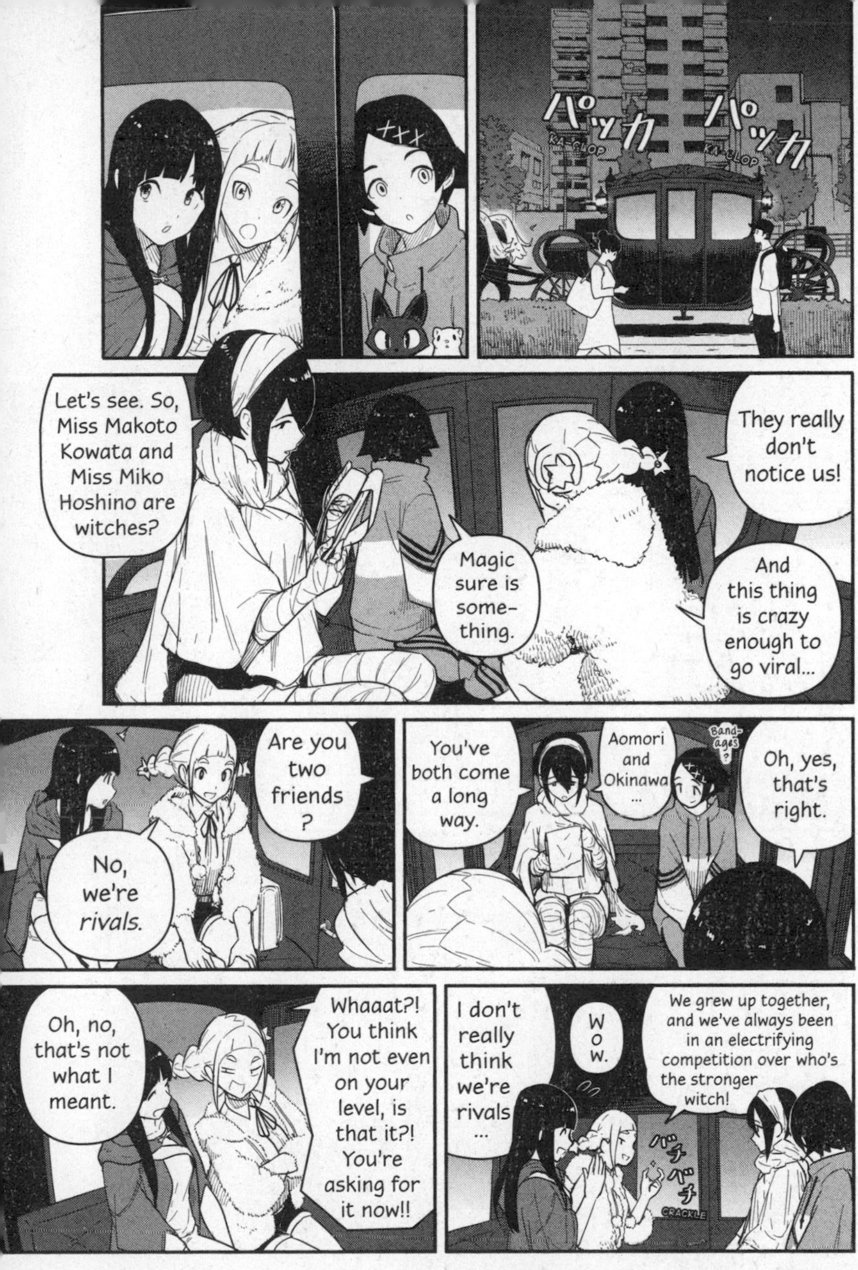
パッカ
KA-CLOP
パッカ
KA-CLOP
They really don't notice us!
And this thing is crazy enough to go viral...
Let's see. So, Miss Makoto Kowata and Miss Miko Hoshino are witches?
Magic sure is something.
Band-ages?
Oh, yes, that's right.
Aomori and Okinawa ...
You've both come a long way.
Are you two friends ?
No, we're *rivals*.
We grew up together, and we've always been in an electrifying competition over who's the stronger witch!
Wow.
バチバチ
CRACKLE
I don't really think we're rivals ...
Whaaat?! You think I'm not even on your level, is that it?! You're asking for it now!!
Oh, no, that's not what I meant.

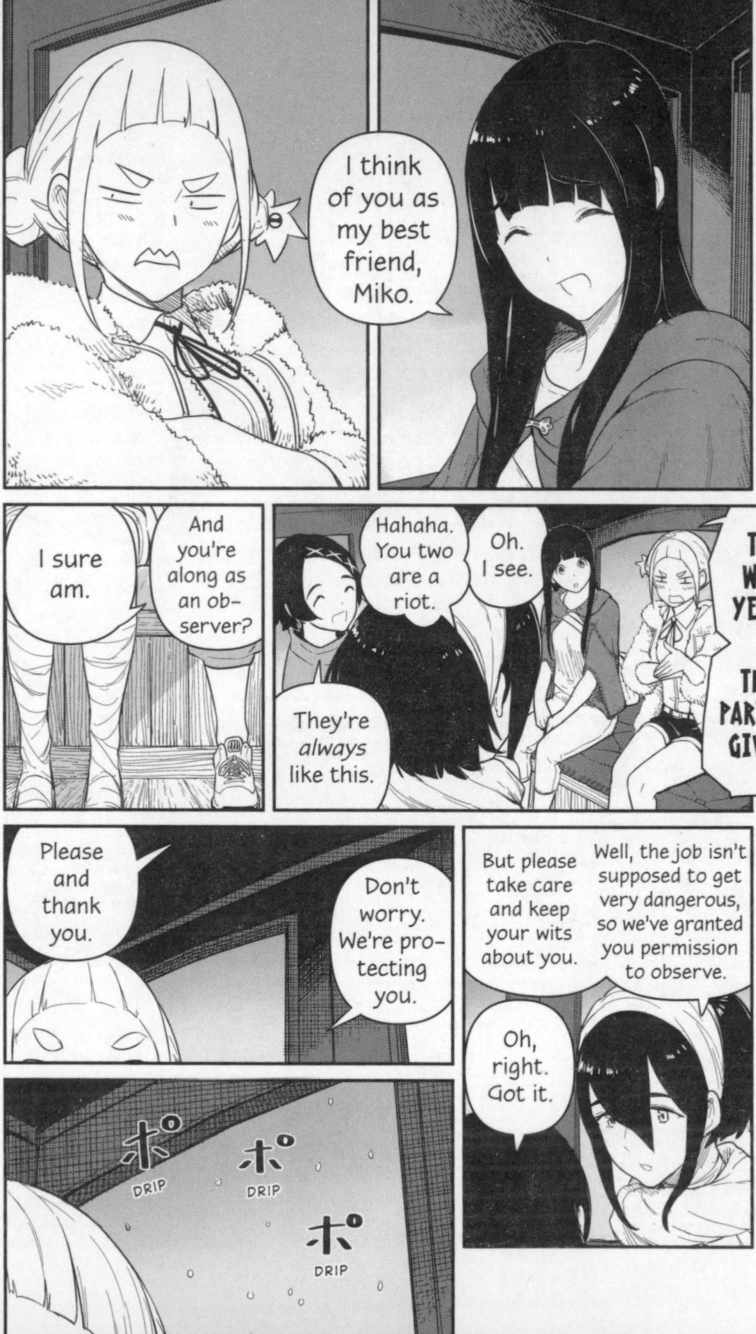

I think of you as my best friend, Miko.
TH... WELL, YEAH...
THAT PART'S A GIVEN.
Oh. I see.
Hahaha. You two are a riot.
They're *always* like this.
And you're along as an ob-server?
I sure am.
Well, the job isn't supposed to get very dangerous, so we've granted you permission to observe.
But please take care and keep your wits about you.
Oh, right. Got it.
Don't worry. We're pro-tecting you.
Please and thank you.
ポ
DRIP
ポ
DRIP
ポ
DRIP

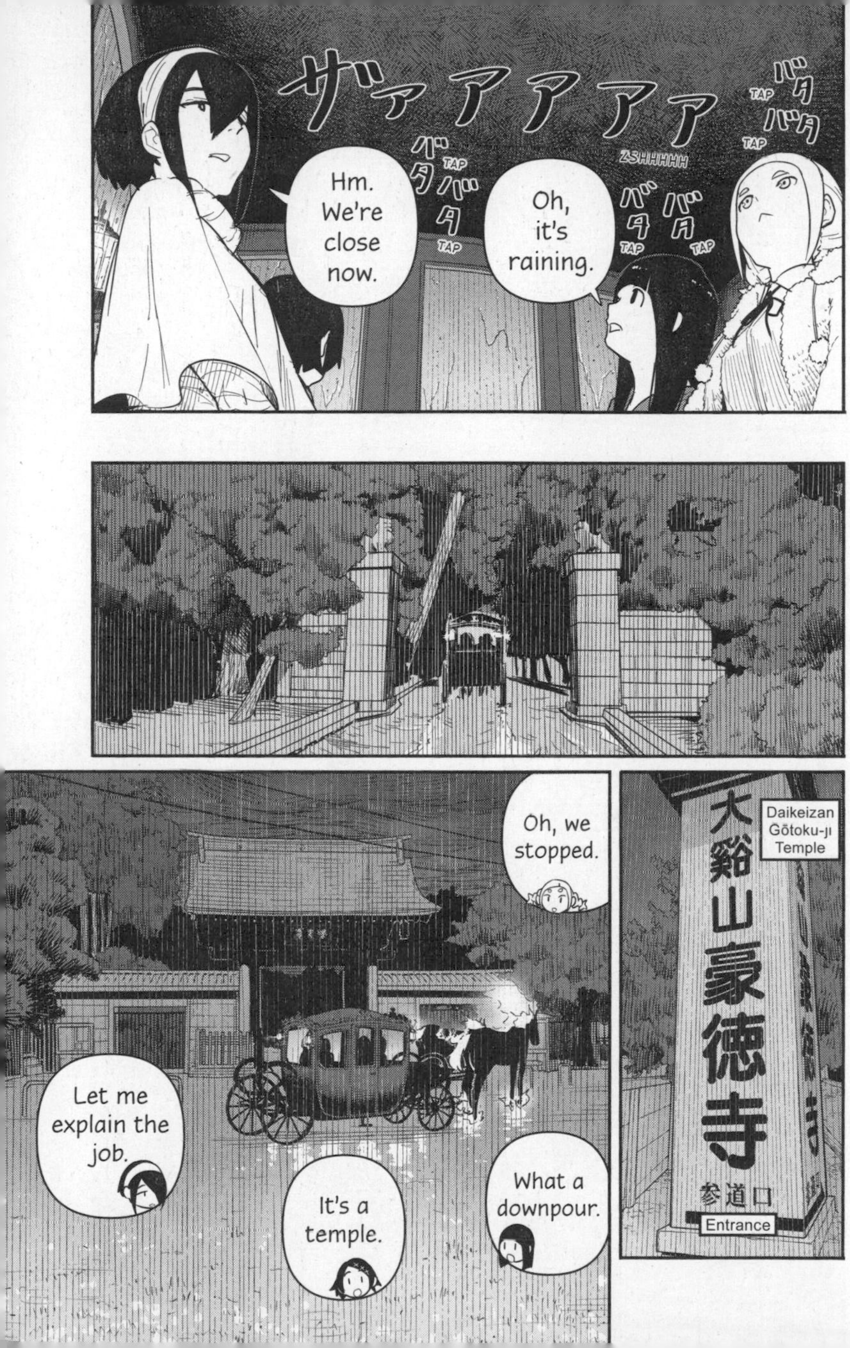
ザァアアアア
ZSHHHHH
バタバタ
TAP TAP
バタバタ
TAP TAP
バタバタ
TAP TAP
Oh, it's raining.
Hm. We're close now.
大谿山豪徳寺
Daikeizan Gōtoku-ji Temple
参道口
Entrance
Oh, we stopped.
What a downpour.
It's a temple.
Let me explain the job.

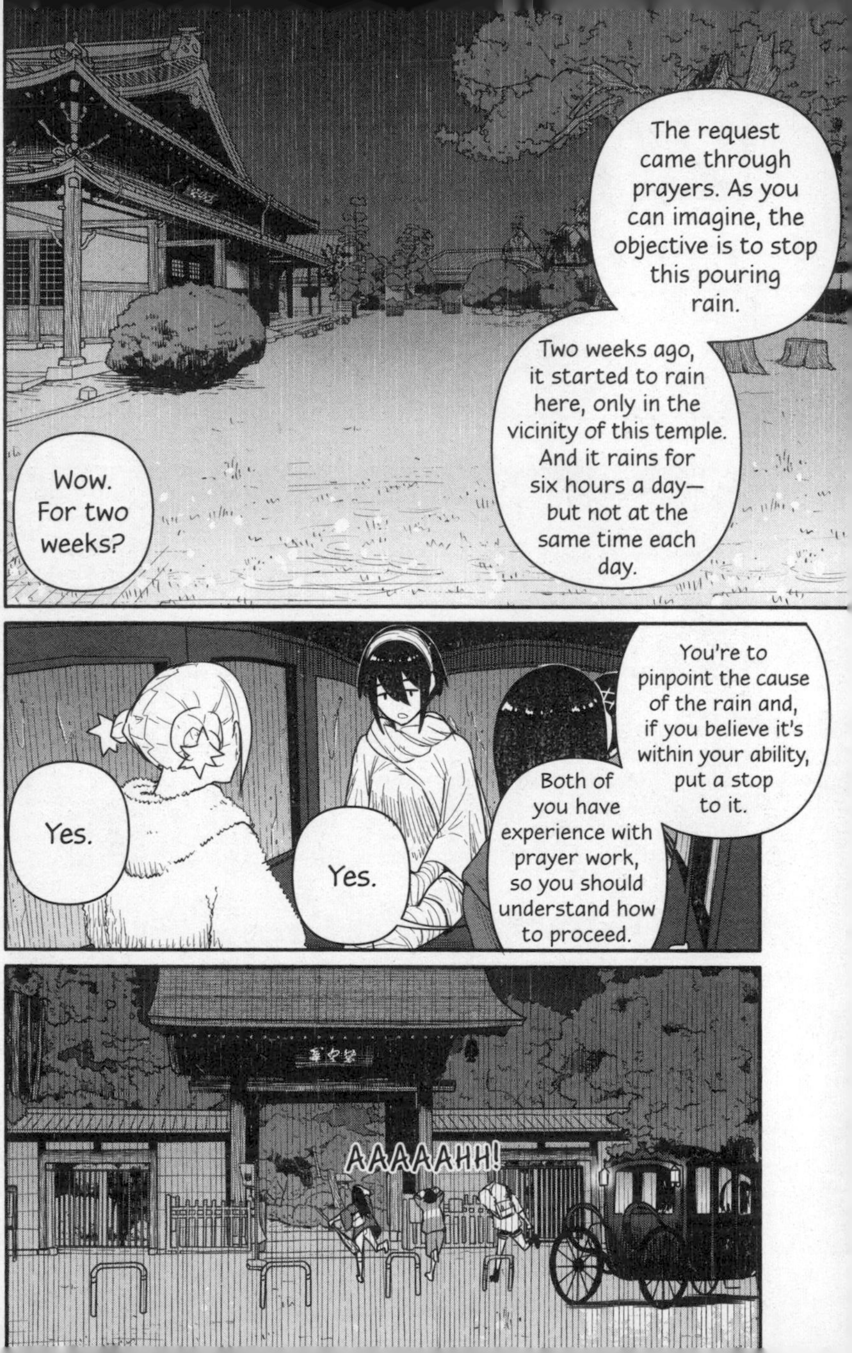
The request came through prayers. As you can imagine, the objective is to stop this pouring rain.
Two weeks ago, it started to rain here, only in the vicinity of this temple. And it rains for six hours a day—but not at the same time each day.
Wow. For two weeks?
You're to pinpoint the cause of the rain and, if you believe it's within your ability, put a stop to it.
Both of you have experience with prayer work, so you should understand how to proceed.
Yes.
Yes.
AAAAAHH!

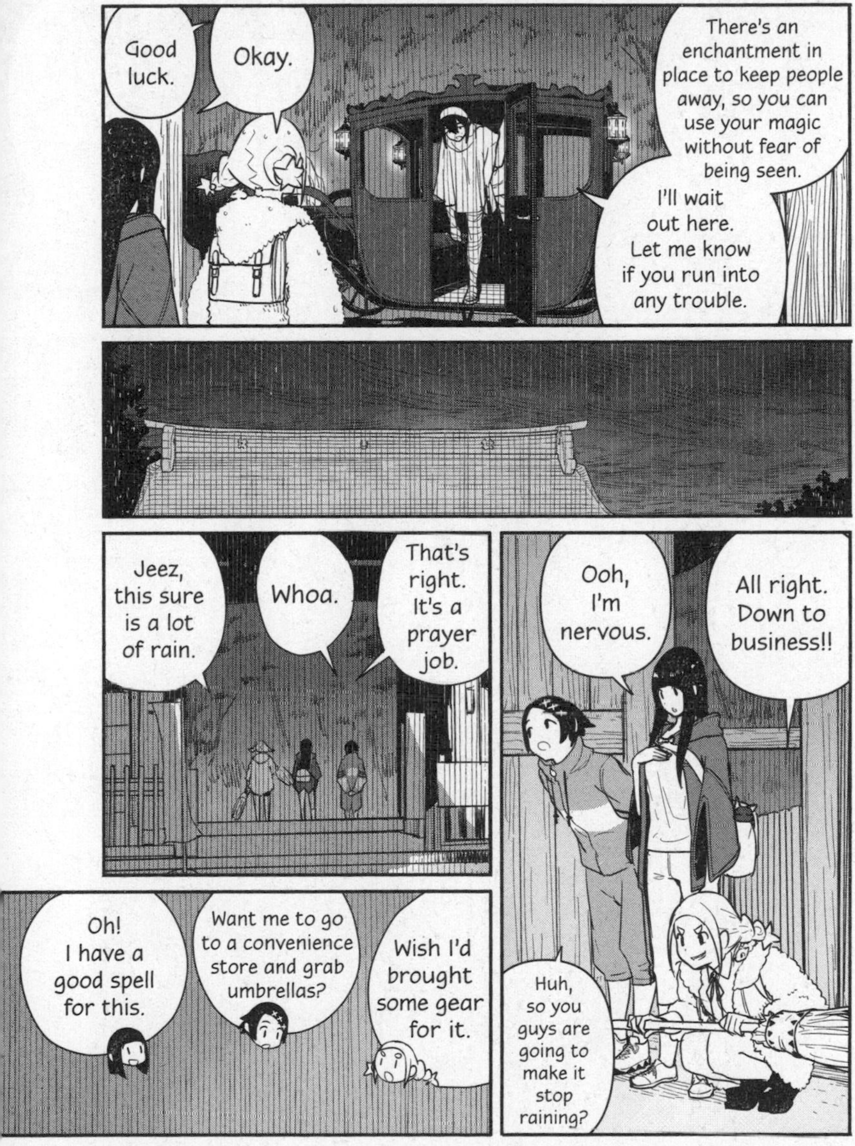
There's an enchantment in place to keep people away, so you can use your magic without fear of being seen.
I'll wait out here. Let me know if you run into any trouble.
Okay.
Good luck.
All right. Down to business!!
Ooh, I'm nervous.
Huh, so you guys are going to make it stop raining?
That's right. It's a prayer job.
Whoa.
Jeez, this sure is a lot of rain.
Wish I'd brought some gear for it.
Want me to go to a convenience store and grab umbrellas?
Oh! I have a good spell for this.

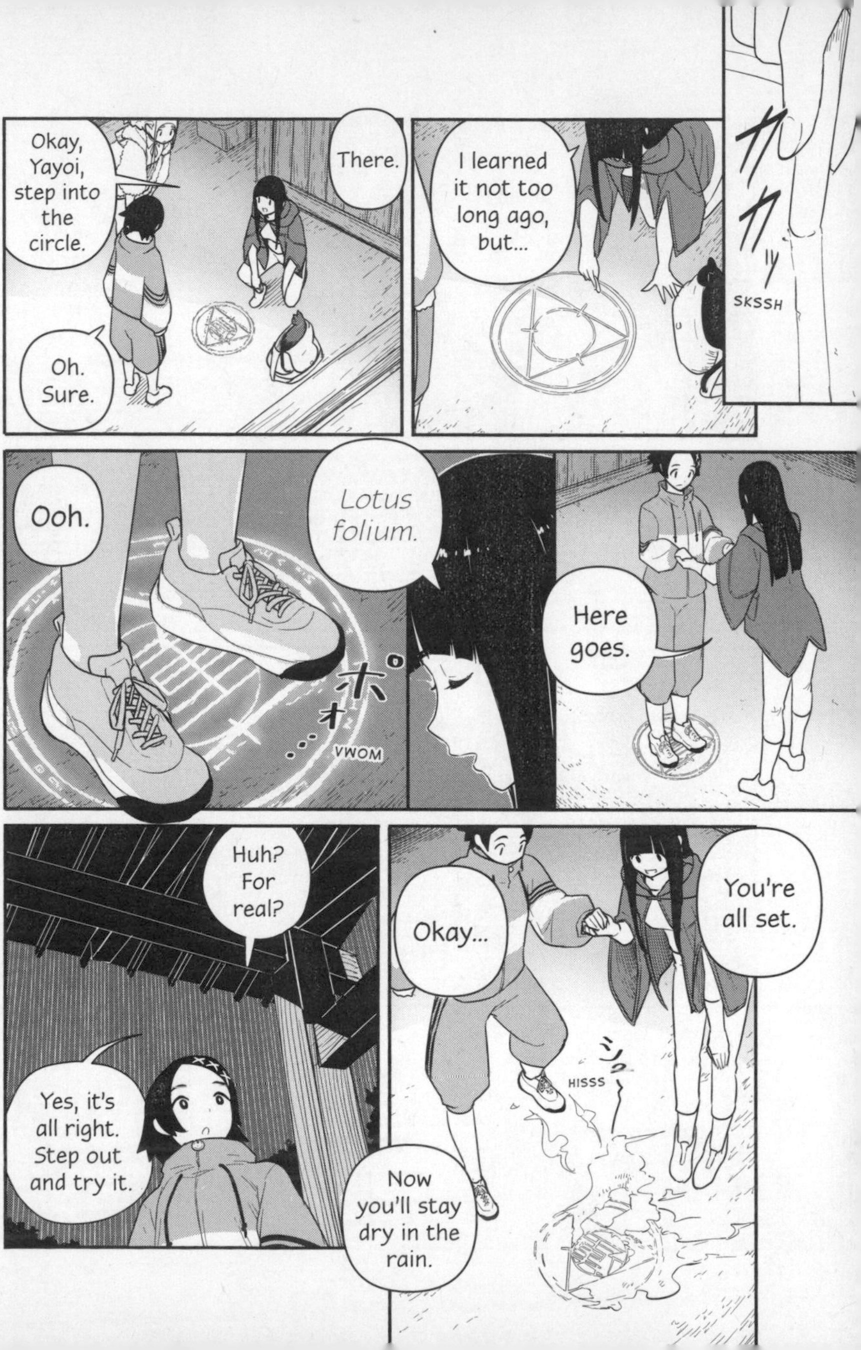

カカカッ
SKSSH
I learned it not too long ago, but...
There.
Okay, Yayoi, step into the circle.
Oh. Sure.
Here goes.
Lotus folium.
Ooh.
VWOM
You're all set.
Okay...
HISSS
Now you'll stay dry in the rain.
Huh? For real?
Yes, it's all right. Step out and try it.

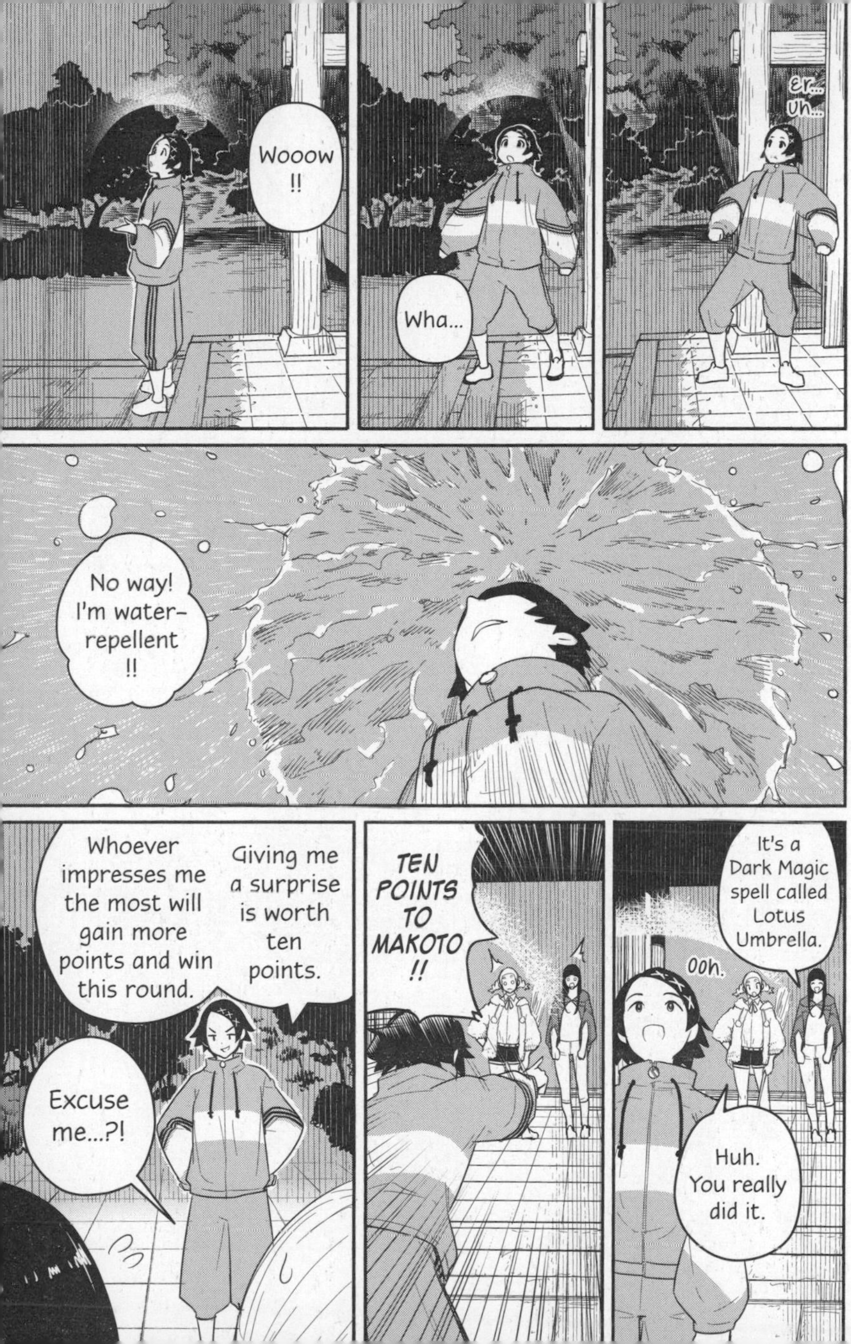
Er... Uh...
Wha...
Wooow !!
No way! I'm water-repellent !!
It's a Dark Magic spell called Lotus Umbrella.
Ooh.
Huh. You really did it.
TEN POINTS TO MAKOTO !!
Giving me a surprise is worth ten points.
Whoever impresses me the most will gain more points and win this round.
Excuse me...?!

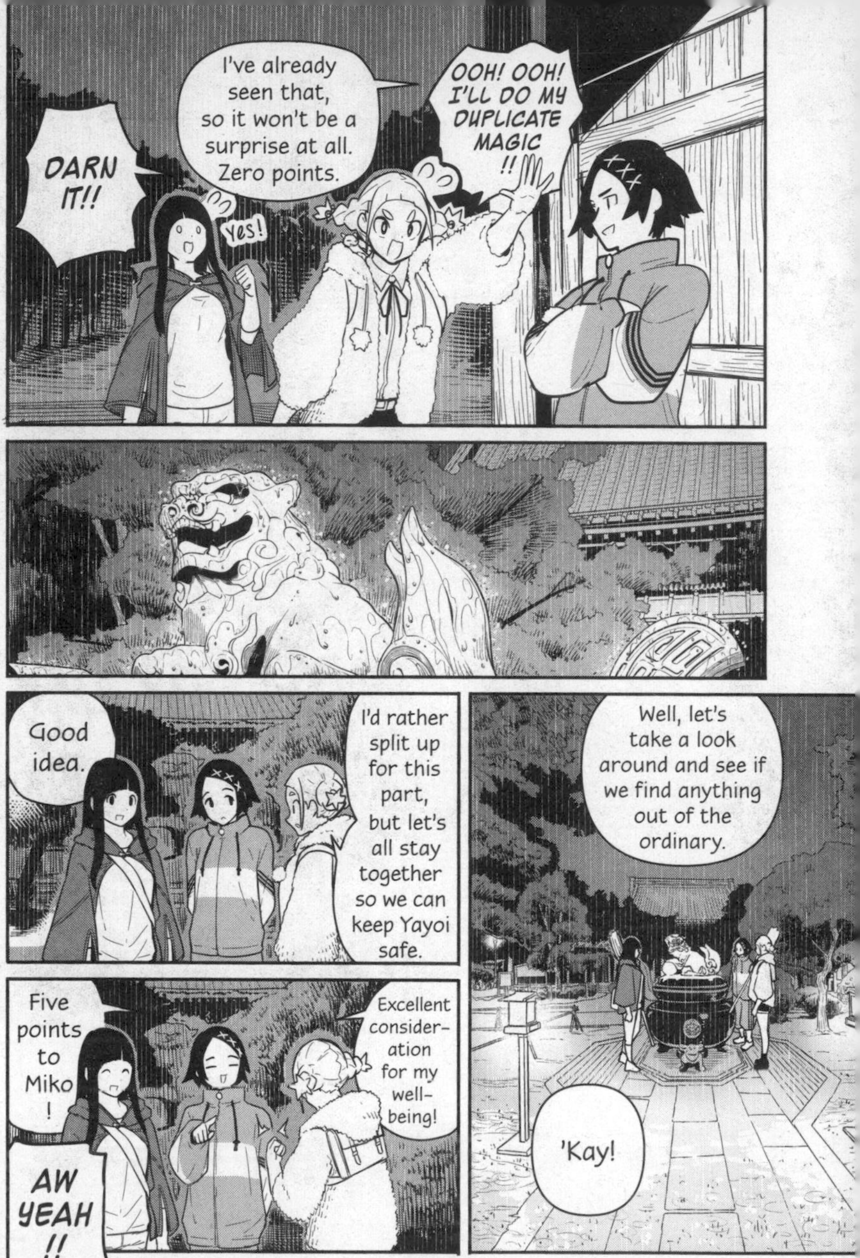
OOH! OOH! I'LL DO MY DUPLICATE MAGIC !!
I've already seen that, so it won't be a surprise at all. Zero points.
Yes!
DARN IT!!
Well, let's take a look around and see if we find anything out of the ordinary.
'Kay!
I'd rather split up for this part, but let's all stay together so we can keep Yayoi safe.
Good idea.
Excellent consider-ation for my well-being!
Five points to Miko !
AW YEAH !!

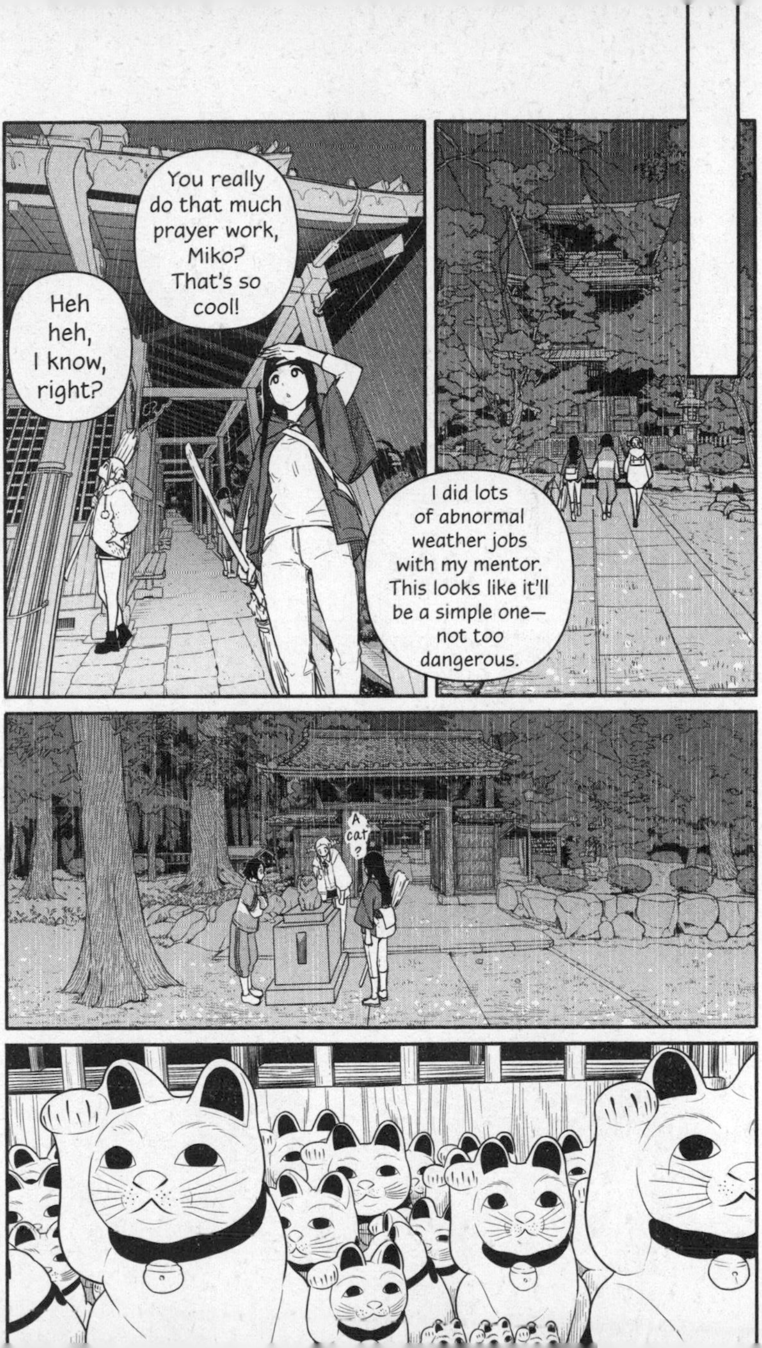
You really do that much prayer work, Miko? That's so cool!
Heh heh, I know, right?
I did lots of abnormal weather jobs with my mentor. This looks like it'll be a simple one—not too dangerous.
A cat?

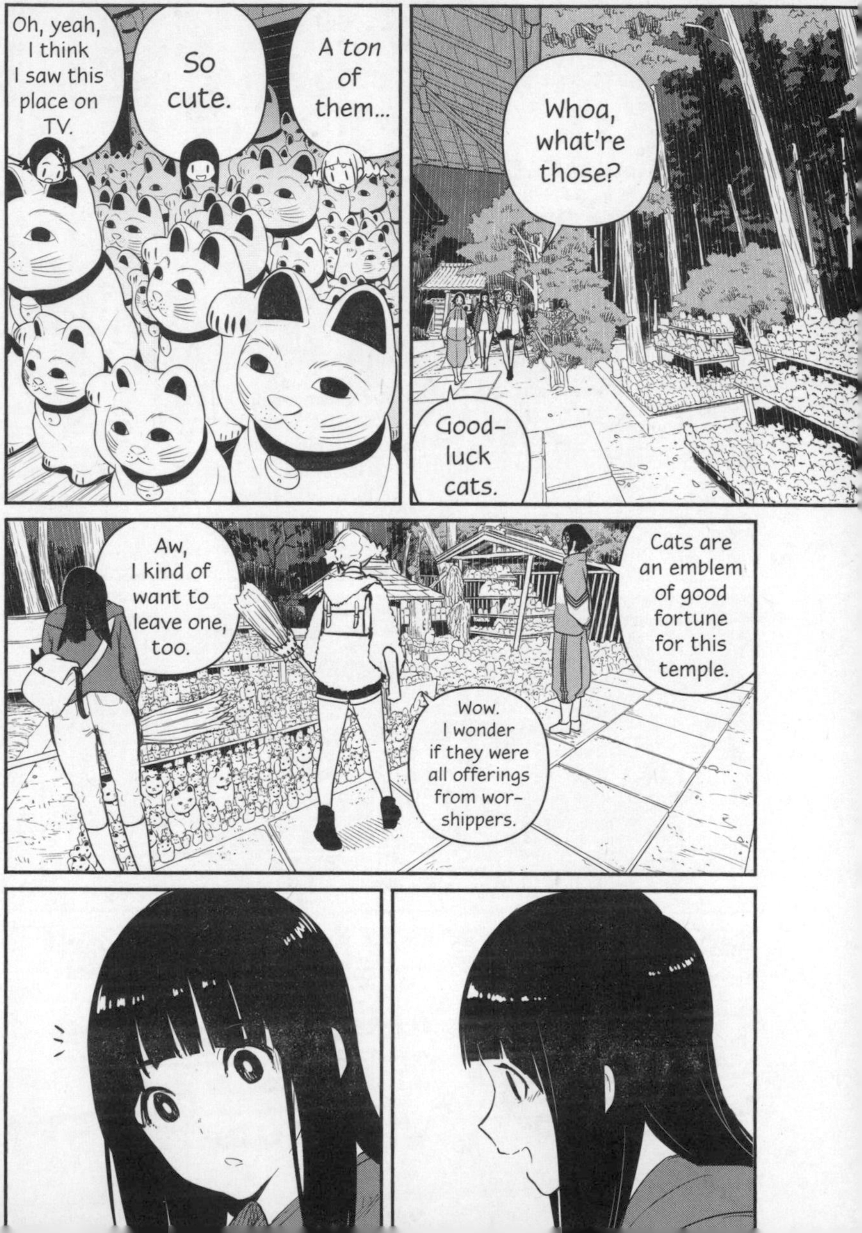
Whoa, what're those?
Good-luck cats.
A *ton* of them...
So cute.
Oh, yeah, I think I saw this place on TV.
Cats are an emblem of good fortune for this temple.
Wow. I wonder if they were all offerings from worshippers.
Aw, I kind of want to leave one, too.

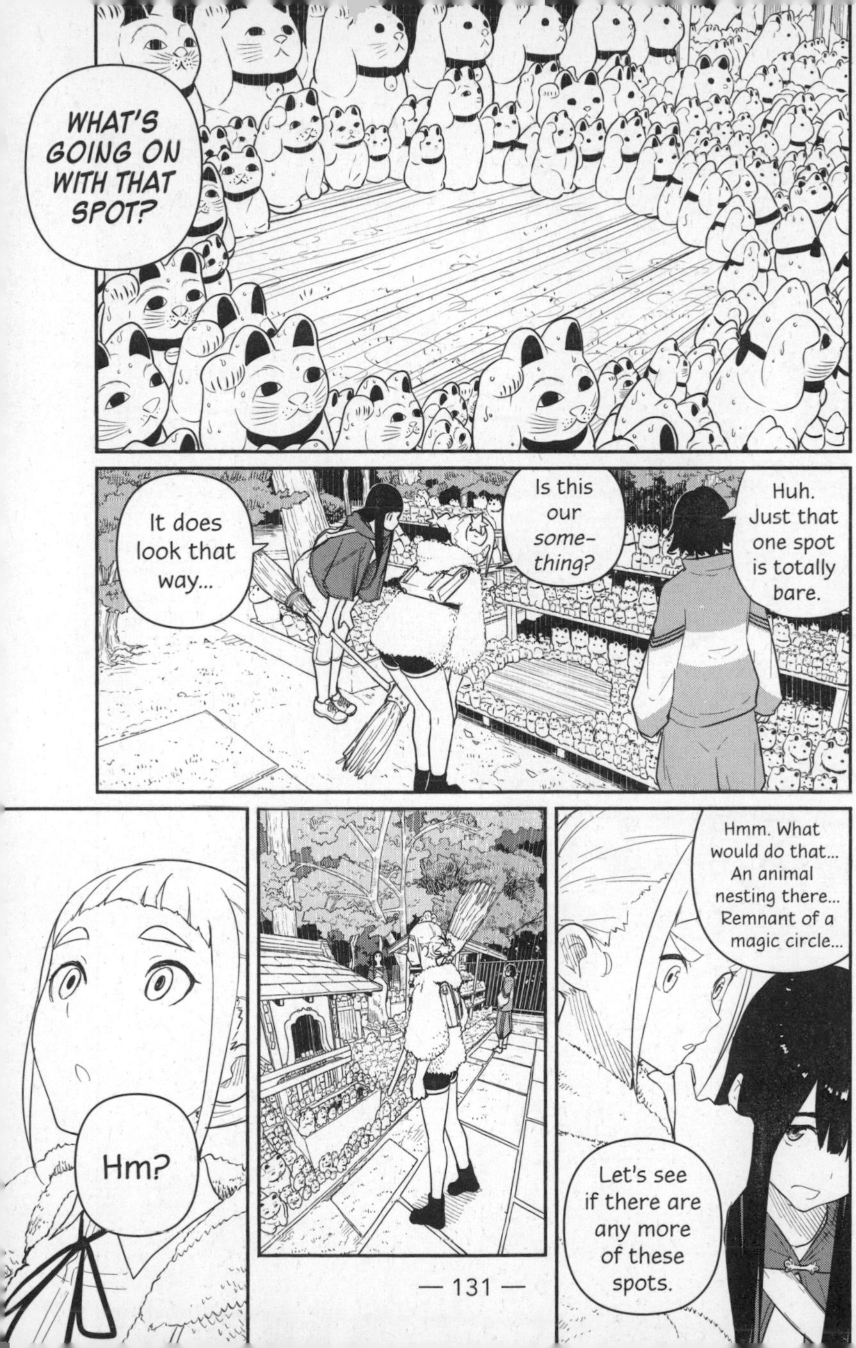
WHAT'S GOING ON WITH THAT SPOT?
Huh. Just that one spot is totally bare.
Is this our *something*?
It does look that way...
Hmm. What would do that... An animal nesting there... Remnant of a magic circle...
Let's see if there are any more of these spots.
Hm?

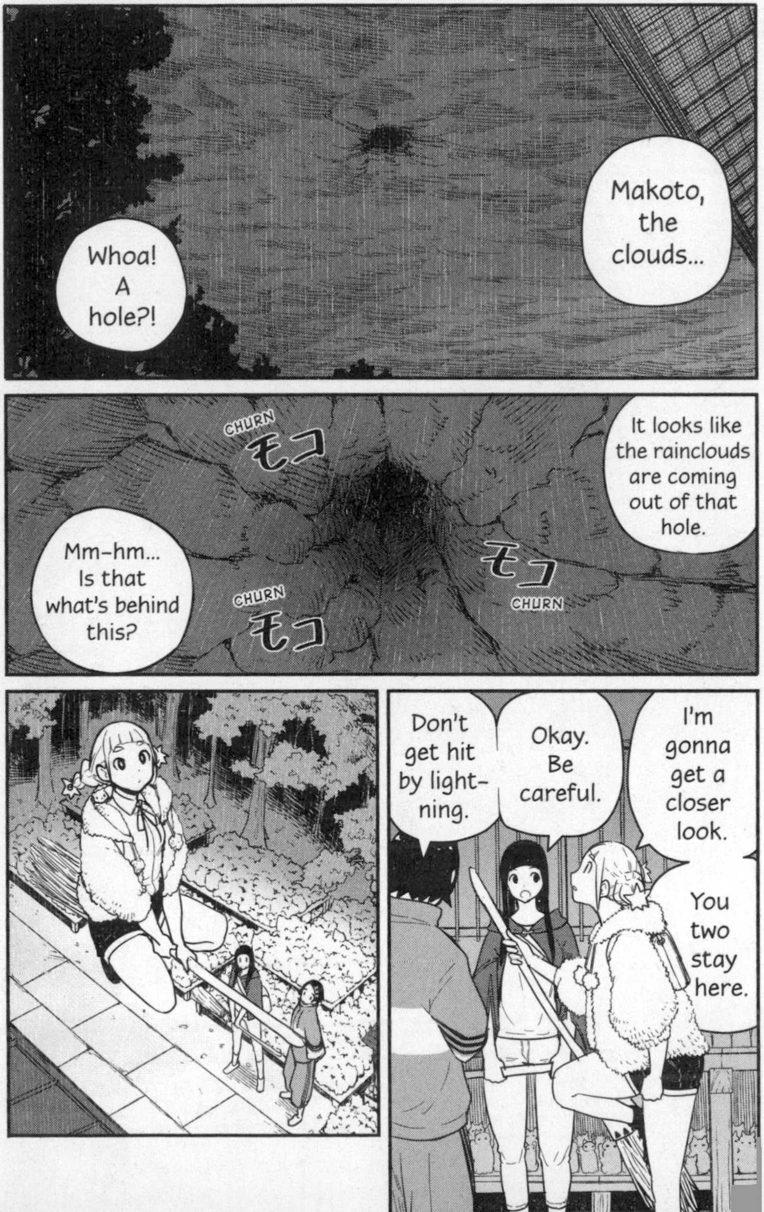
Makoto, the clouds...
Whoa! A hole?!
It looks like the rainclouds are coming out of that hole.
CHURN
モコ
CHURN
モコ
CHURN
モコ
Mm-hm... Is that what's behind this?
I'm gonna get a closer look.
You two stay here.
Okay. Be careful.
Don't get hit by light-ning.

Ten points for bravery.

Hm?

It sure looks like a hole in the sky, but...

CHURN
モコ

CHURN
モコ

モコ
CHURN

Hmmm.

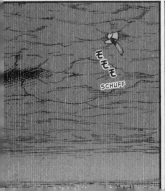

モモモ
SCHUFF

Maybe if I take a look from above...

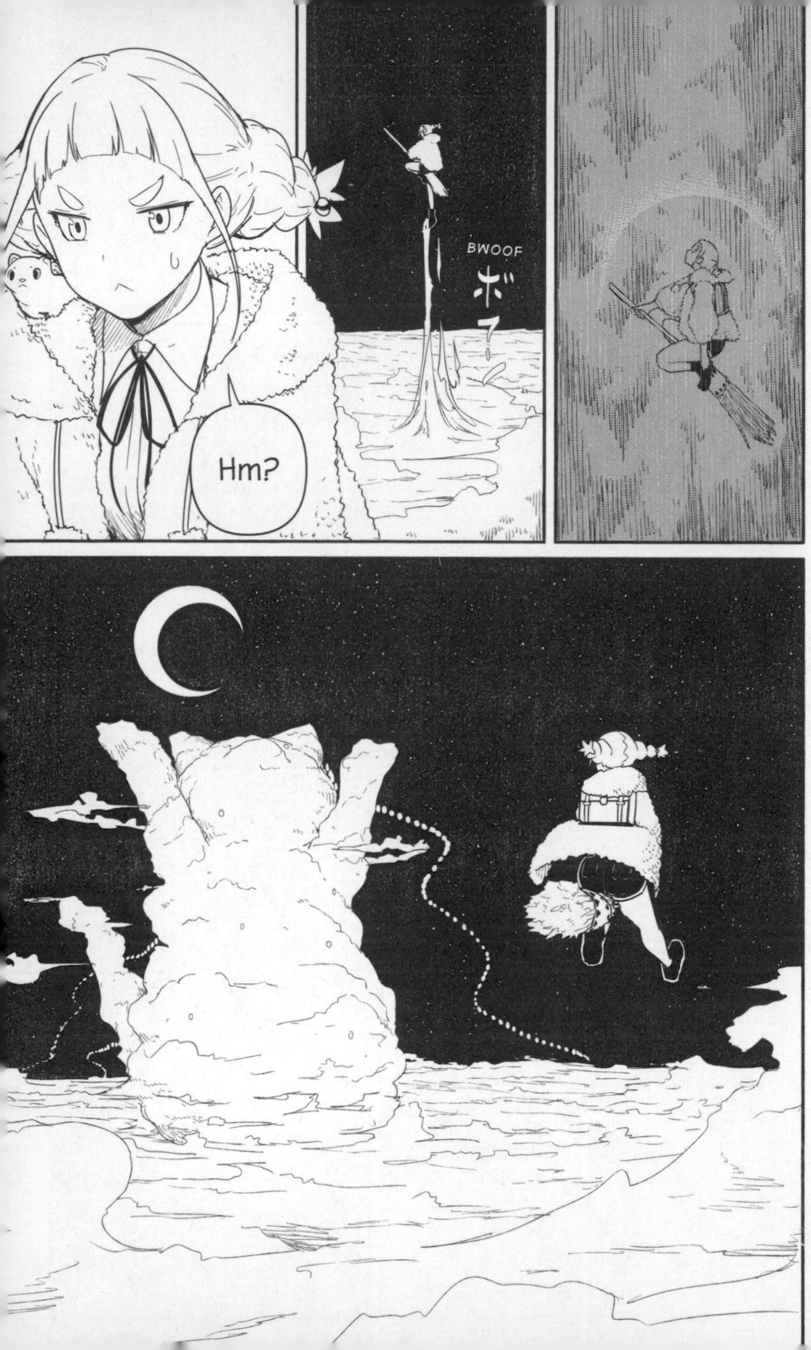
BWOOF
ボフ
Hm?

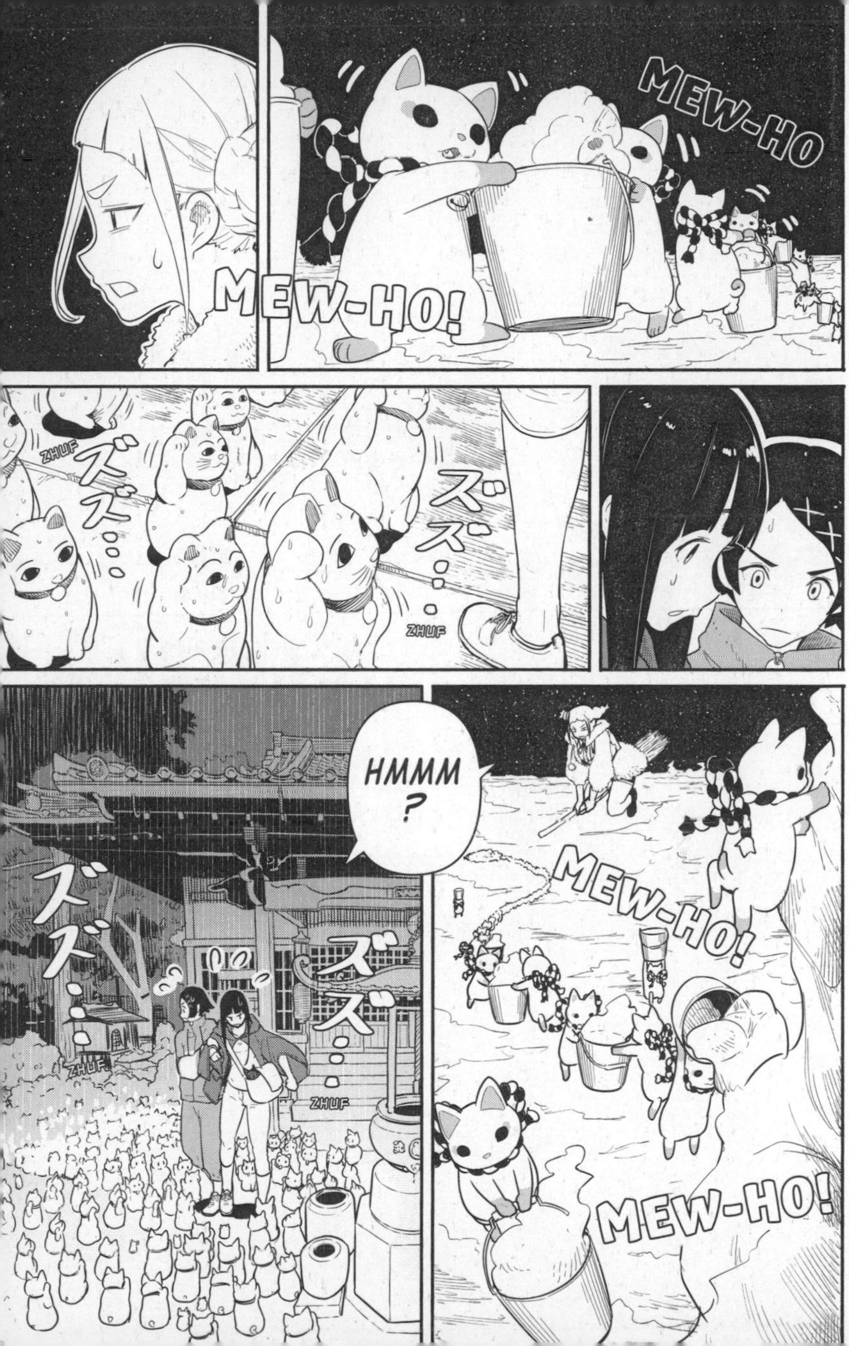

MEW-HO
MEW-HO!
ズズ…
ZHUF
ズズ…
ZHUF
HMMM ?
MEW-HO!
MEW-HO!
ズズ…
ZHUF
ズズ…
ZHUF

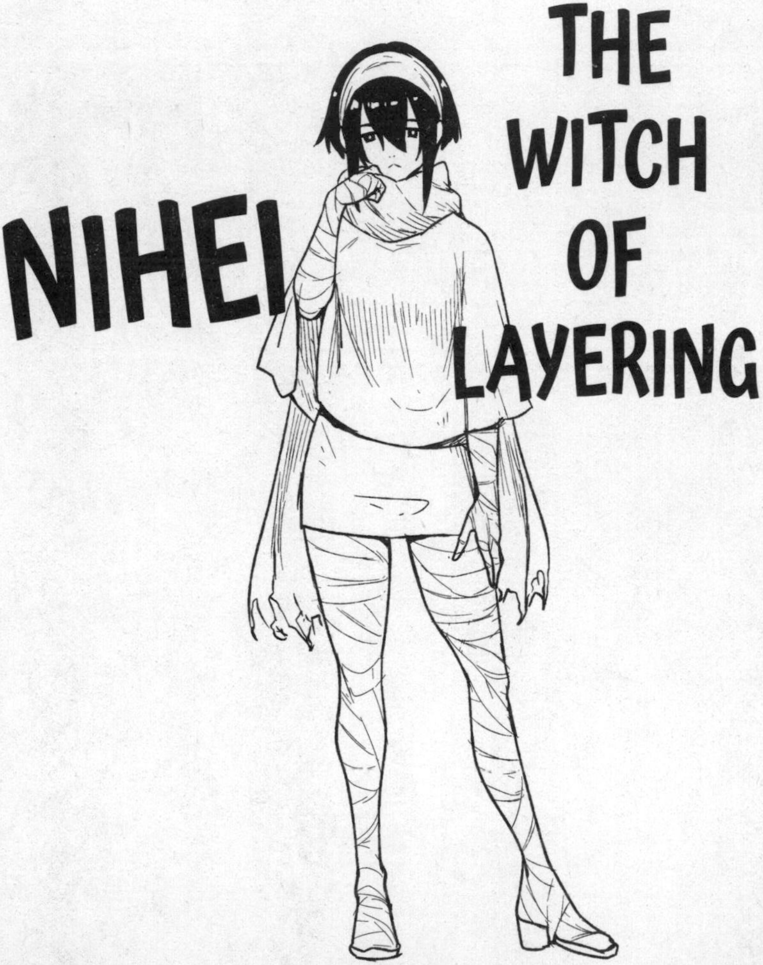
NIHEI
THE WITCH OF LAYERING

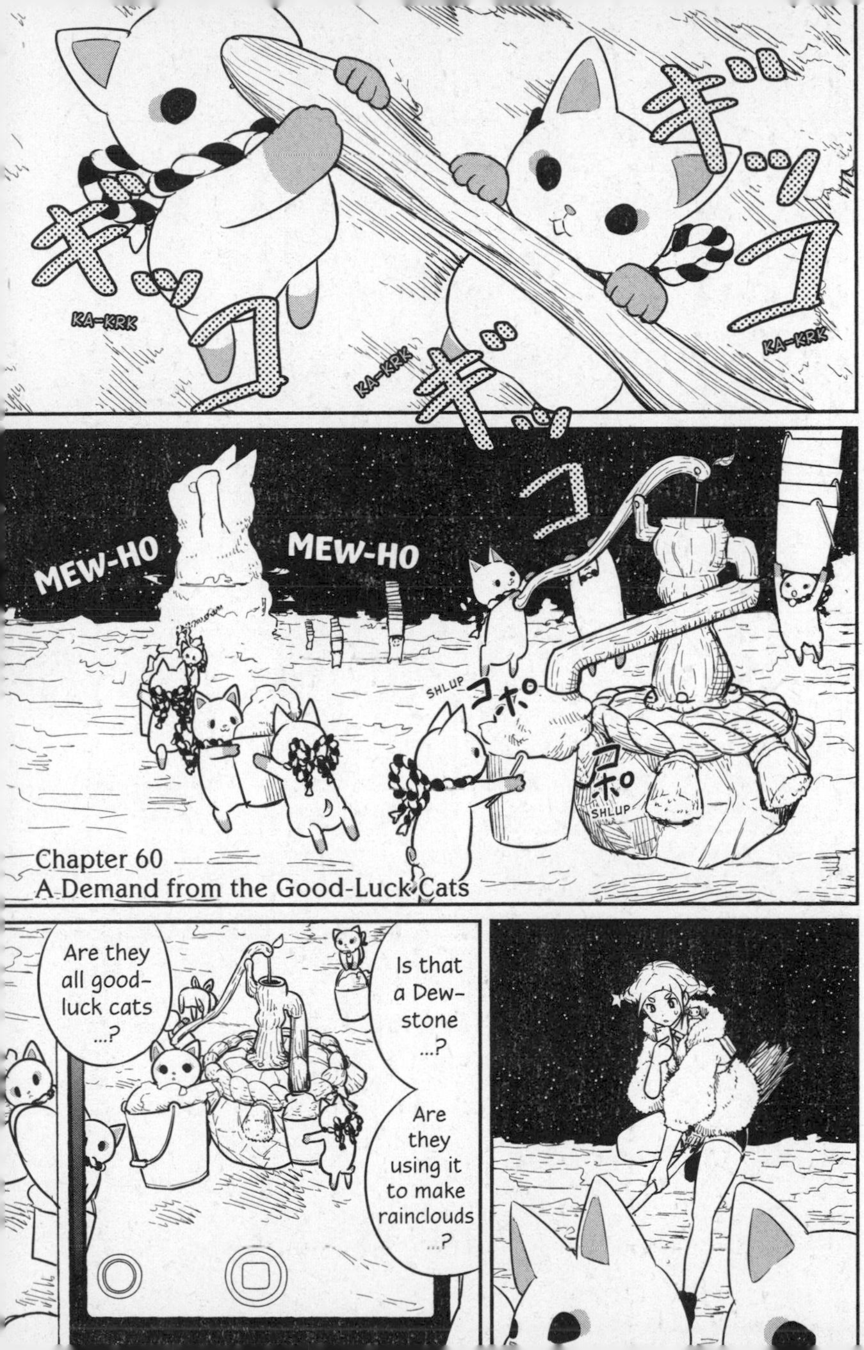
ギッコ
KA-KRK
ギッコ
KA-KRK
KA-KRK
MEW-HO
MEW-HO
SHLUP
SHLUP
Chapter 60
A Demand from the Good-Luck Cats
Is that a Dew-stone ...?
Are they using it to make rainclouds ...?
Are they all good-luck cats ...?

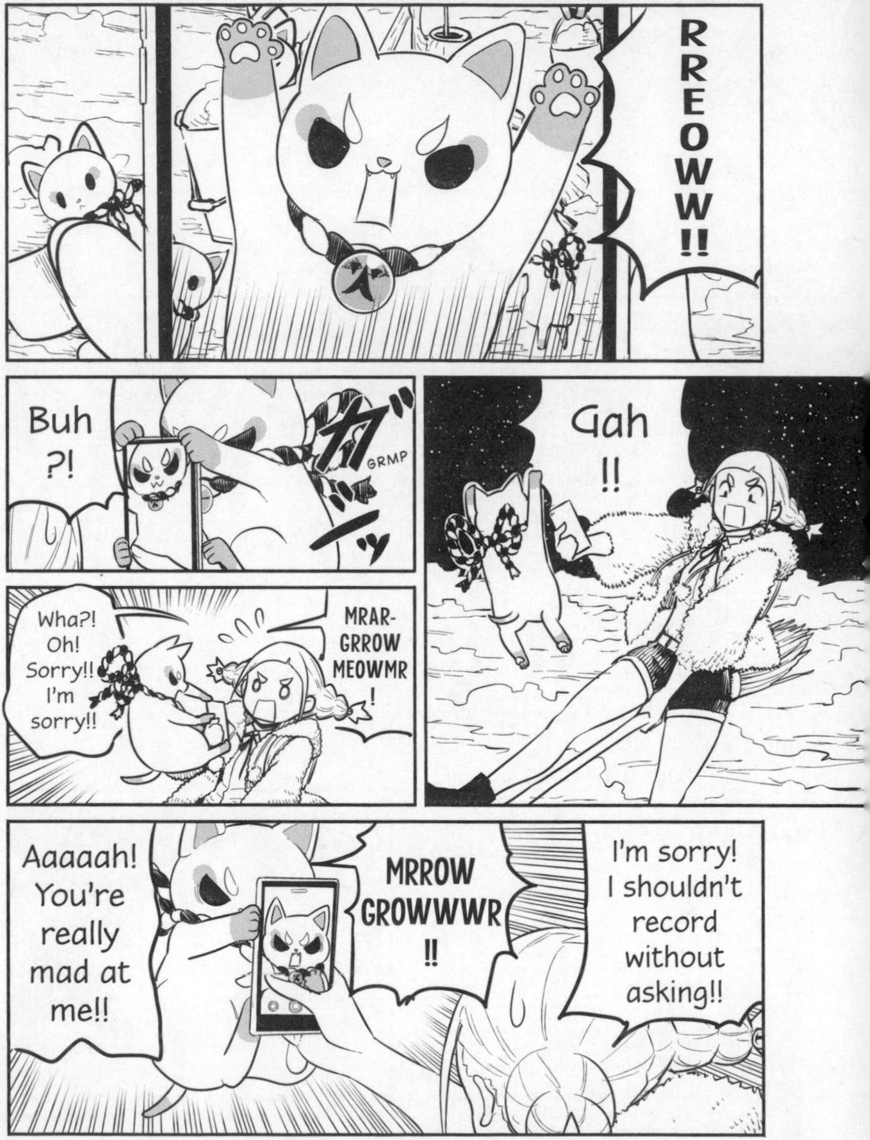
RREOWW!!
Gah!!
Buh?!
ガブッ
GRMP
MRAR-GRROW MEOWMR!
Wha?! Oh! Sorry!! I'm sorry!!
I'm sorry! I shouldn't record without asking!!
MRROW GROWWWR!!
Aaaaah! You're really mad at me!!

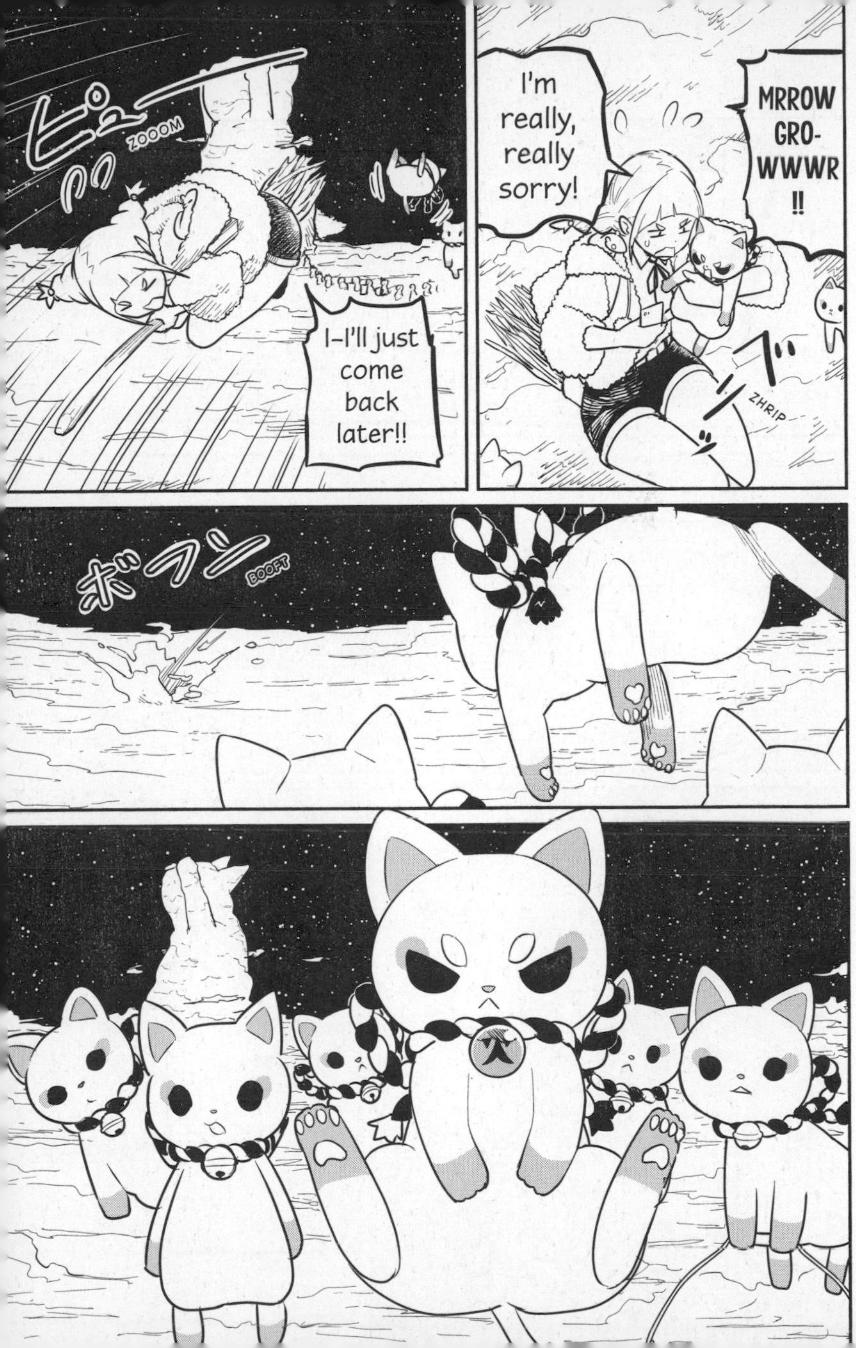
MRROW GRO-WWWR!!
I'm really, really sorry!
ZHRIP
ZOOOM
I-I'll just come back later!!
BOOFT

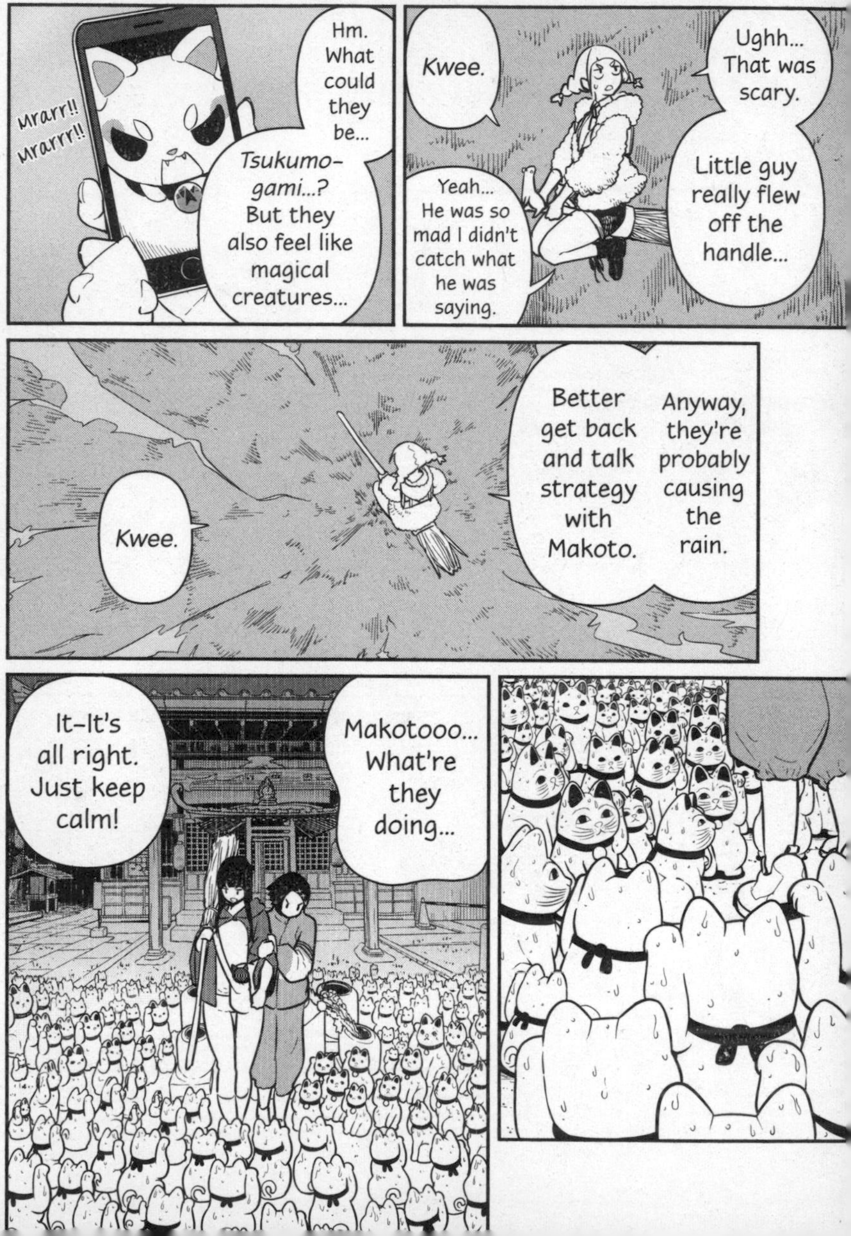
Ughh... That was scary.
Kwee.
Little guy really flew off the handle...
Yeah... He was so mad I didn't catch what he was saying.
Hm. What could they be...
Mrarr!! Mrarrr!!
Tsukumo-gami...? But they also feel like magical creatures...
Anyway, they're probably causing the rain.
Better get back and talk strategy with Makoto.
Kwee.
Makotooo... What're they doing...
It-It's all right. Just keep calm!

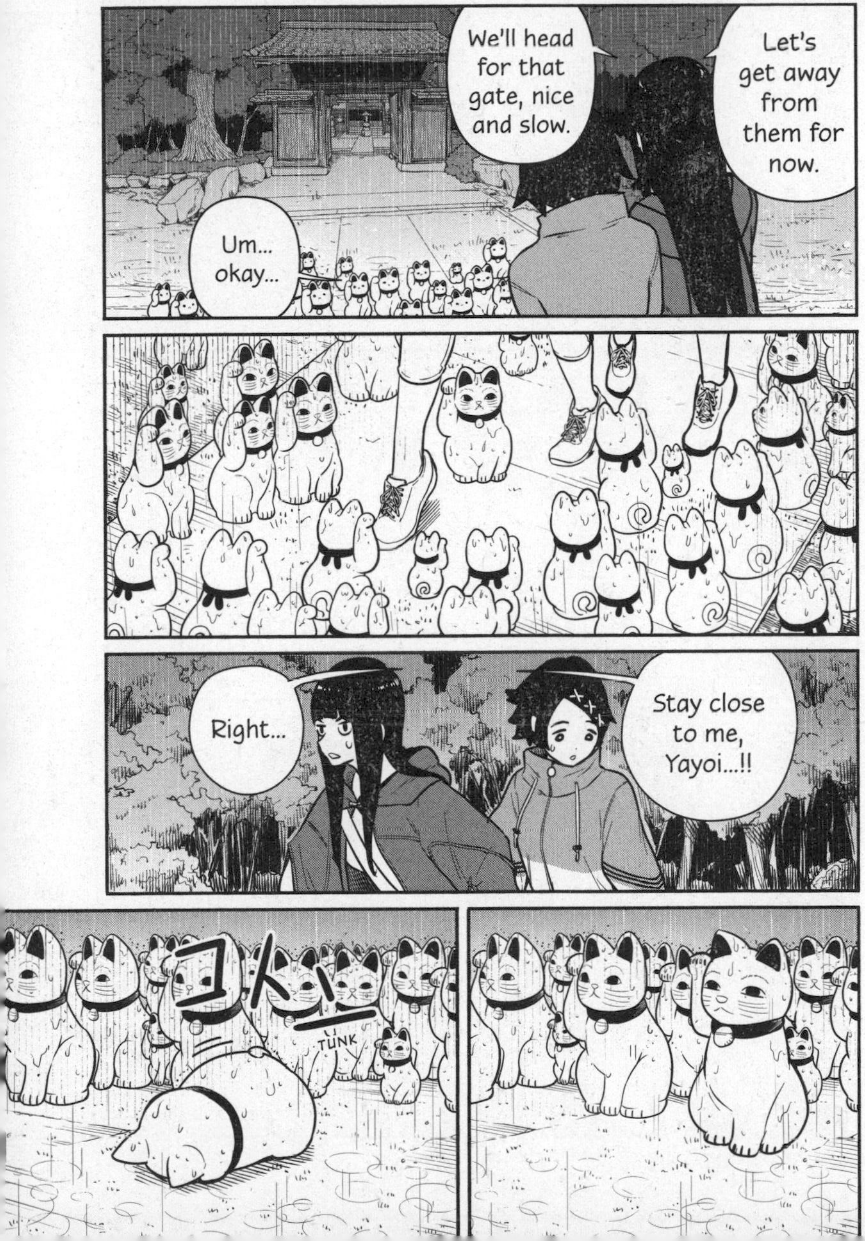
Let's get away from them for now.
We'll head for that gate, nice and slow.
Um... okay...
Stay close to me, Yayoi...!!
Right...
TUNK

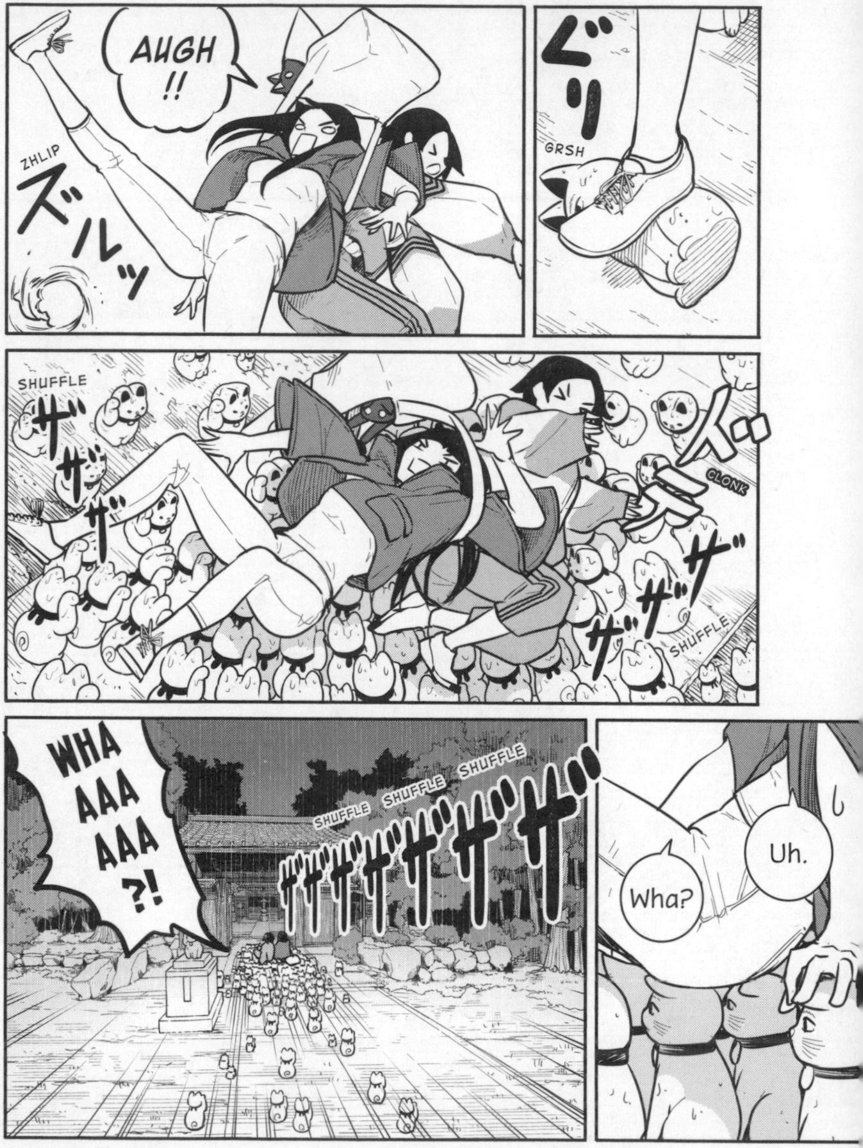
ぐり
GRSH
AUGH !!
ZHLIP
ズルッ
CLONK
ザザザ
SHUFFLE
SHUFFLE
ザザザ
Uh.
Wha?
SHUFFLE SHUFFLE SHUFFLE
ザザザザザザ
WHA AAA AAA ?!

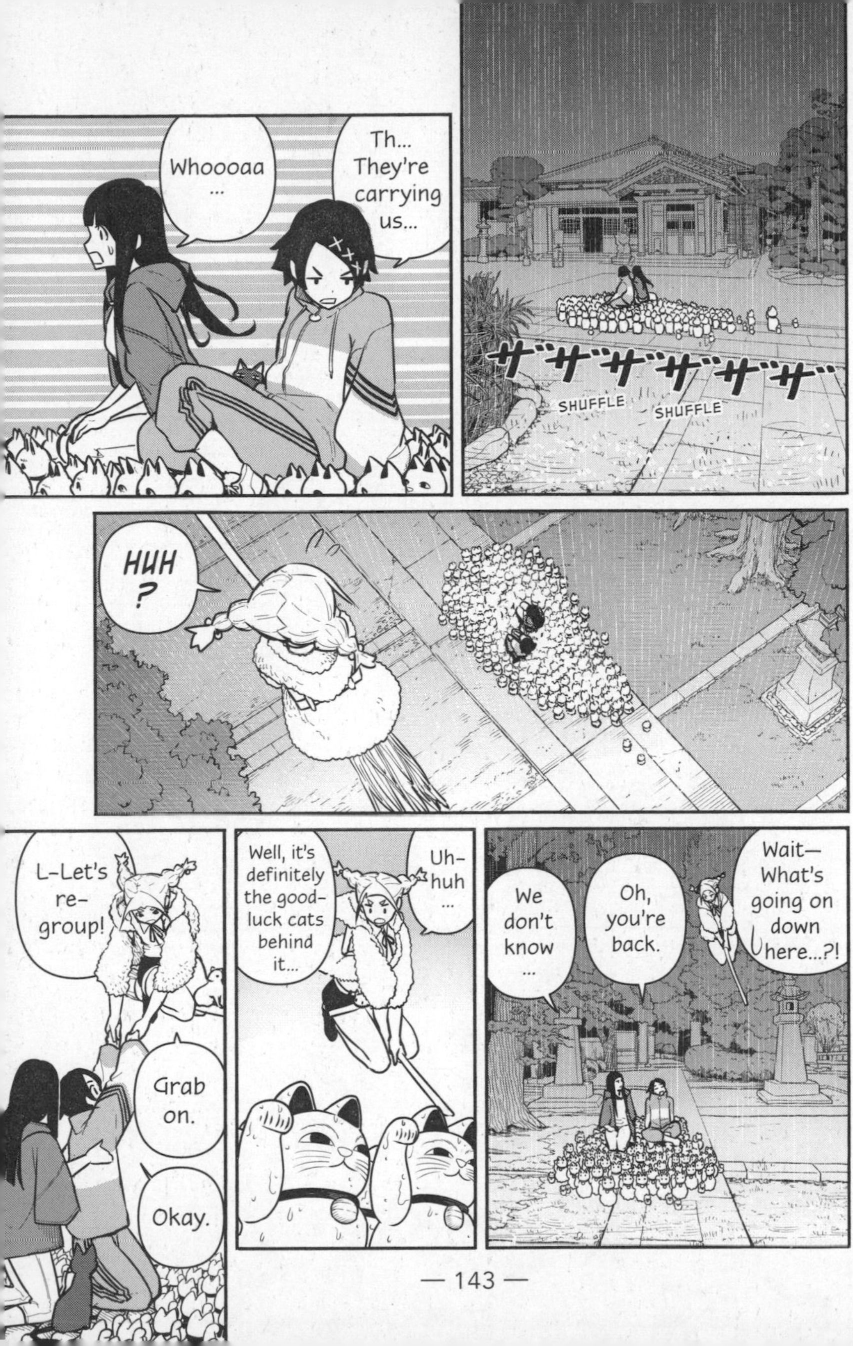
ザザザザザ
SHUFFLE
SHUFFLE
Th... They're carrying us...
Whoooaa ...
HUH ?
Wait— What's going on down here...?!
Oh, you're back.
We don't know ...
Uh-huh ...
Well, it's definitely the good-luck cats behind it...
L-Let's re-group!
Grab on.
Okay.

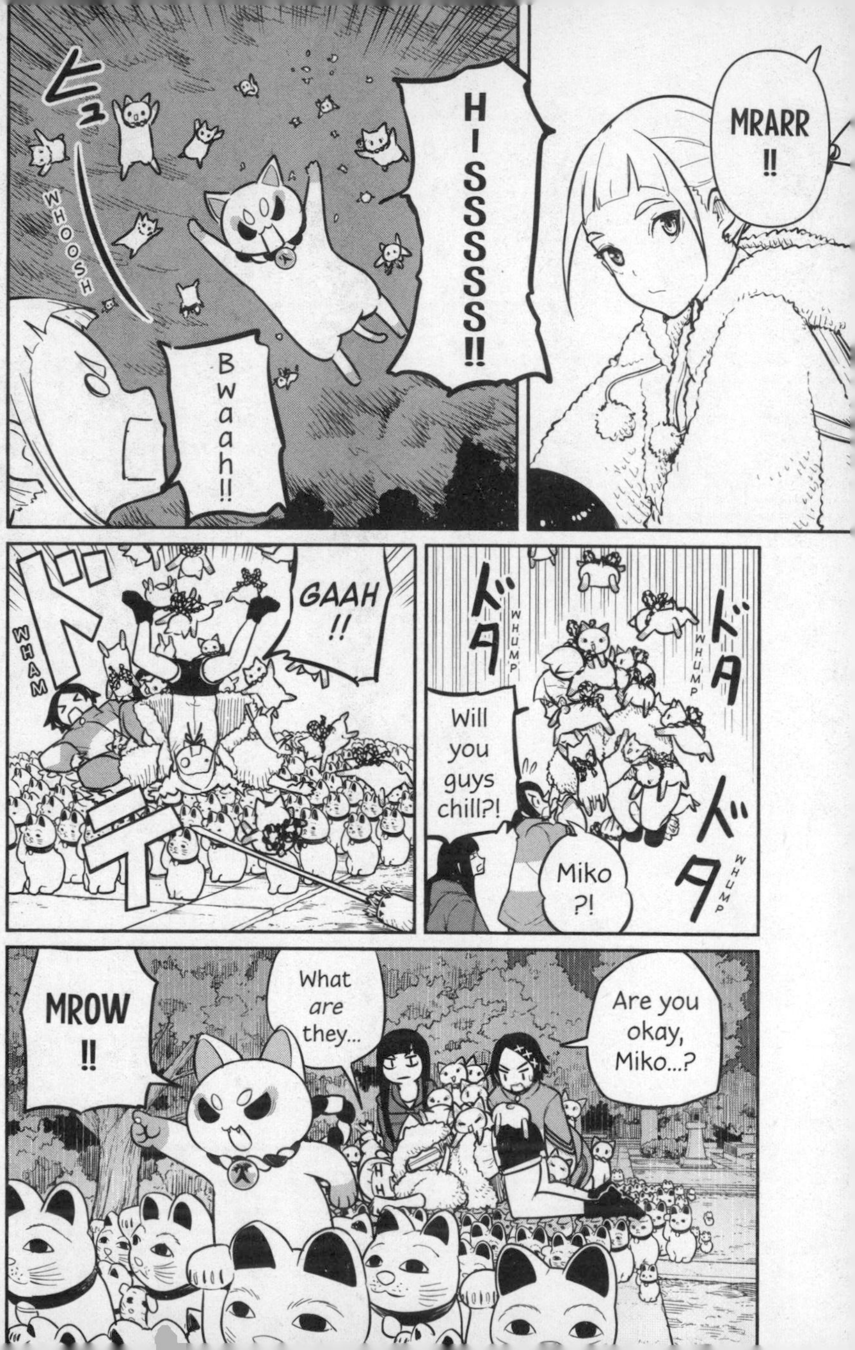
MRARR !!
HISSSSSS!!
ヒュ
WHOOSH
Bwaah!!
ドタ
WHUMP
ドタ
WHUMP
Will you guys chill?!
Miko ?!
ドタ
WHUMP
GAAH !!
WHAM
Are you okay, Miko...?
What *are* they...
MROW !!

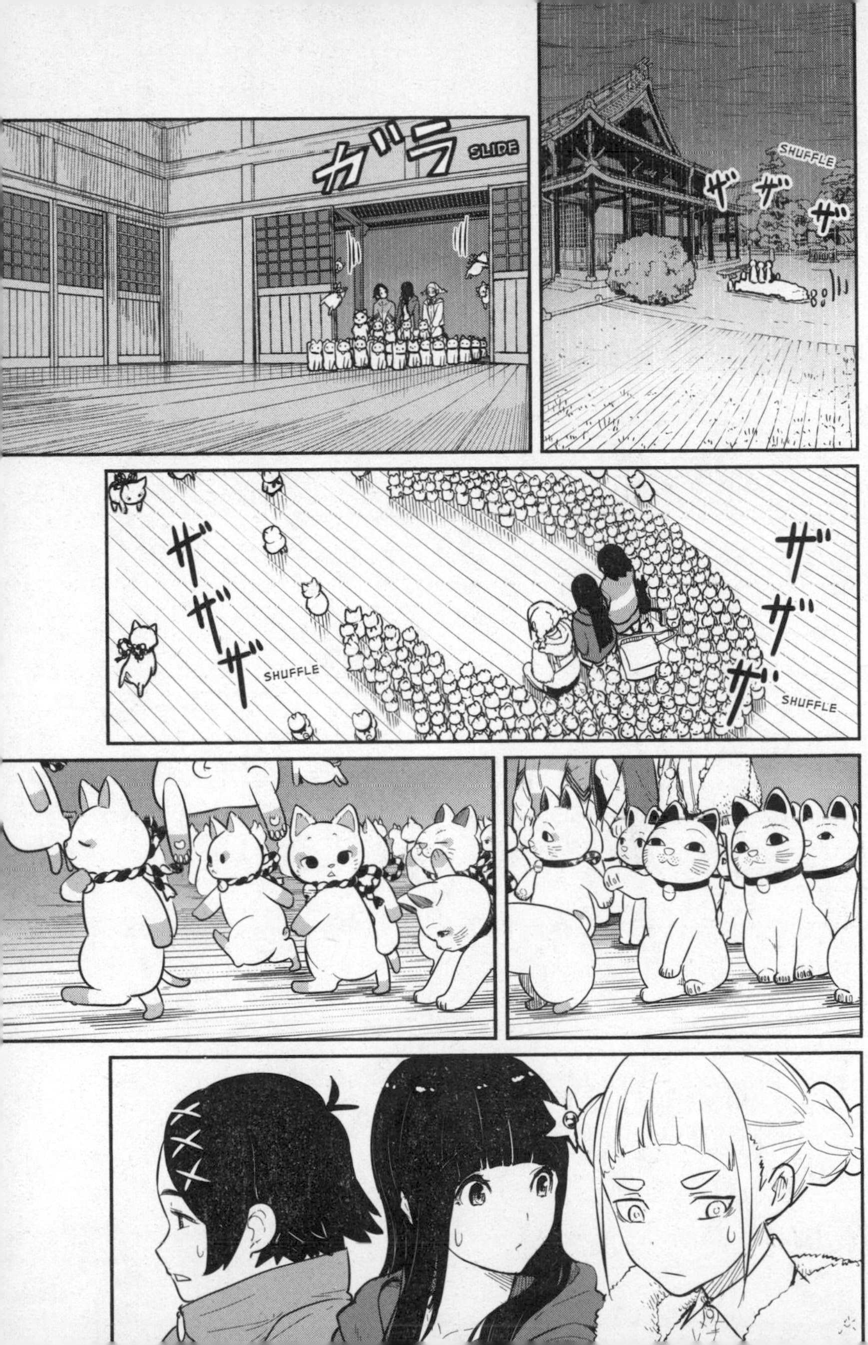
SHUFFLE
ザ ザ ザ
ガラ
SLIDE
ザ ザ ザ
SHUFFLE
ザ ザ ザ
SHUFFLE

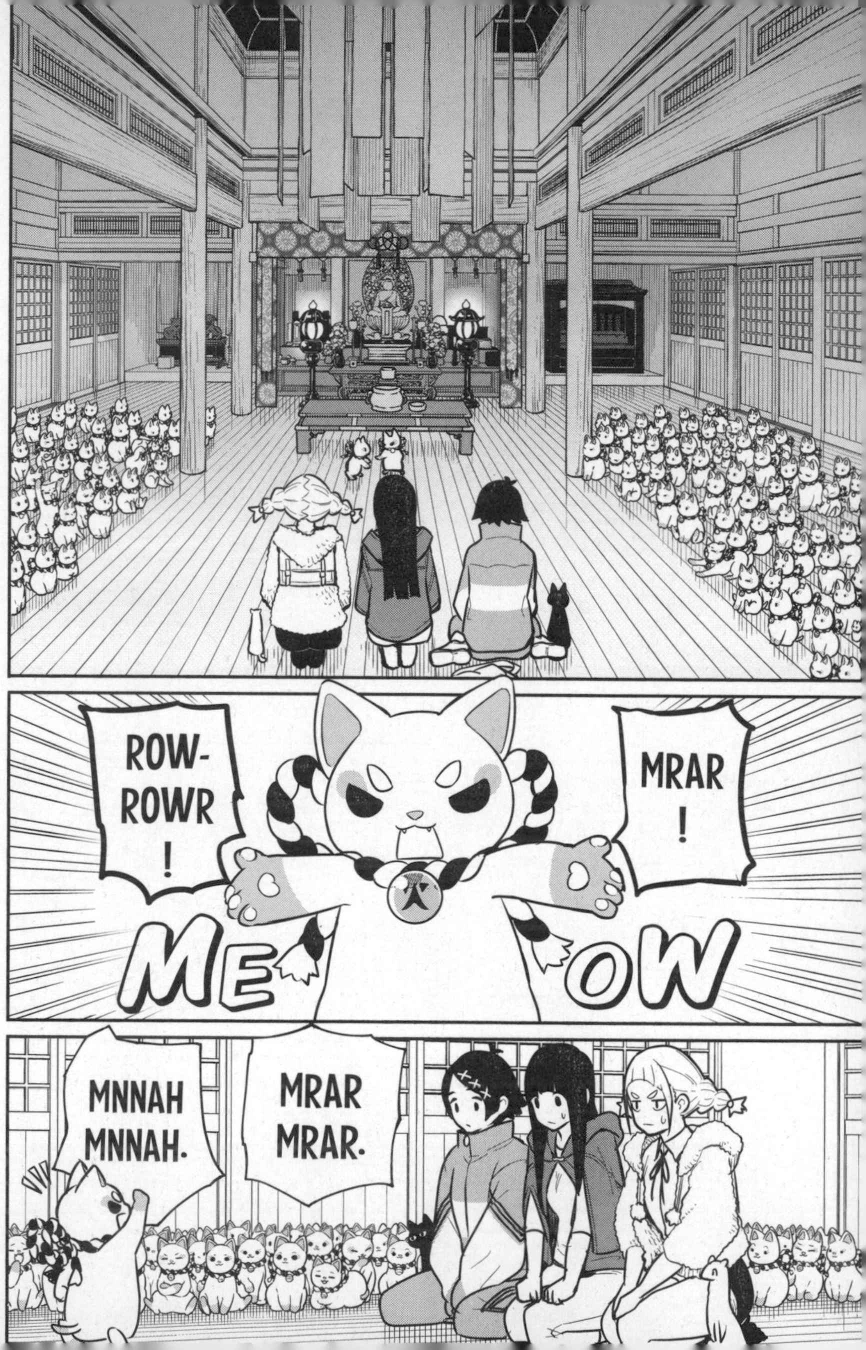
MRAR!
ROW-ROWR!
MEOW
MRAR MRAR.
MNNAH MNNAH.

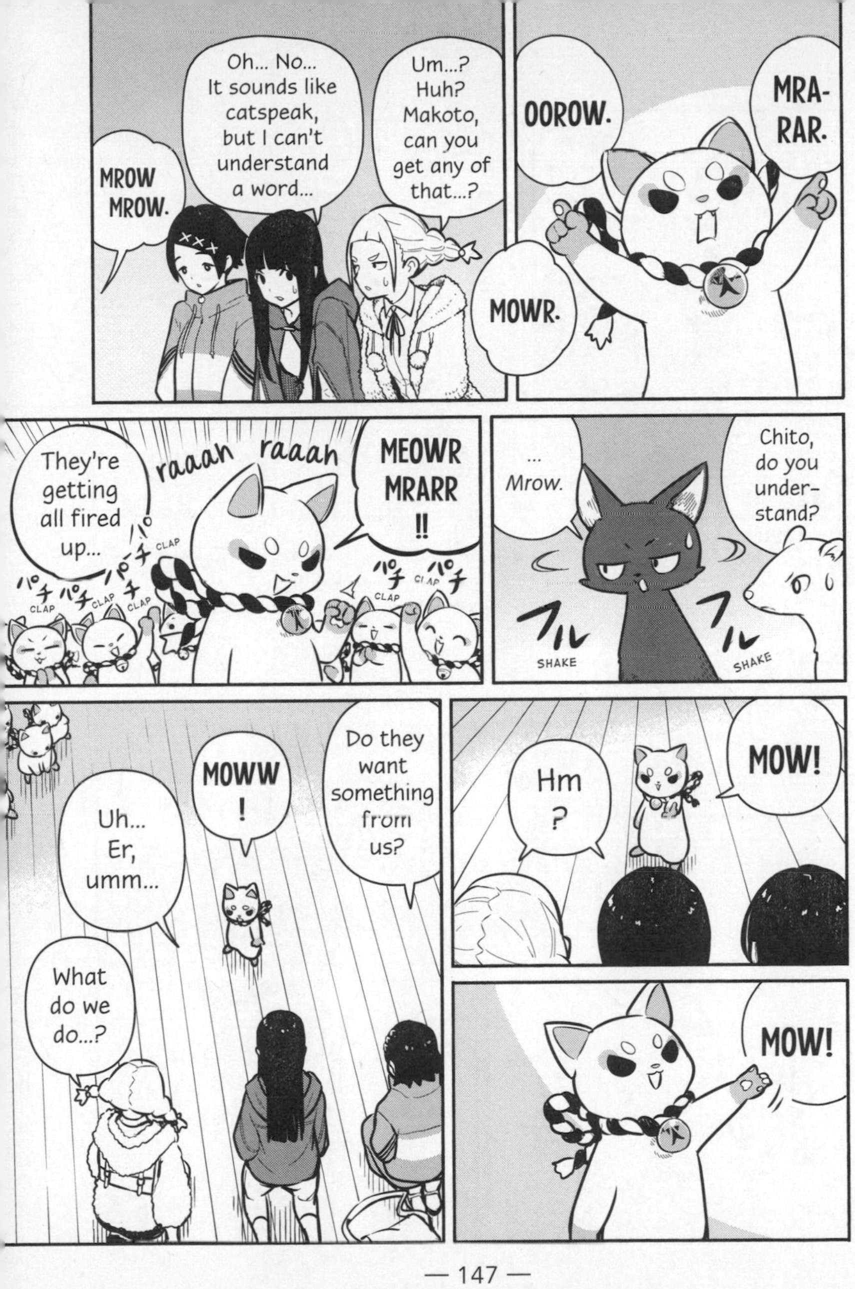
MRA-RAR.
OOROW.
MOWR.
Um...? Huh? Makoto, can you get any of that...?
Oh... No... It sounds like catspeak, but I can't understand a word...
MROW MROW.
Chito, do you under-stand?
... Mrow.
フル SHAKE
フル SHAKE
MEOWR MRARR !!
raaah raaah
They're getting all fired up...
パチ CLAP
パチ CLAP
パチ CLAP
パチ CLAP
パチ CLAP
パチ CLAP
MOW!
Hm ?
MOW!
Do they want something from us?
MOWW !
Uh... Er, umm...
What do we do...?

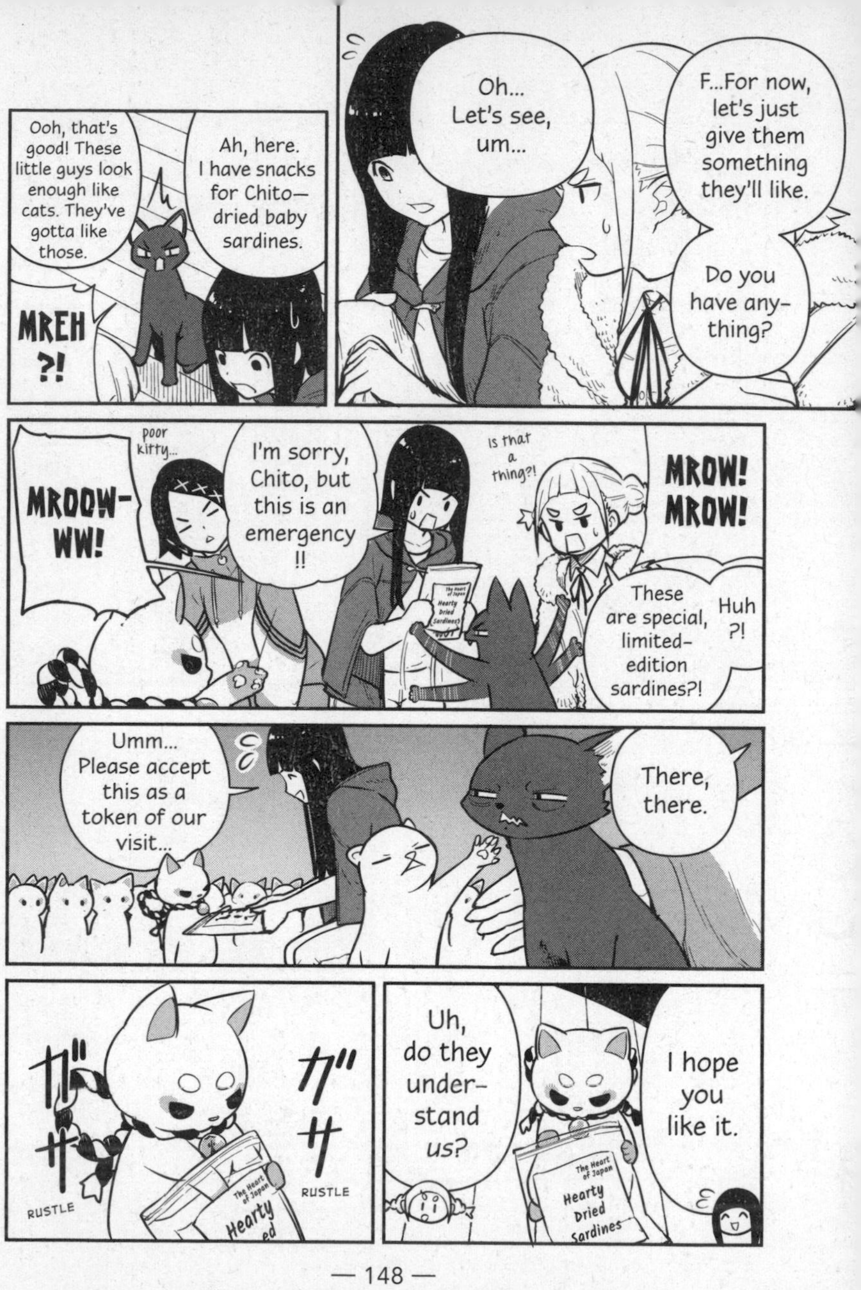
F...For now, let's just give them something they'll like.
Do you have anything?
Oh... Let's see, um...
Ah, here. I have snacks for Chito—dried baby sardines.
Ooh, that's good! These little guys look enough like cats. They've gotta like those.
MREH ?!
MROW! MROW!
These are special, limited-edition sardines?!
Huh ?!
is that a thing?!
I'm sorry, Chito, but this is an emergency !!
The Heart of Japan Hearty Dried Sardines
poor kitty...
MROOW-WW!
There, there.
Umm... Please accept this as a token of our visit...
I hope you like it.
Uh, do they understand us?
The Heart of Japan Hearty Dried Sardines
ガサ
RUSTLE
ガサ
RUSTLE
The Heart of Japan Hearty

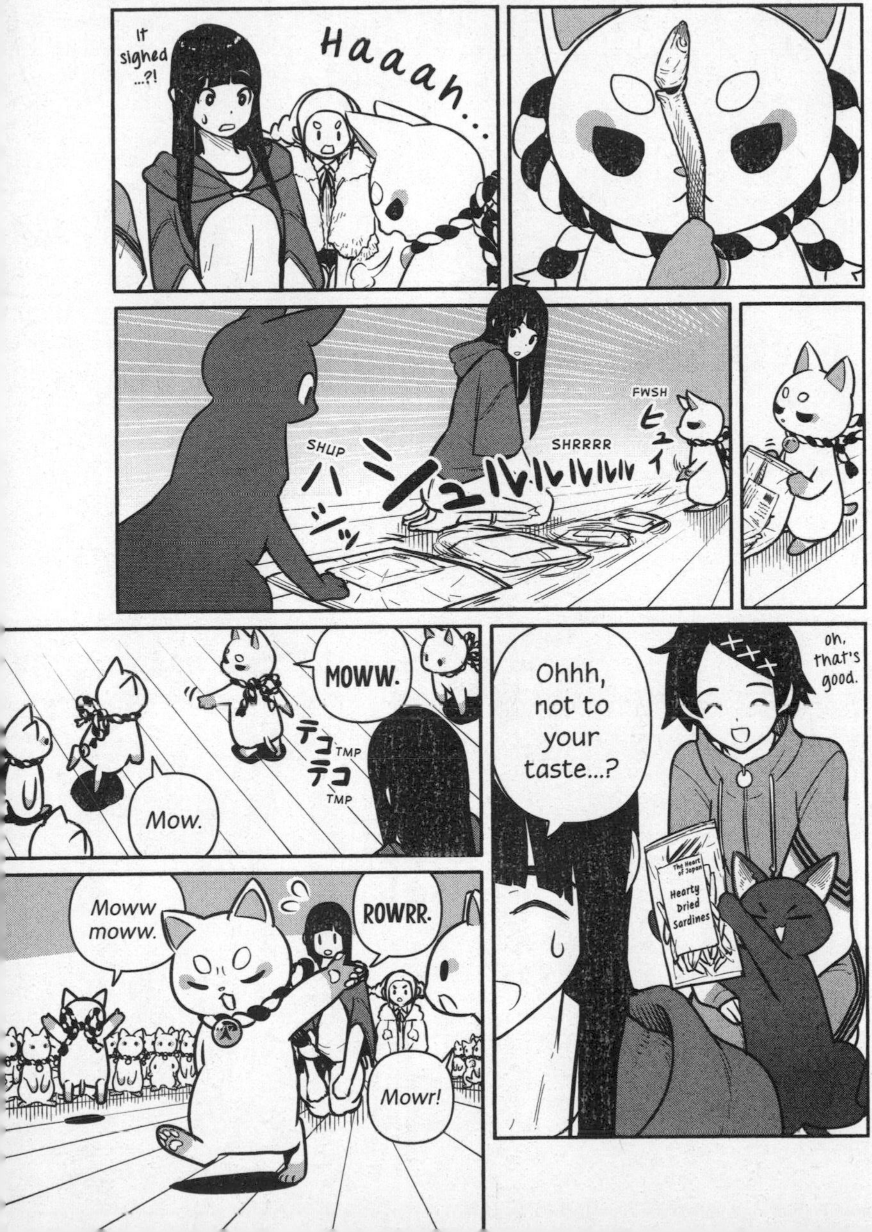
Haaaah...
It signed ...?!
FWSH
ヒュイ
SHRRRR
SHUP
oh, that's good.
Ohhh, not to your taste...?
The Heart of Japan
Hearty Dried Sardines
MOWW.
テコ TMP
テコ TMP
Mow.
ROWRR.
Moww moww.
Mowr!

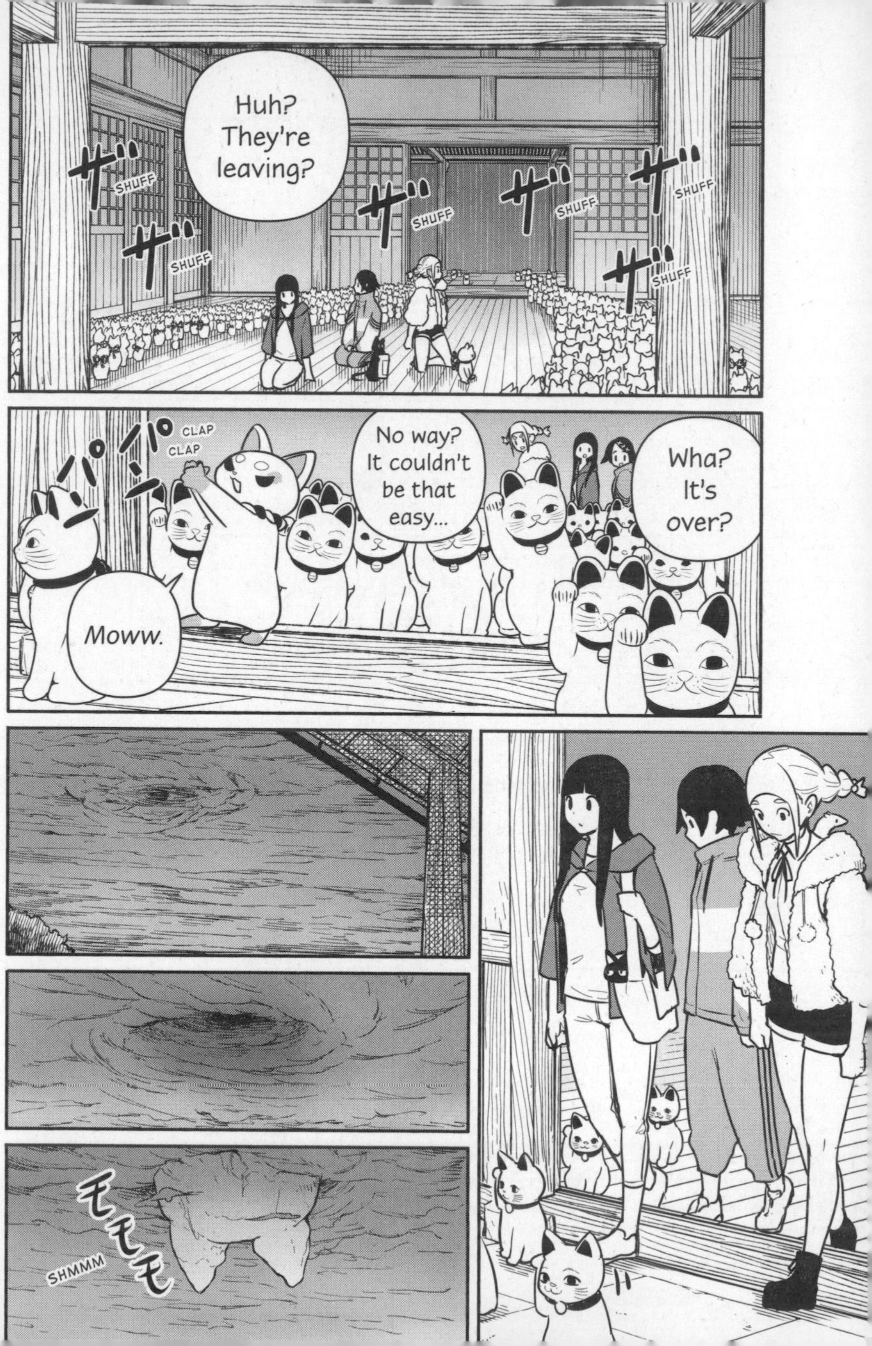
ザ SHUFF
ザ SHUFF
ザ SHUFF
Huh? They're leaving?
ザ SHUFF
ザ SHUFF
ザ SHUFF
Wha? It's over?
No way? It couldn't be that easy...
パン CLAP CLAP
Moww.
モモモ SHMMM

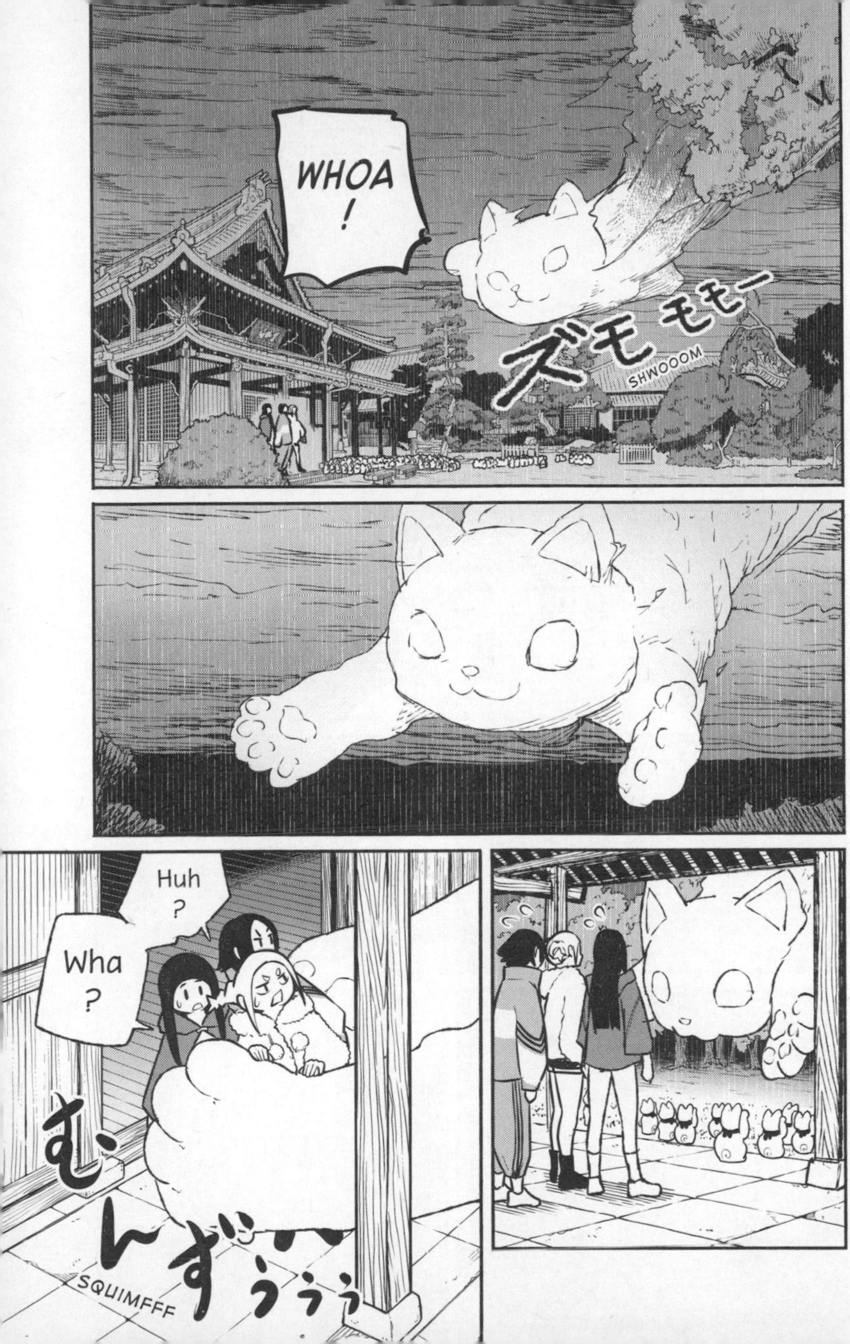
WHOA!
ズモモモー
SHWOOOM
Huh?
Wha?
SQUIMFFF

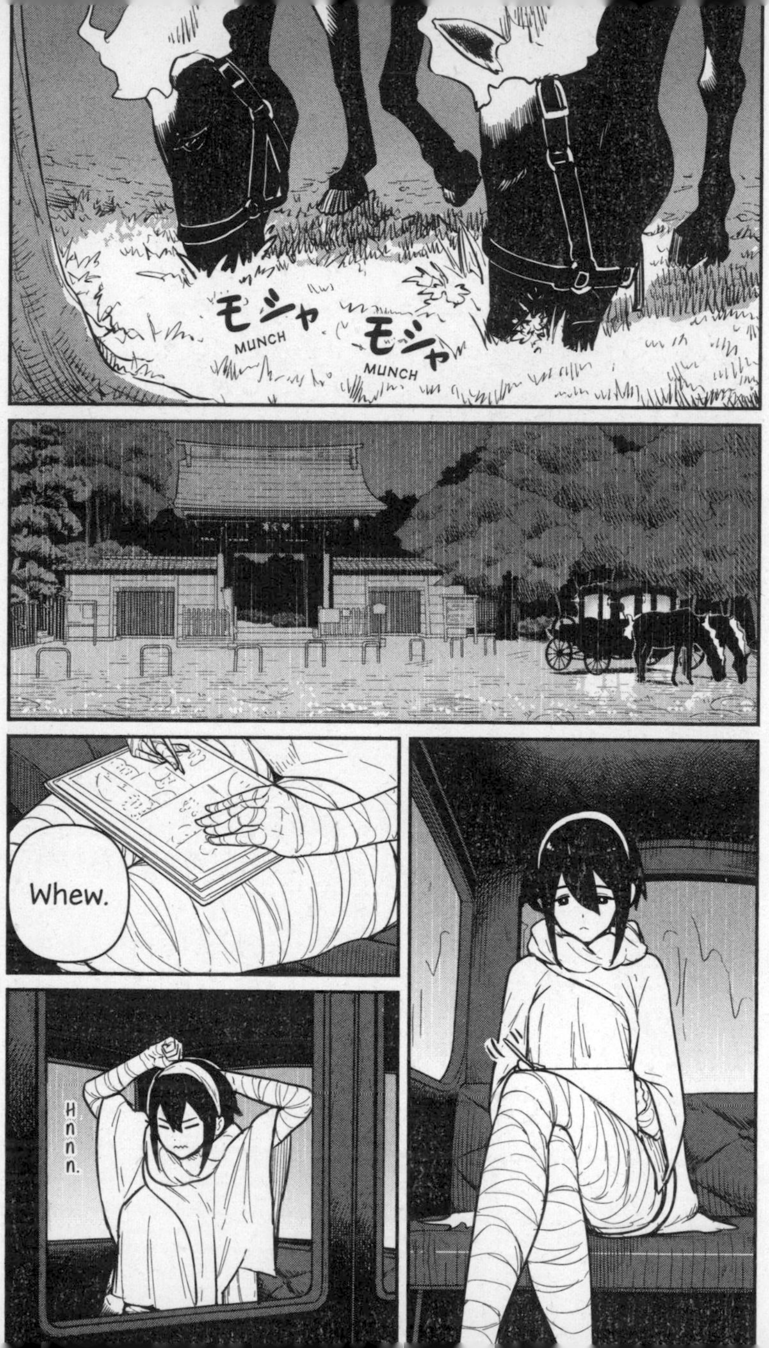
モシャ
MUNCH
モシャ
MUNCH
Whew.
Hnnn.

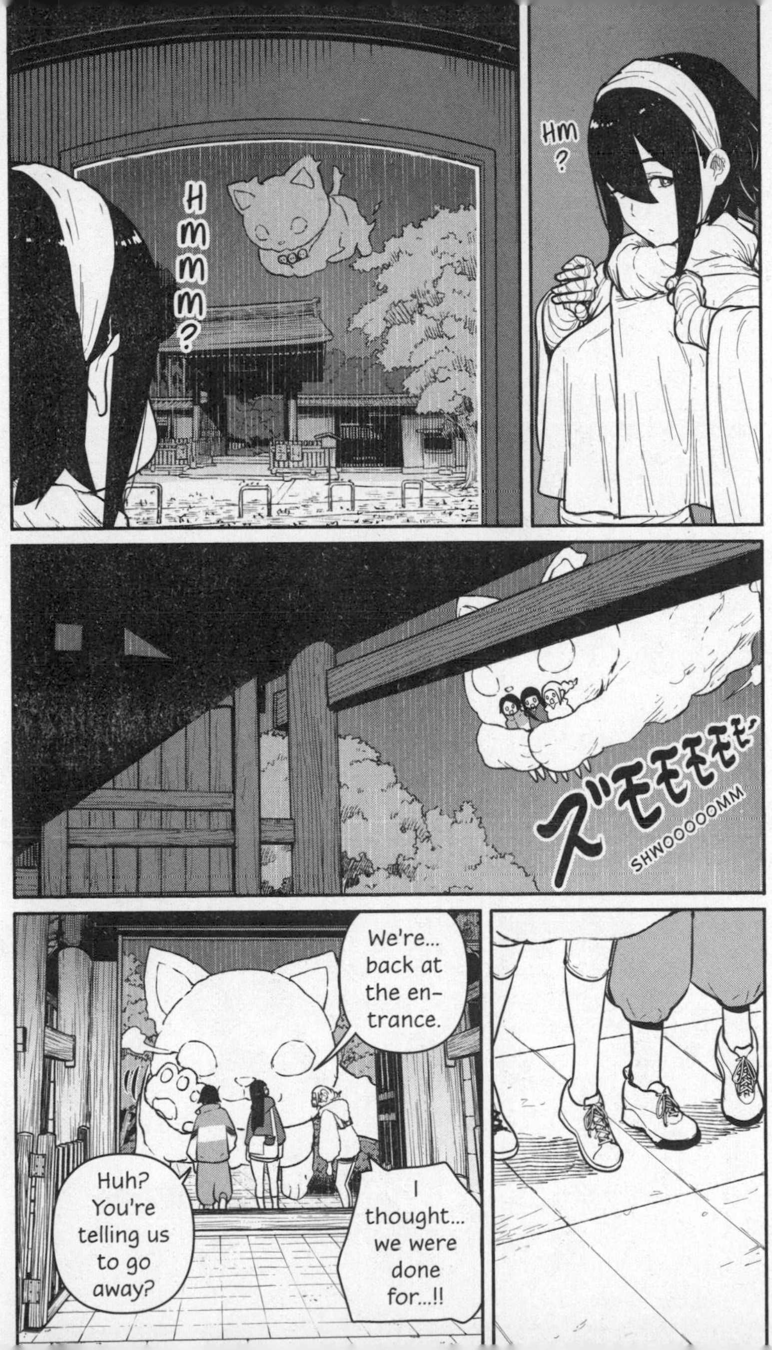
Hm ?
Hmmmm?
ズモモモモモ
SHWOOOOOMM
We're... back at the en-trance.
I thought... we were done for...!!
Huh? You're telling us to go away?

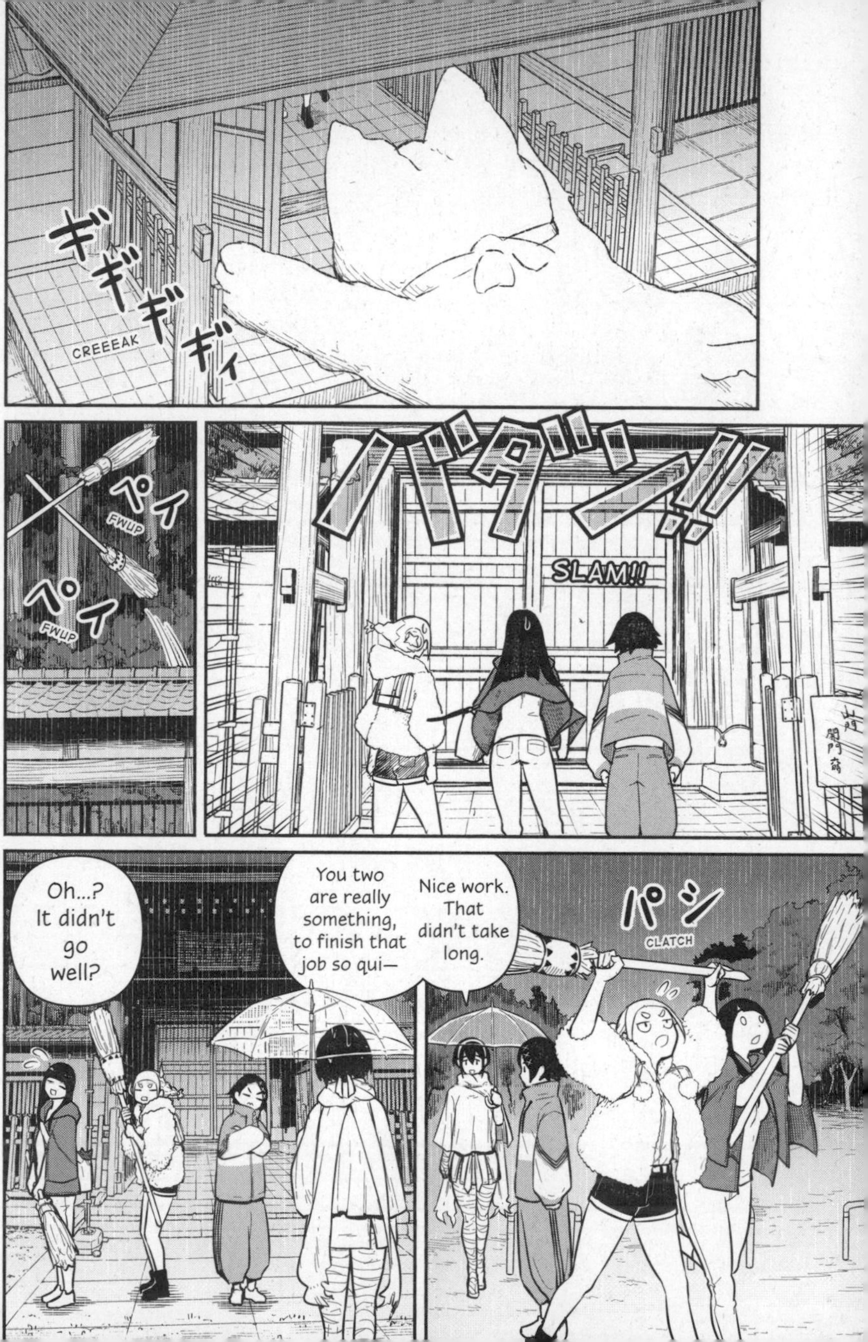
ギギギィ
CREEEAK
バタン!!
SLAM!!
ペイ
FWUP
ペイ
FWUP
パシ
CLATCH
Nice work. That didn't take long.
You two are really something, to finish that job so qui—
Oh...? It didn't go well?

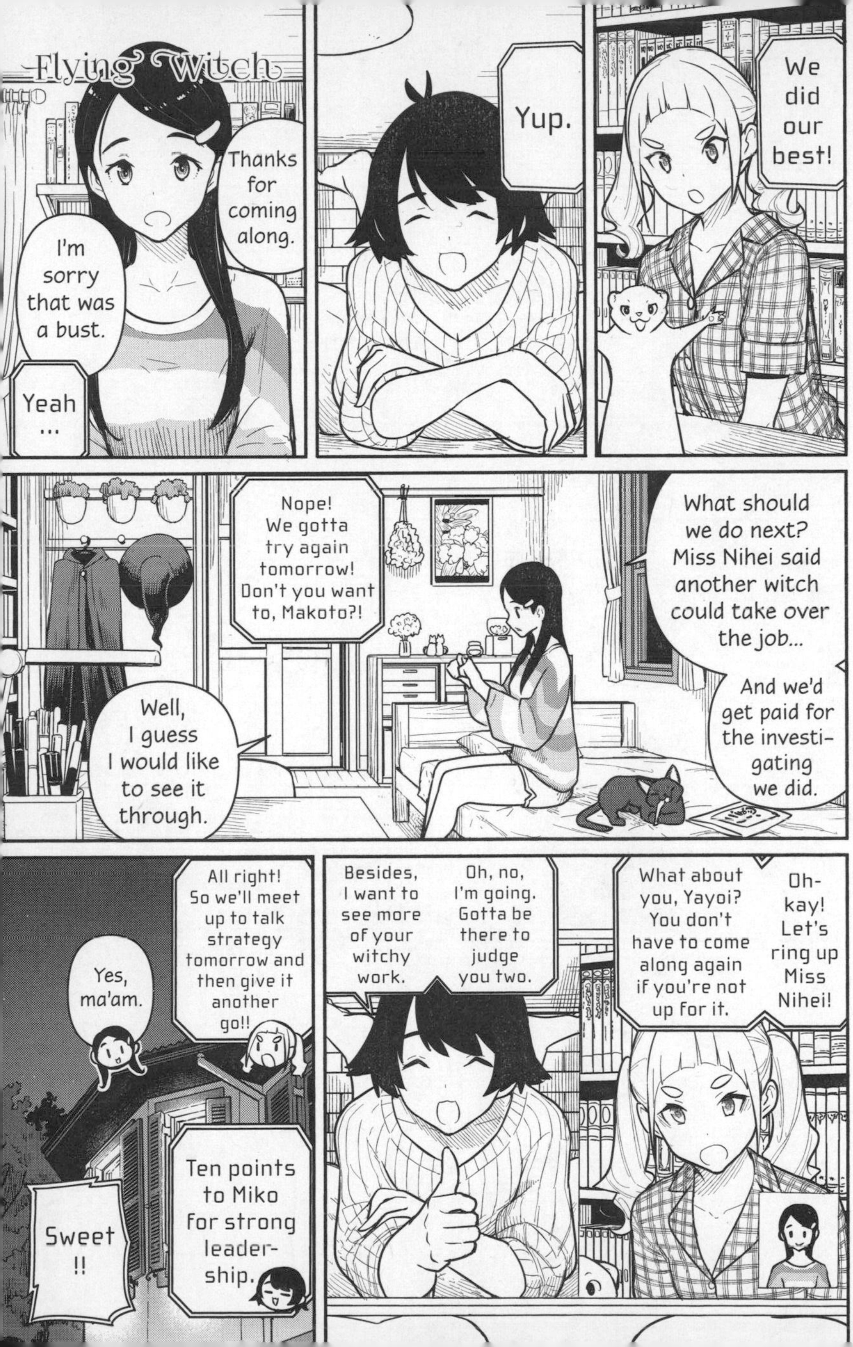
We did our best!
Yup.
Thanks for coming along.
I'm sorry that was a bust.
Yeah ...
What should we do next? Miss Nihei said another witch could take over the job...
And we'd get paid for the investigating we did.
Nope! We gotta try again tomorrow! Don't you want to, Makoto?!
Well, I guess I would like to see it through.
Oh-kay! Let's ring up Miss Nihei!
What about you, Yayoi? You don't have to come along again if you're not up for it.
Oh, no, I'm going. Gotta be there to judge you two.
Besides, I want to see more of your witchy work.
All right! So we'll meet up to talk strategy tomorrow and then give it another go!!
Yes, ma'am.
Ten points to Miko for strong leadership.
Sweet !!

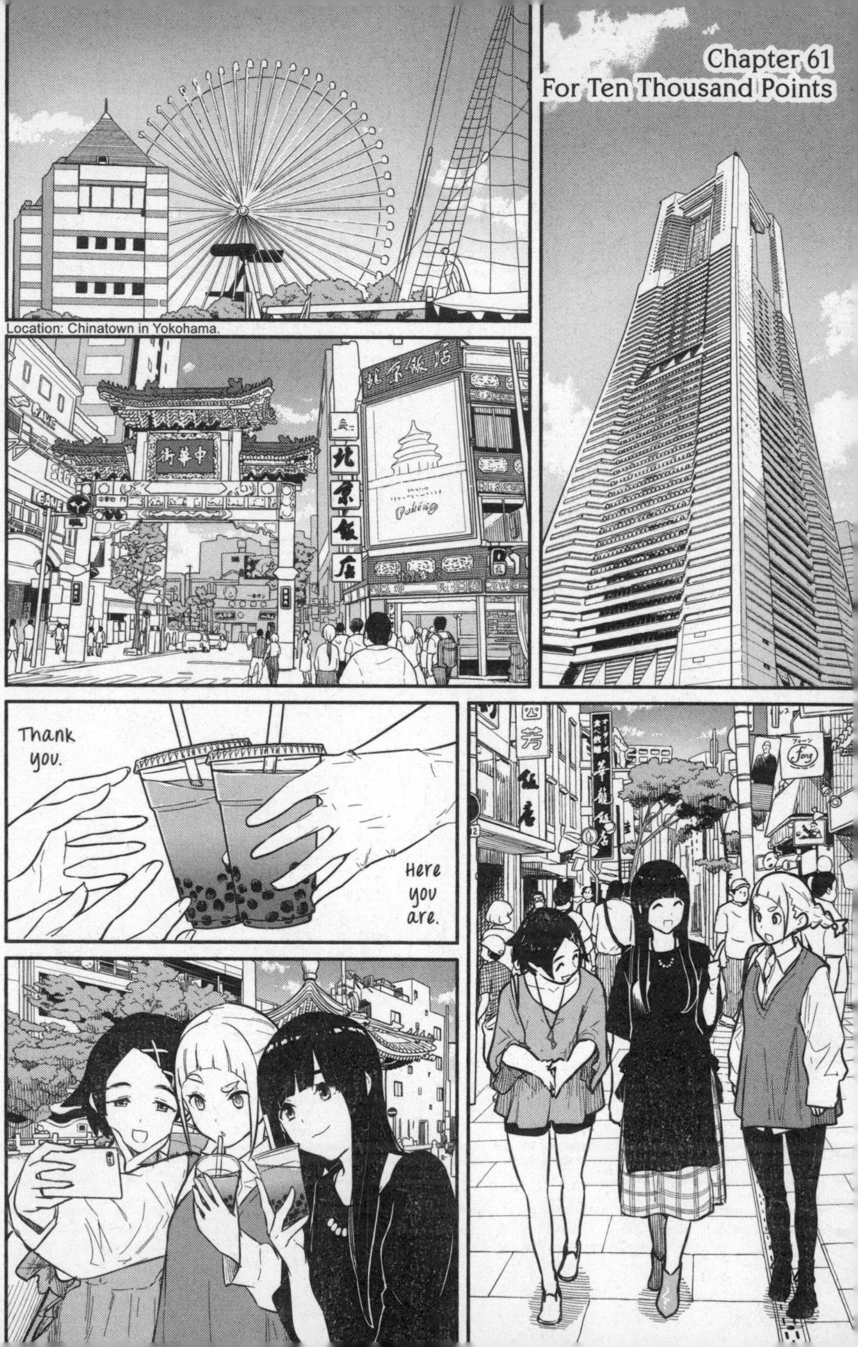
Chapter 61
For Ten Thousand Points
Location: Chinatown in Yokohama.
北京飯店
Here you are.
Thank you.

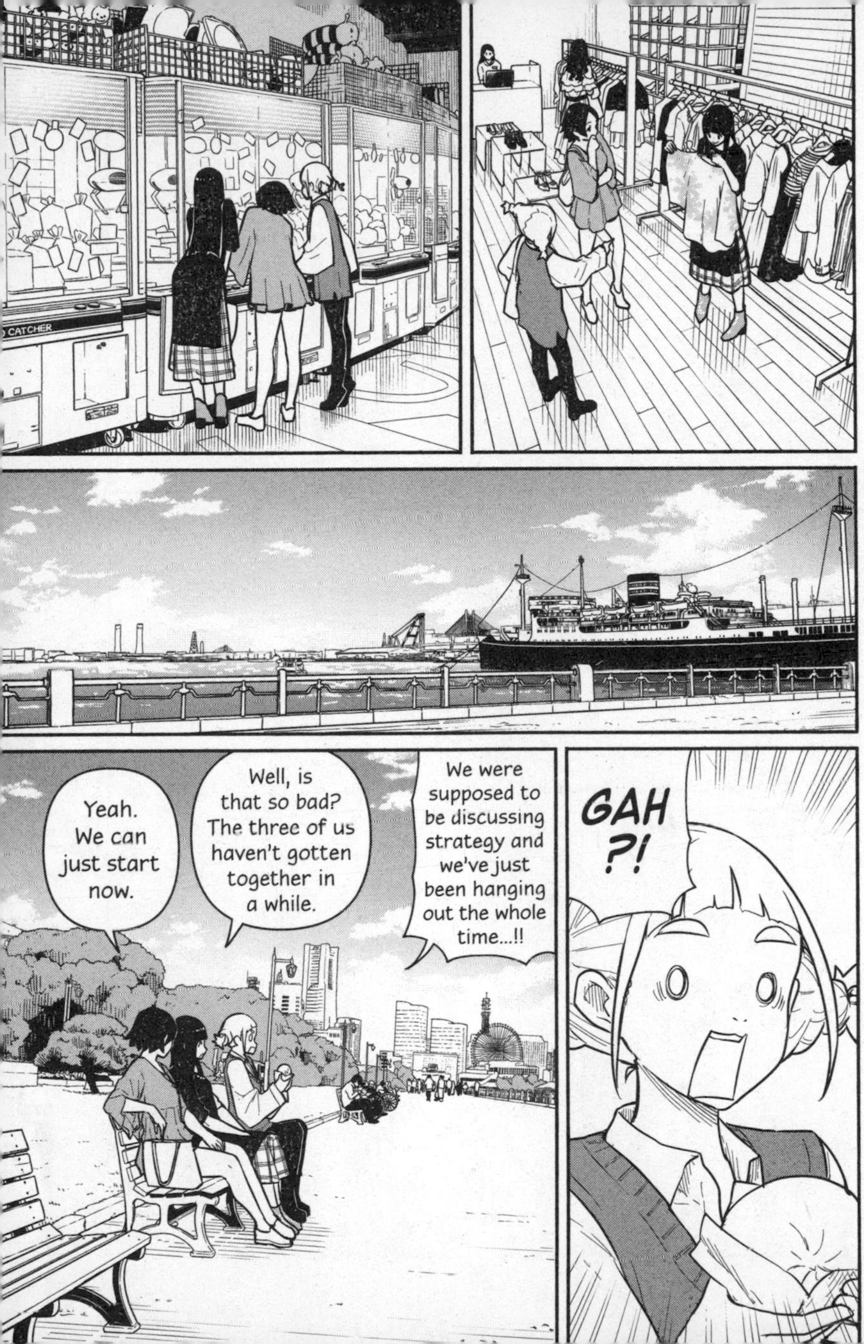
GAH ?!
We were supposed to be discussing strategy and we've just been hanging out the whole time...!!
Well, is that so bad? The three of us haven't gotten together in a while.
Yeah. We can just start now.

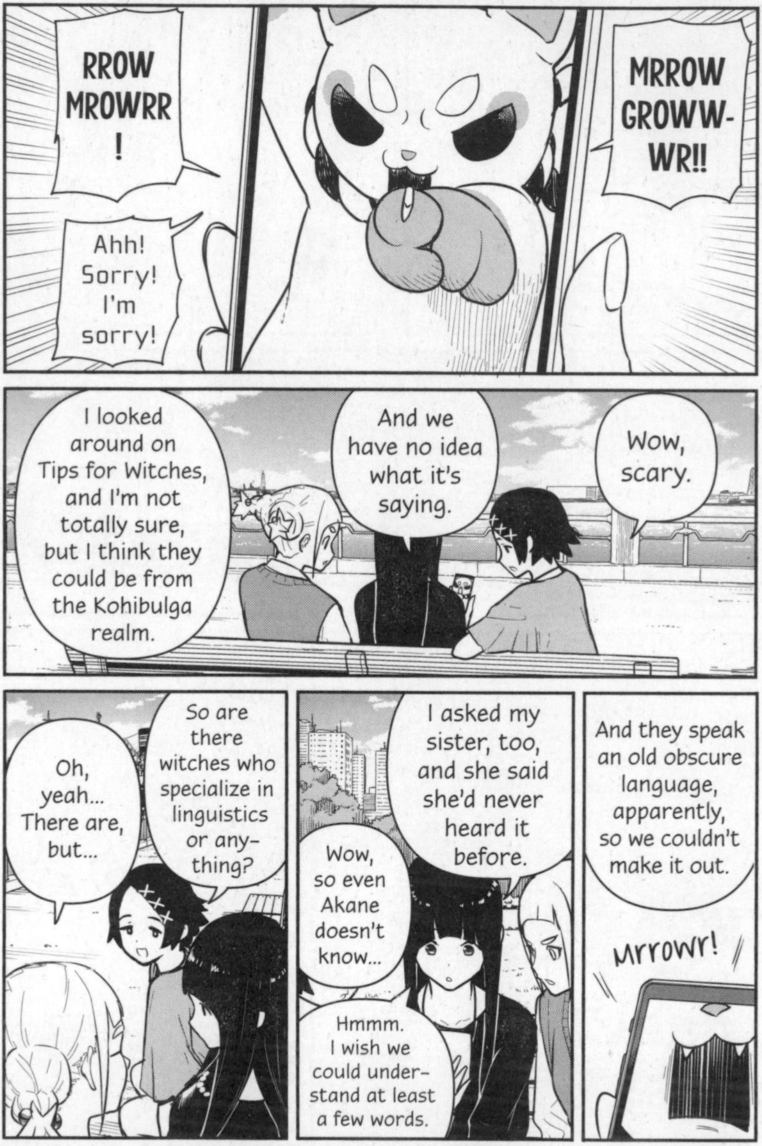
MRROW GROWW-WR!!
RROW MROWRR !
Ahh! Sorry! I'm sorry!
Wow, scary.
And we have no idea what it's saying.
I looked around on Tips for Witches, and I'm not totally sure, but I think they could be from the Kohibulga realm.
And they speak an old obscure language, apparently, so we couldn't make it out.
Mrrowr!
I asked my sister, too, and she said she'd never heard it before.
Wow, so even Akane doesn't know...
Hmmm. I wish we could understand at least a few words.
So are there witches who specialize in linguistics or any-thing?
Oh, yeah... There are, but...

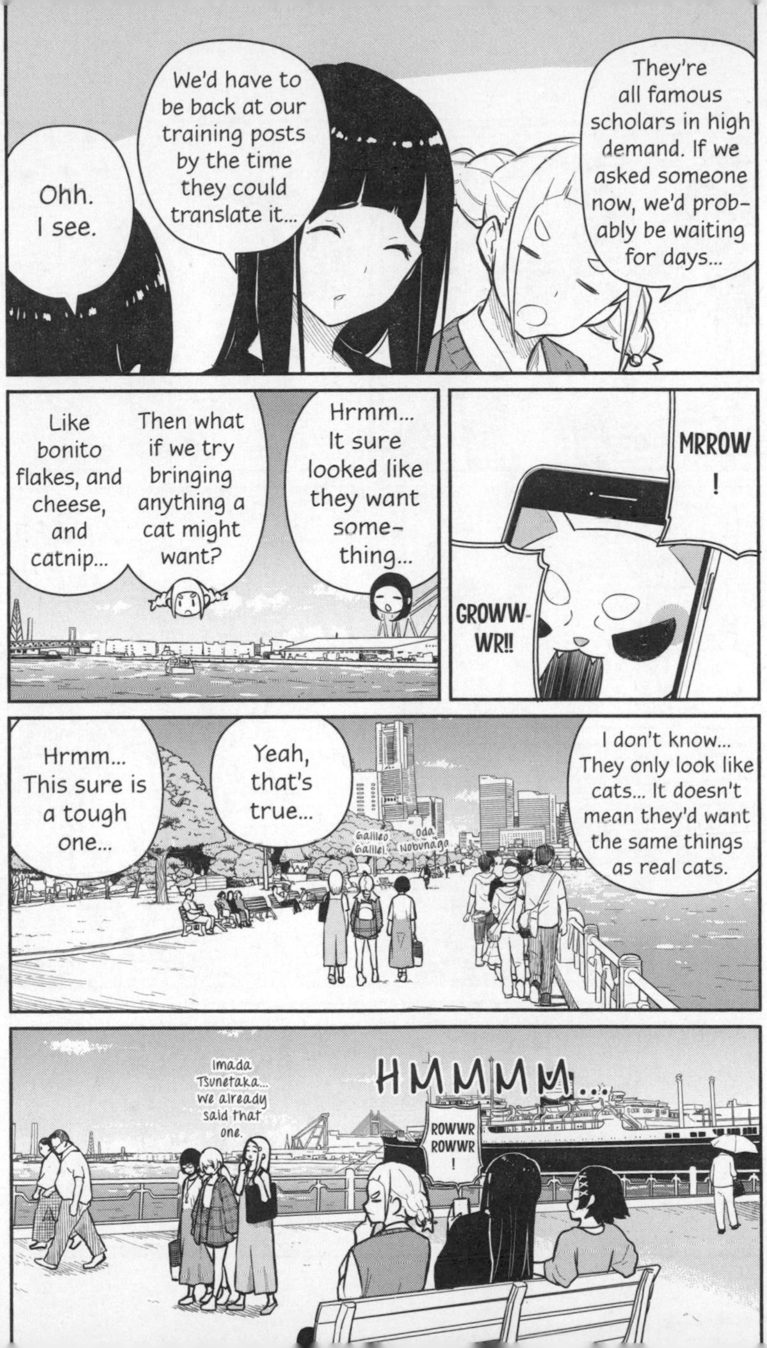
They're all famous scholars in high demand. If we asked someone now, we'd probably be waiting for days...
We'd have to be back at our training posts by the time they could translate it...
Ohh. I see.
MRROW !
GROWW-WR!!
Hrmm... It sure looked like they want something...
Then what if we try bringing anything a cat might want?
Like bonito flakes, and cheese, and catnip...
I don't know... They only look like cats... It doesn't mean they'd want the same things as real cats.
Oda Nobunaga
Galileo Galilei
Yeah, that's true...
Hrmm... This sure is a tough one...
HMMMM...
ROWWR ROWWR !
Imada Tsunetaka... we already said that one.

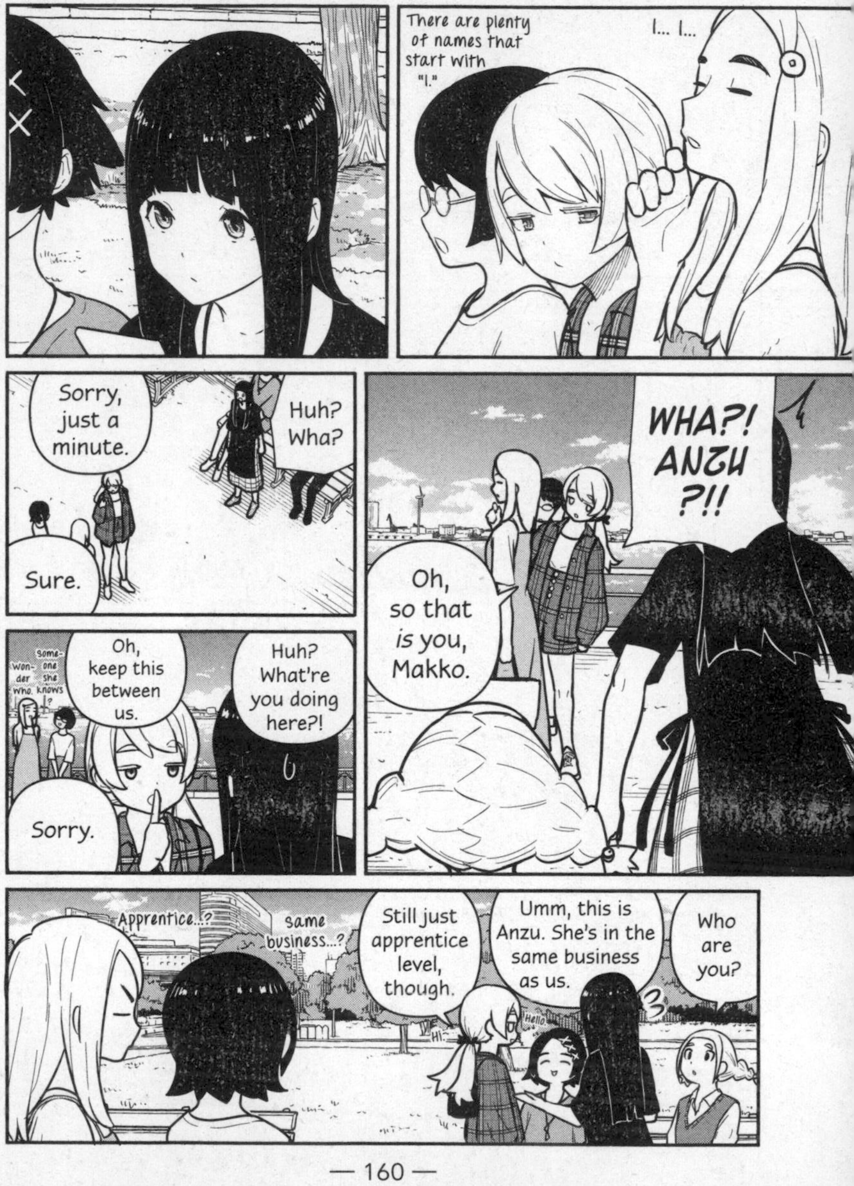
I... I...
There are plenty of names that start with "I."
WHA?! ANZU?!!
Oh, so that is you, Makko.
Huh? Wha?
Sorry, just a minute.
Sure.
Huh? What're you doing here?!
Oh, keep this between us.
Someone she knows?
Wonder who.
Sorry.
Who are you?
Umm, this is Anzu. She's in the same business as us.
Hello.
Hi!
Still just apprentice level, though.
same business...?
Apprentice...?

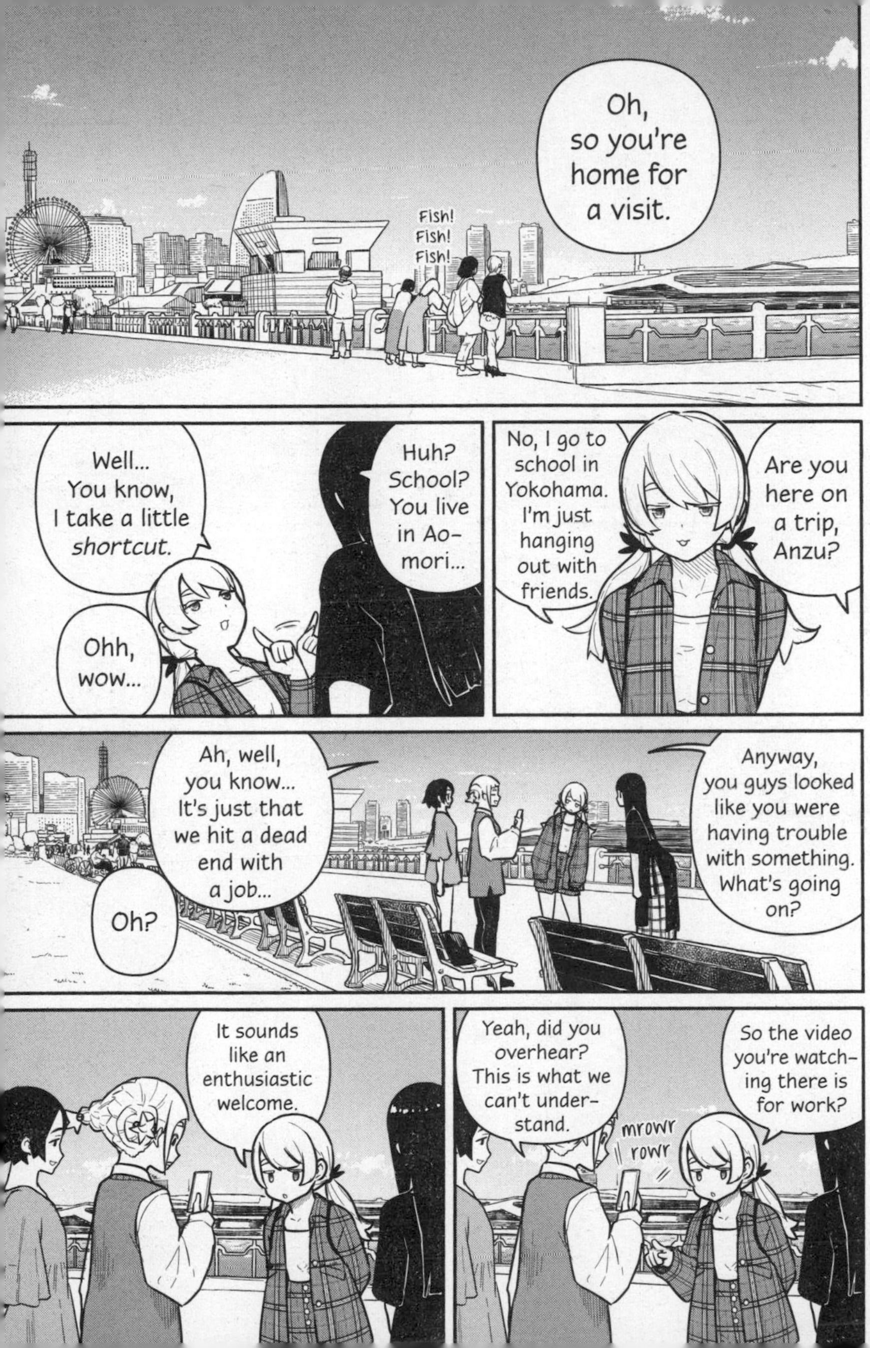
Oh, so you're home for a visit.
Fish! Fish! Fish!
Are you here on a trip, Anzu?
No, I go to school in Yokohama. I'm just hanging out with friends.
Huh? School? You live in Ao-mori...
Well... You know, I take a little *shortcut*.
Ohh, wow...
Anyway, you guys looked like you were having trouble with something. What's going on?
Ah, well, you know... It's just that we hit a dead end with a job...
Oh?
So the video you're watching there is for work?
Yeah, did you overhear? This is what we can't under-stand.
mrowr rowr
It sounds like an enthusiastic welcome.

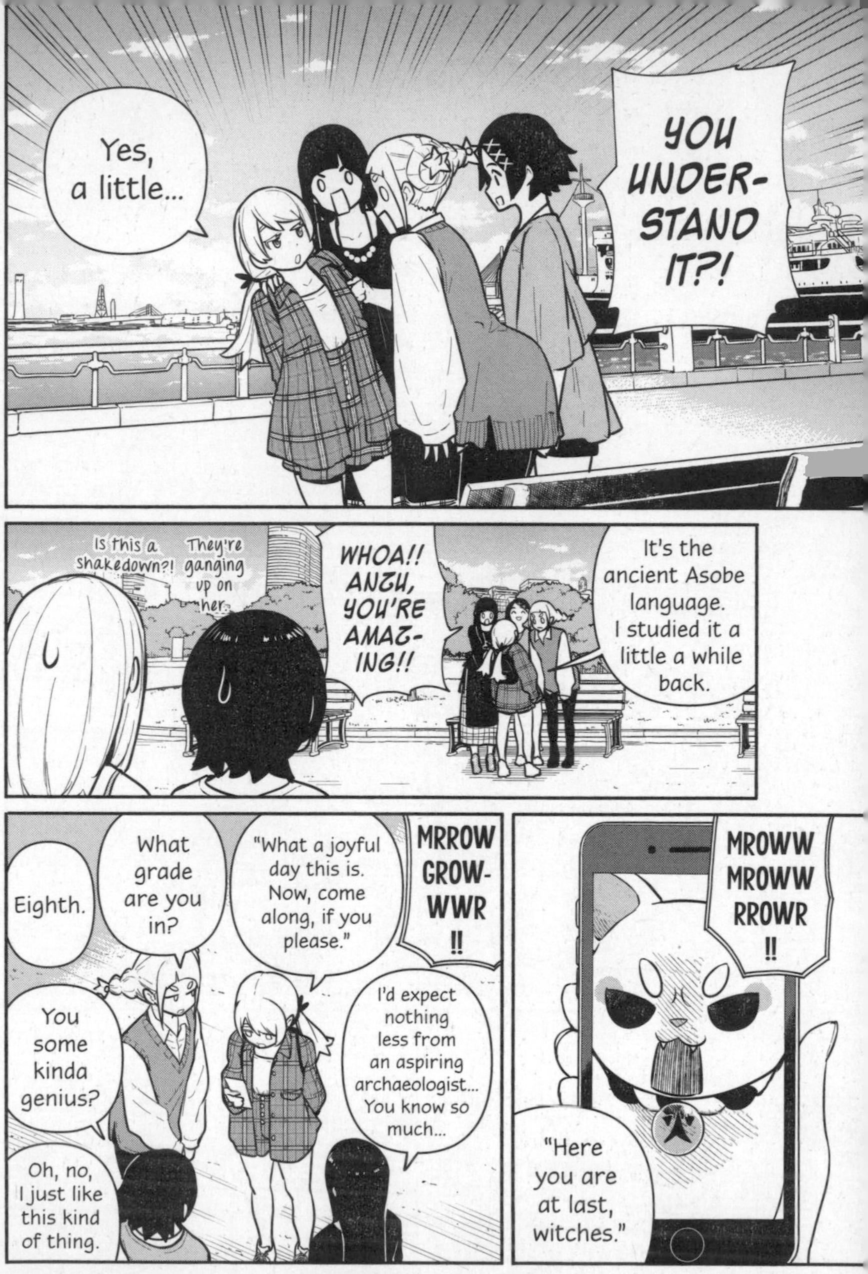
YOU UNDER-STAND IT?!
Yes, a little...
It's the ancient Asobe language. I studied it a little a while back.
WHOA!! ANZU, YOU'RE AMAZ-ING!!
They're ganging up on her.
Is this a shakedown?!
MROWW MROWW RROWR !!
"Here you are at last, witches."
MRROW GROW-WWR !!
"What a joyful day this is. Now, come along, if you please."
What grade are you in?
Eighth.
I'd expect nothing less from an aspiring archaeologist... You know so much...
You some kinda genius?
Oh, no, I just like this kind of thing.

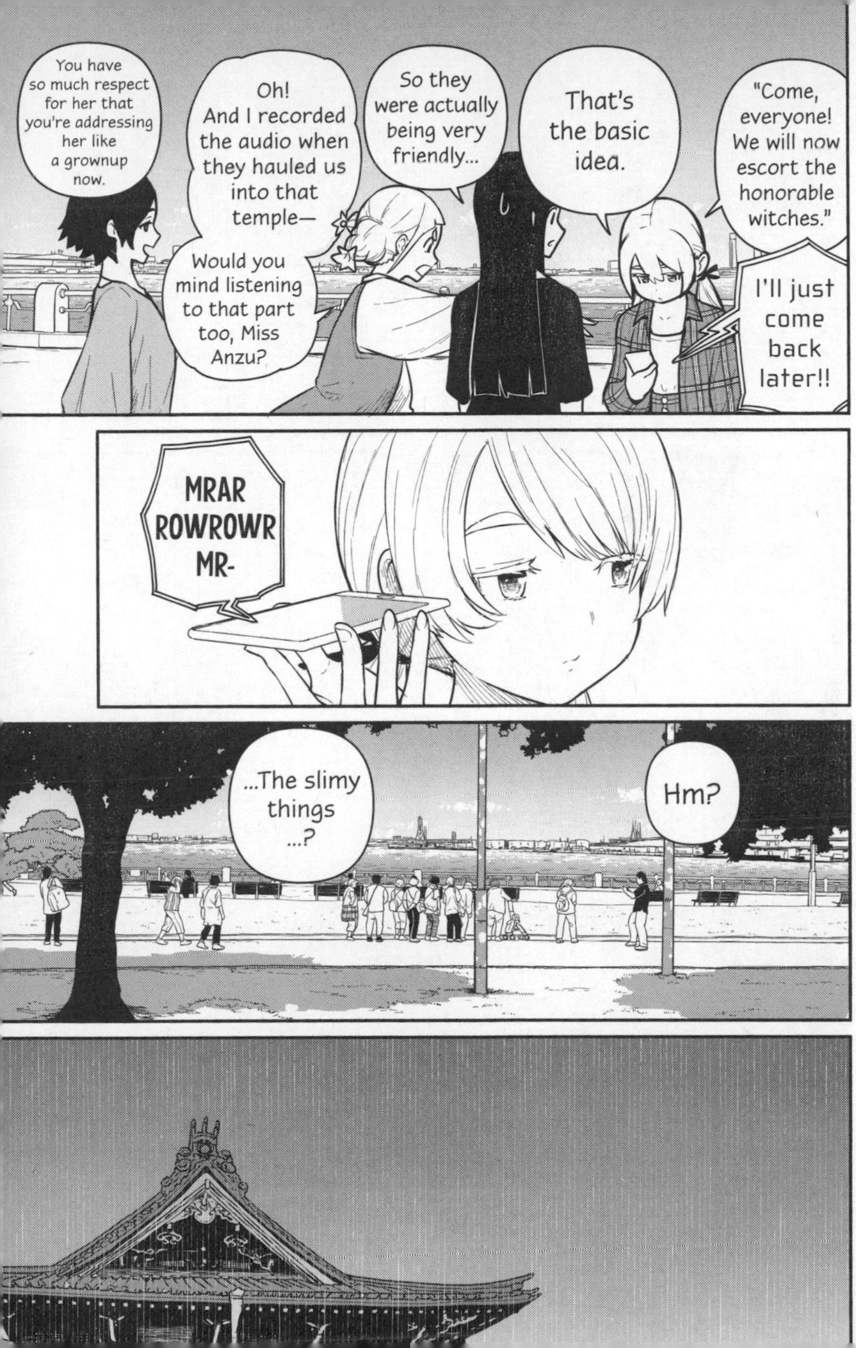
"Come, everyone! We will now escort the honorable witches."
I'll just come back later!!
That's the basic idea.
So they were actually being very friendly...
Oh! And I recorded the audio when they hauled us into that temple—
Would you mind listening to that part too, Miss Anzu?
You have so much respect for her that you're addressing her like a grownup now.
MRAR ROWROWR MR-
Hm?
...The slimy things ...?

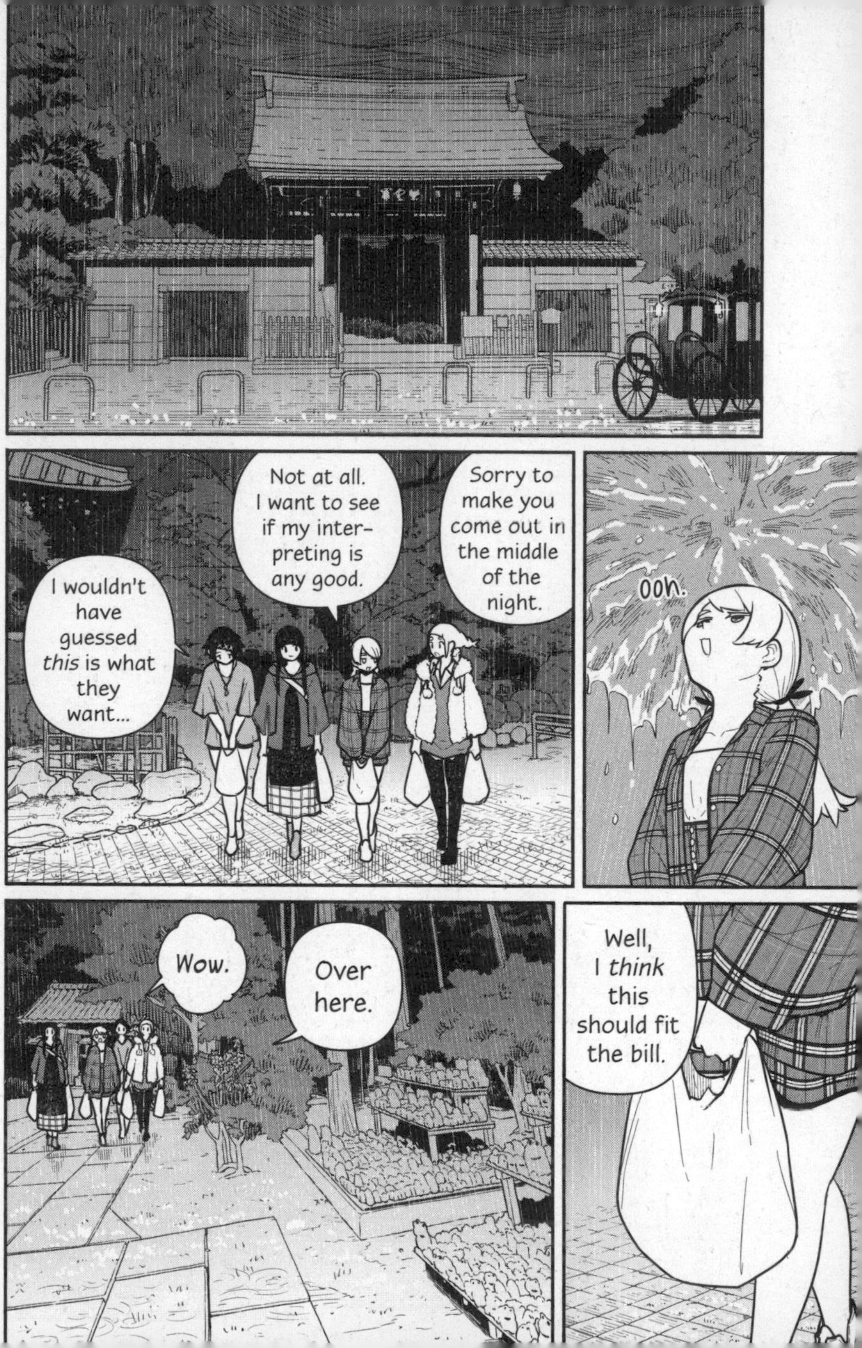
Ooh.
Sorry to make you come out in the middle of the night.
Not at all. I want to see if my interpreting is any good.
I wouldn't have guessed *this* is what they want...
Well, I *think* this should fit the bill.
Over here.
Wow.

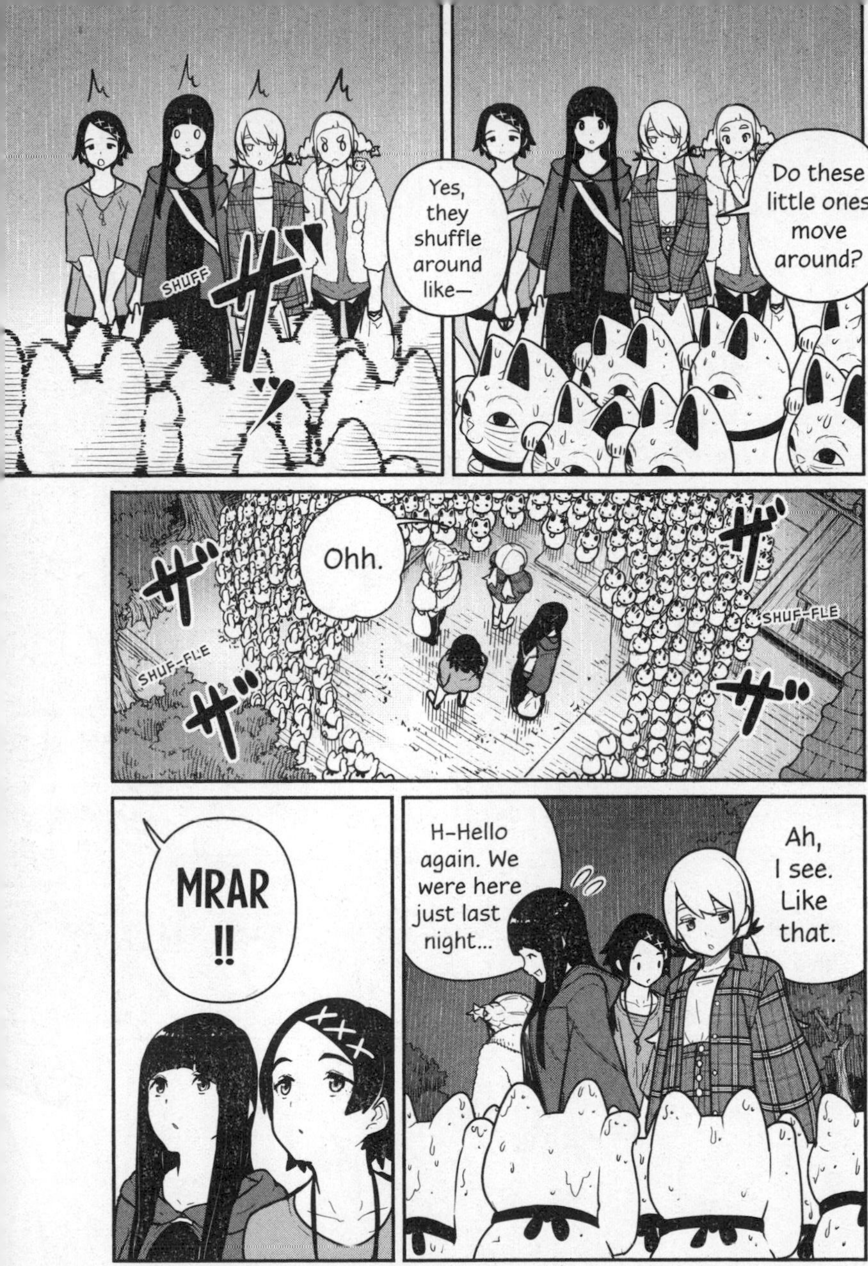
Do these little ones move around?
Yes, they shuffle around like—
SHUFF
Ohh.
SHUF-FLE
SHUF-FLE
Ah, I see. Like that.
H-Hello again. We were here just last night...
MRAR !!

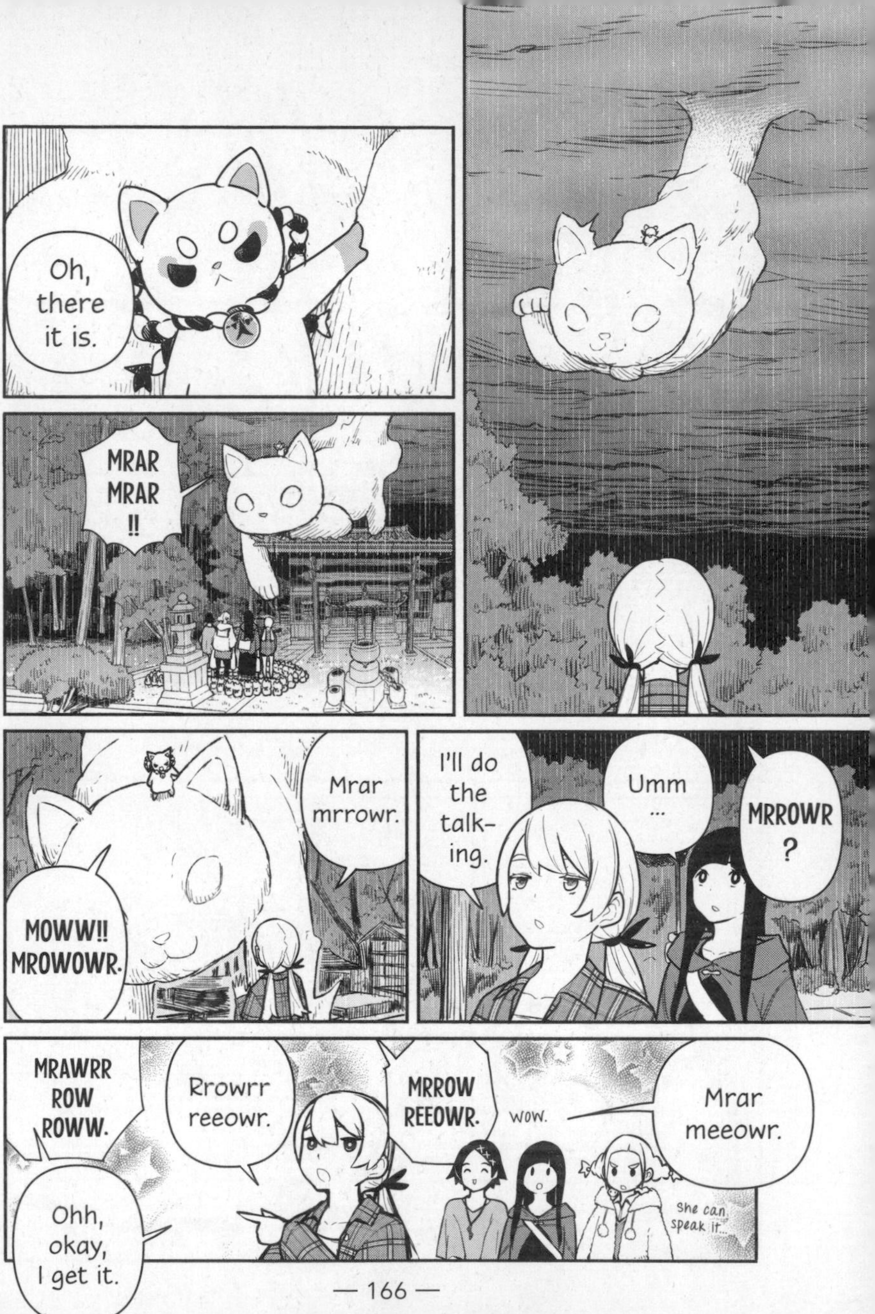
Oh, there it is.
MRAR MRAR !!
MRROWR ?
Umm ...
I'll do the talk-ing.
Mrar mrrowr.
MOWW!! MROWOWR.
Mrar meeowr.
wow.
She can speak it...
MRROW REEOWR.
Rrowrr reeowr.
MRAWRR ROW ROWW.
Ohh, okay, I get it.

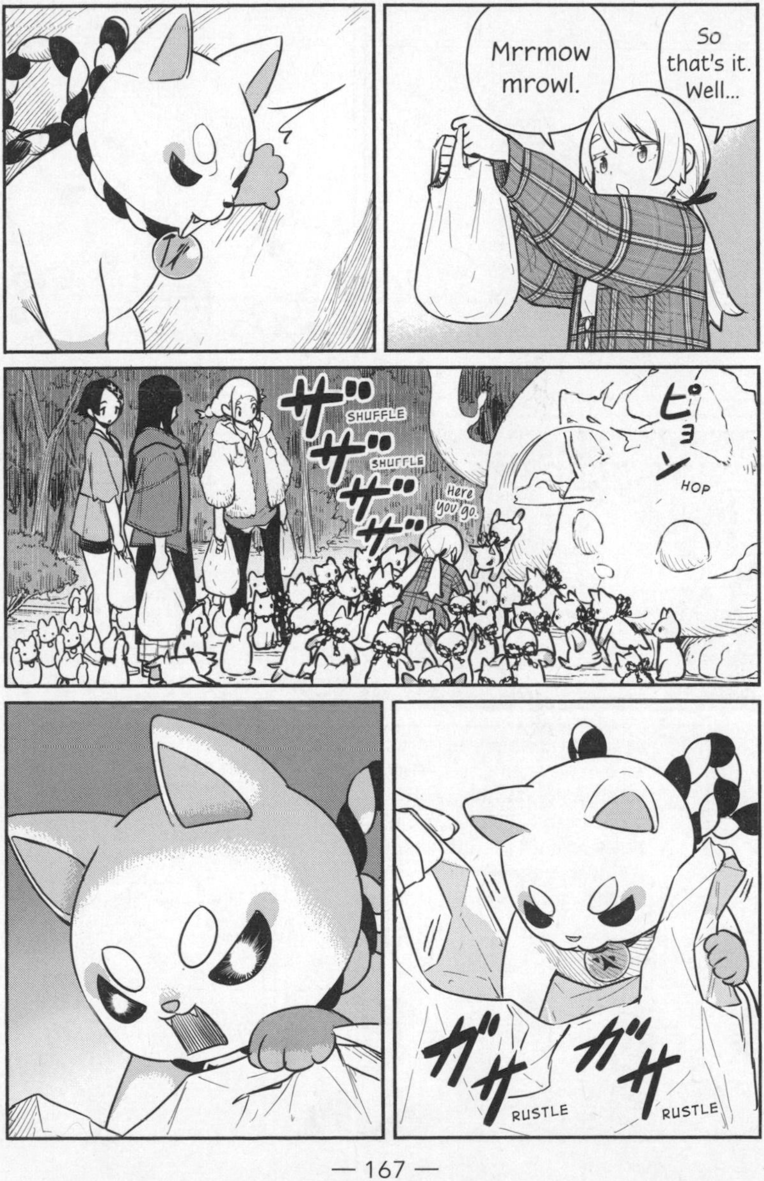
So that's it. Well...
Mrrmow mrowl.
ピョン
HOP
Here you go.
ザザザザ
SHUFFLE
SHUFFLE
ガサ
RUSTLE
ガサ
RUSTLE

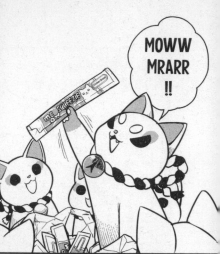

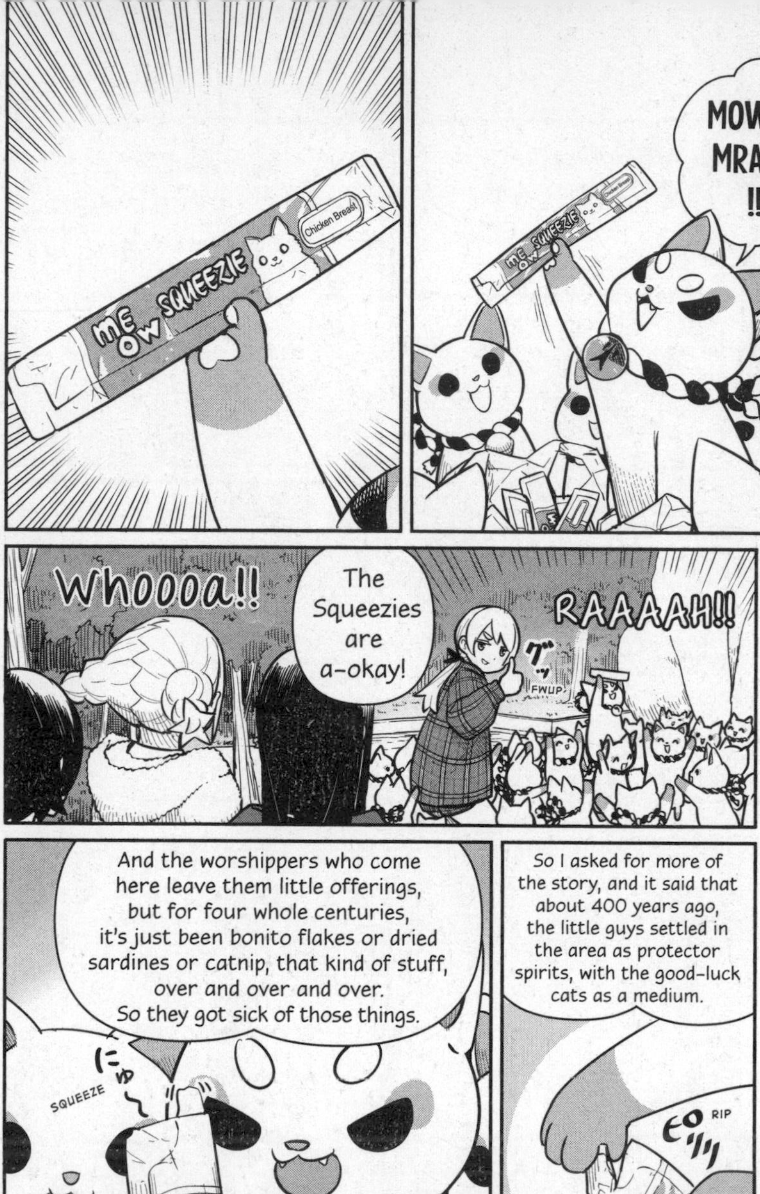
MOWW MRARR !!
ME OW SQUEEZIE
Chicken Breast
ME OW SQUEEZIE
Chicken Breast!
RAAAAH!!
グッ
FWUP
The Squeezies are a-okay!
Whoooa!!
So I asked for more of the story, and it said that about 400 years ago, the little guys settled in the area as protector spirits, with the good-luck cats as a medium.
ビリッ
RIP
And the worshippers who come here leave them little offerings, but for four whole centuries, it's just been bonito flakes or dried sardines or catnip, that kind of stuff, over and over and over. So they got sick of those things.
にゅ〜
SQUEEZE

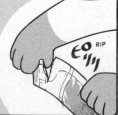

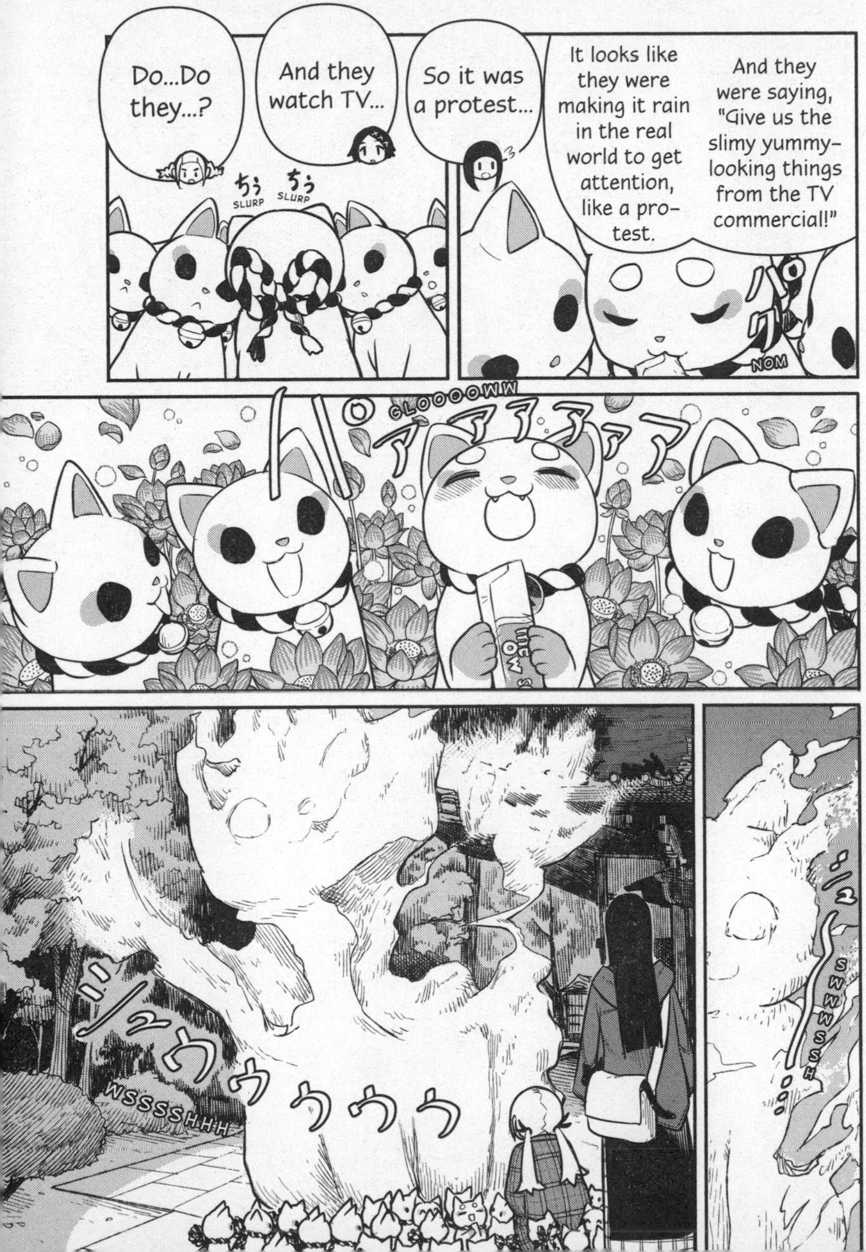
And they were saying, "Give us the slimy yummy-looking things from the TV commercial!"
It looks like they were making it rain in the real world to get attention, like a pro-test.
NOM
So it was a protest...
And they watch TV...
SLURP
SLURP
Do...Do they...?
GLOOOOWW
SWWWSSH
WSSSSHHH

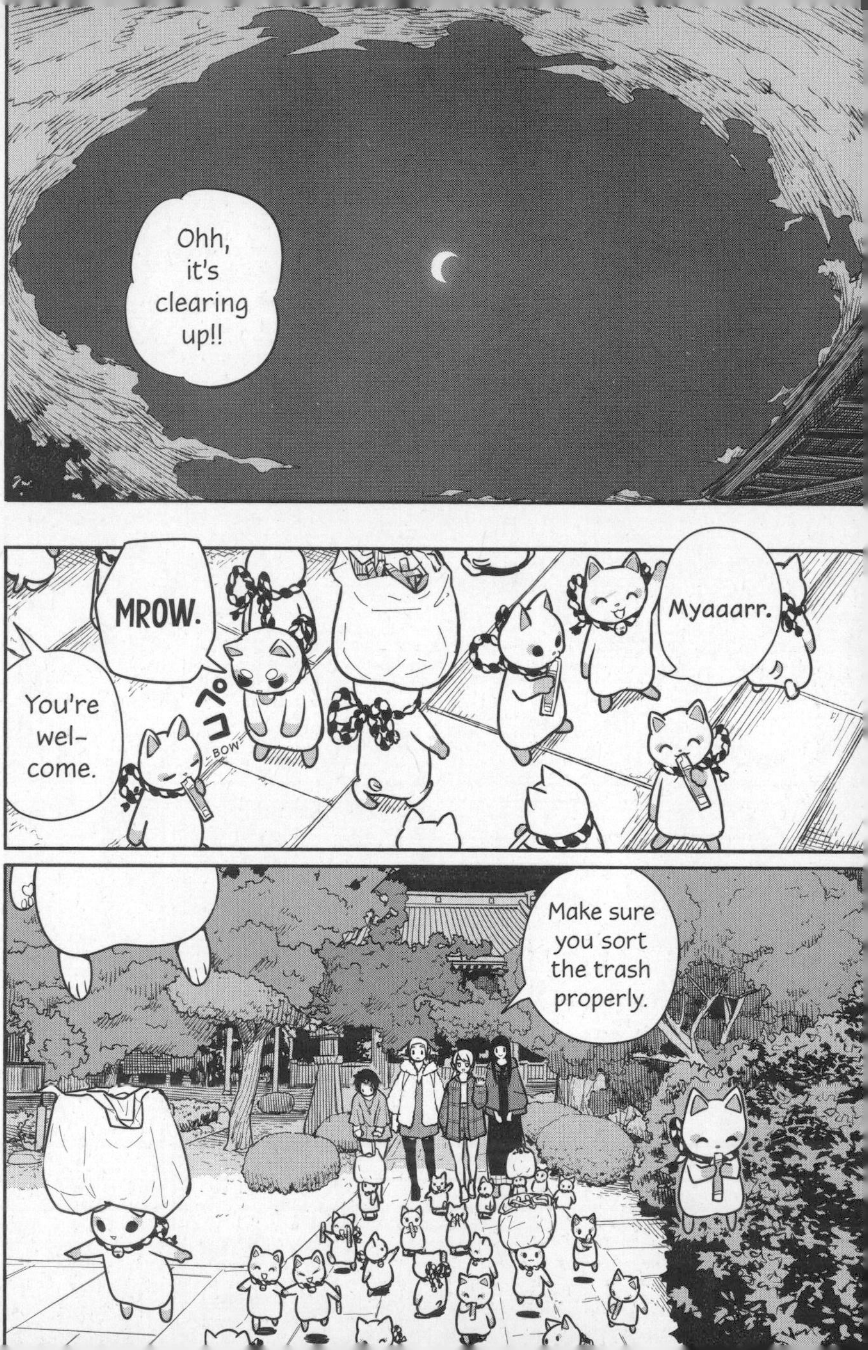
Ohh, it's clearing up!!
Myaaarr.
MROW.
ペコ
BOW
You're wel- come.
Make sure you sort the trash properly.

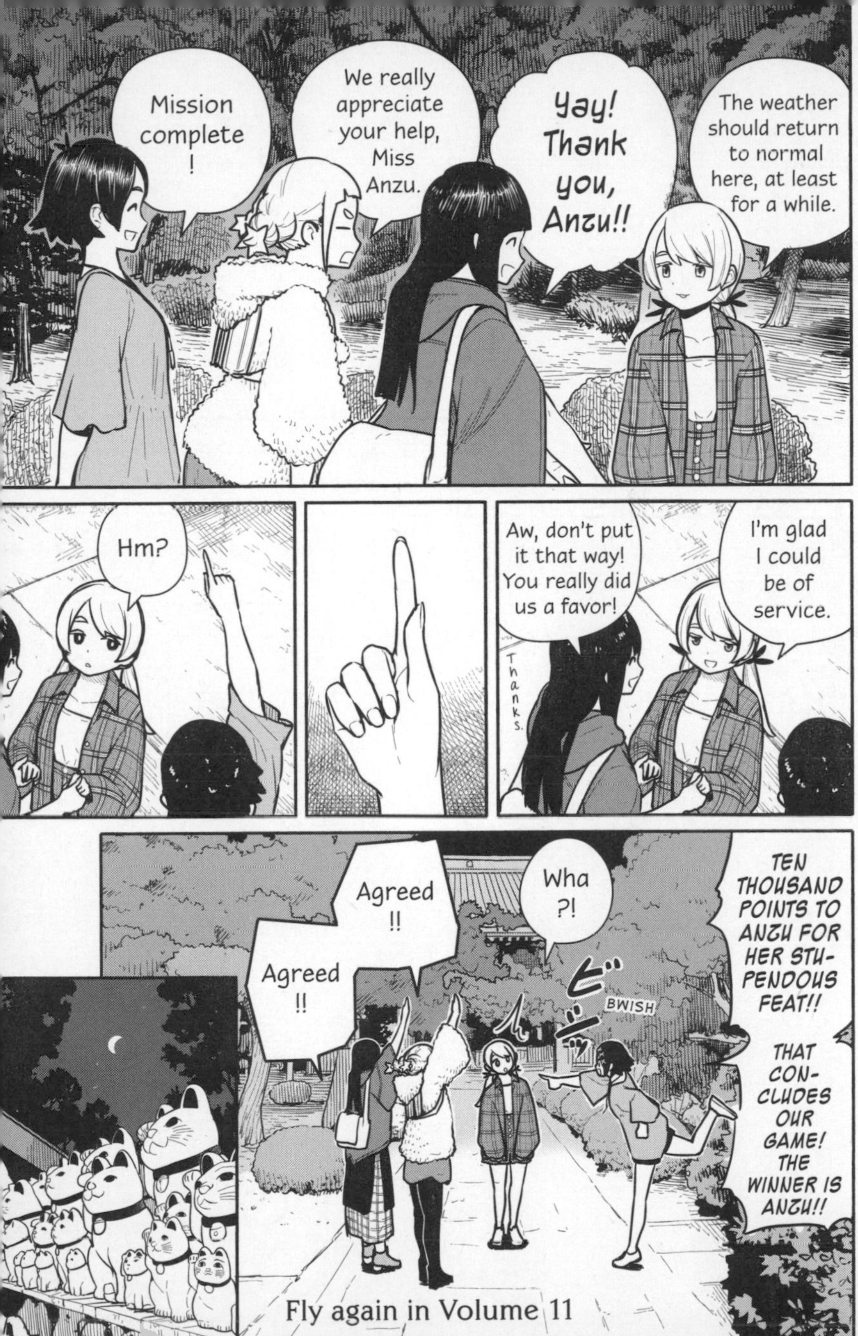
The weather should return to normal here, at least for a while.
Yay! Thank you, Anzu!!
We really appreciate your help, Miss Anzu.
Mission complete!
I'm glad I could be of service.
Aw, don't put it that way! You really did us a favor!
Thanks.
Hm?
TEN THOUSAND POINTS TO ANZU FOR HER STUPENDOUS FEAT!!
THAT CONCLUDES OUR GAME! THE WINNER IS ANZU!!
Wha?!
BWISH
Agreed!!
Agreed!!

Fly again in Volume 11

Flying
Witch

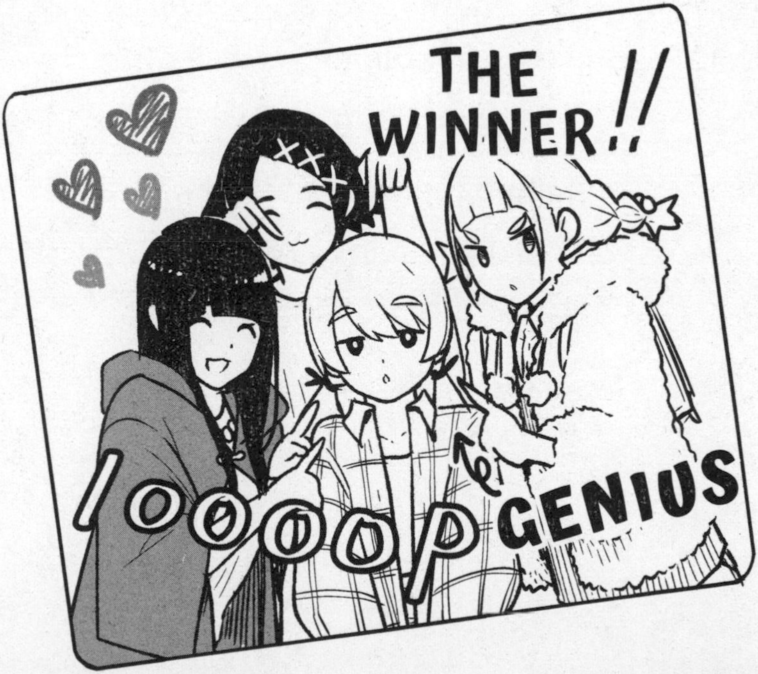
THE WINNER!!
1000000p
GENIUS

Back home at last.

It really is relaxing to spend some time in the place where you grew up.

And I'm allowed to take on jobs as a witch here, so I feel like I've been able to make a little progress during my stay.

In the meantime, Kei tells me that Chinatsu is taking her own steps toward becoming a witch.

I can't wait to see them all again!

flying witch ✷ kcm flying witch preview for next volume ✷ flying witch ✷ kcm
Volume 11 preview

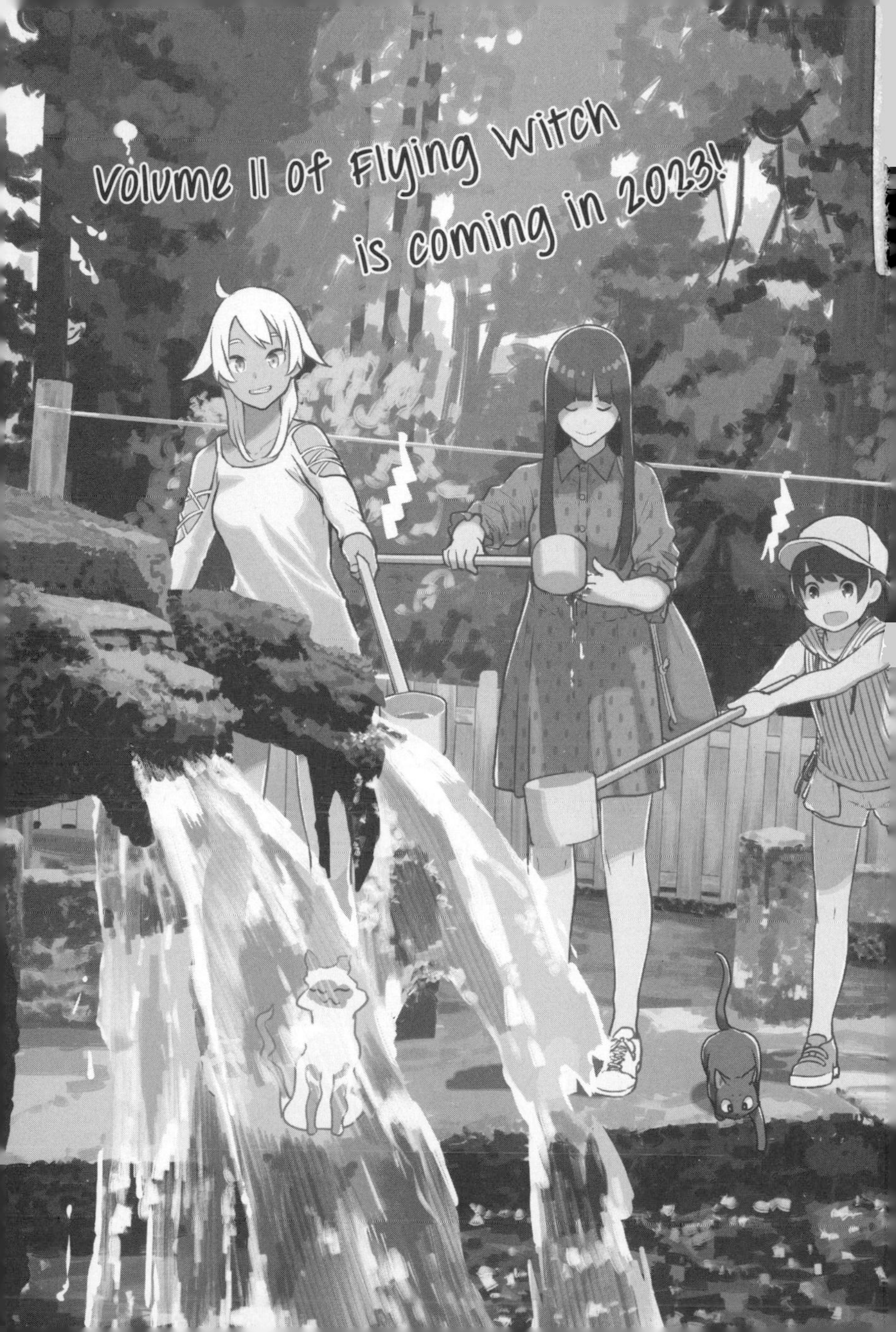
Volume 11 of Flying Witch
is coming in 2023!

Flying Witch 10

Editor - Ajani Oloye
Translation - Melissa Tanaka
Production - Grace Lu
Shirley Fang
Tomoe Tsutsumi

First published in Japan in 2021 by Kodansha, Ltd., Tokyo
Publication for this English edition arranged through Kodansha, Ltd., Tokyo
English language version produced by Vertical Comics,
an imprint of Kodansha USA Publishing, LLC

Translation provided by Vertical Comics, 2022
Published by Kodansha USA Publishing, LLC, New York

Originally published in Japanese as *Flying Witch 10* by Kodansha, Ltd., 2021
Flying Witch first serialized in *Bessatsu Shonen Magazine*, Kodansha, Ltd., 2013-

ISBN: 978-1-64729-048-1

Manufactured in the United States of America

First Edition

Kodansha USA Publishing, LLC
451 Park Avenue South, 7th Floor
New York, NY 10016
www.kodansha.us

Vertical books are distributed through Penguin-Random House Publisher Services.